Zheng He

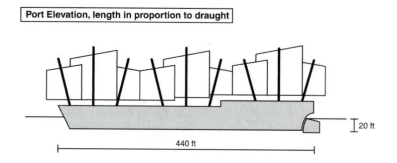

20 ft

440 ft

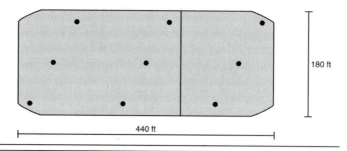

180 ft

440 ft

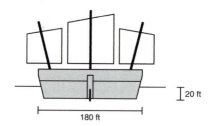

20 ft

180 ft

The actual appearance of Zheng He's treasure ships is unknown, but this drawing illustrates the dimensions reported in the sources, along with the possible off-center and off-vertical arrangement of the nine masts. With their broad beams and flat bottoms, the treasure ships would have resembled enormous river barges rather than true oceangoing ships.

Edward L. Dreyer

Zheng He

China and the Oceans in the
Early Ming Dynasty, 1405–1433

The Library of World Biography

Series Editor: Peter N. Stearns

PEARSON
Longman

New York   Boston   San Francisco
London   Toronto   Sydney   Tokyo   Singapore   Madrid
Mexico City   Munich   Paris   Cape Town   Hong Kong   Montreal

Senior Acquisitions Editor: Janet Lanphier
Executive/Senior/Marketing Manager: Sue Westmoreland
Production Manager: Virginia Riker
Senior Cover Design Manager/Cover Designer: Nancy Danahy
Cover Photo: © ChinaStock
Manufacturing Buyer: Lucy Hebard
Electronic Page Makeup: Alison Barth Burgoyne
Printer and Binder: RR Donnelley Harrisonburg
Cover Printer: Coral Graphics Services, Inc.

Library of Congress Cataloging-in-Publication Data

Dreyer, Edward L.
   Zheng He : China and the oceans in the early Ming dynasty,
1405/1433 / Edward L. Dreyer.
      p. cm. -- (The library of world biography)
   Includes bibliographical references and index.
   ISBN 0-321-08443-8 (alk. paper)
   1. Zheng, He, 1371–1435--Travel. 2. China--History--Ming
dynasty, 1368–1644. 3. Southeast Asia--Relations--China. 4.
China--Relations--Southeast Asia. I. Title. II. Title: China and
the oceans in the early Ming dynasty, 1405/1433. III. Series.

DS753.6.Z47D74 2006
951'.026092--dc22   2006007923

Please visit us at www.ablongman.com

ISBN 0-321-08443-8

1 2 3 4 5 6 7 8 9 10—DOH—09 08 07 06

Contents

Editor's Preface

"Biography is history seen through the prism of a person."

—Louis Fischer

It is often challenging to identify the roles and experiences of individuals in world history. Larger forces predominate. Yet biography provides important access to world history. It shows how individuals helped shape the society around them. Biography also offers concrete illustrations of larger patterns in political and intellectual life, in family life, and in the economy.

The Longman Library of World Biography series seeks to capture the individuality and drama that mark human character. It deals with individuals operating in one of the main periods of world history, while also reflecting issues in the particular society around them. Here, the individual illustrates larger themes of time and place. The interplay between the personal and the general is always the key to using biography in history, and world history is no exception. Always, too, there is the question of personal agency: how much do individuals, even great ones, shape their own lives and environment, and how much are they shaped by the world around them?

Peter N. Stearns

Author's Preface

The eunuch and military commander Zheng He, who lived from 1371 to 1433, served the third Ming emperor, Yongle. From 1405 until his death he commanded Chinese fleets in seven unprecedented voyages into the Indian Ocean. His fleets included more and larger ships than those of the Spanish Armada of 1588, and his voyages have become an important symbol of past Chinese success in oceanic exploration and other maritime activities.

When modern interest in Zheng He began early in the twentieth century, China was at a low point in a long period of national humiliation caused by defeats at the hands of European powers and Japan. China's naval weakness was a major element in these defeats. For the Chinese, and for foreign admirers of Chinese civilization, the fact of Zheng He's voyages and the great size of the "treasure ships" that were the main units of Zheng He's fleets became a way of salvaging national pride. By the 1900s, historians of European descent had identified maritime exploration, the conquest of non-European peoples allegedly discovered by the explorers, and the creation of overseas colonial regimes as key elements in the early modern transformation of the world. This transformation had originated in Western Europe, and China seemed backward in comparison. But Zheng He's voyages clearly demonstrated that, during the early decades of the Ming Dynasty (1368–1644), China certainly had the wealth and the shipbuilding and navigational skills to equal or surpass any European maritime accomplishments. And there was a moral dimension, too: the Chinese fleets supposedly paid peaceful visits to other countries, in contrast to the death and destruction meted out by Spanish and

Portuguese conquistadores. For modern historians, both Chinese and Western, the great question about the voyages was why they ended so abruptly in 1433. The answer these historians gave was to blame the inward-looking narrow-mindedness of China's traditional educated elite, who had been obstacles to reform and progress in the fifteenth century as they were in later times.

The concept of Zheng He's voyages as peaceful and as exploration thus fits into a long tradition of sentimentalizing Chinese history to create a preferred alternative to some aspect of European history. The government of the People's Republic of China took up this theme in 2005, commemorating the six hundredth anniversary of Zheng He's first voyage as the start of a series of peaceful voyages of exploration in the early Ming period that paralleled their slogan of "China's peaceful rise" in recent times.

When I accepted the assignment of writing a biography of Zheng He for the Longman Library of World Biography, I already knew that Zheng He's ships and fleets were too large for voyages of exploration, and that he and his men did too much fighting for the voyages to be entirely peaceful. That meant that I would need to engage and modify the standard narrative of Zheng He as a peaceful explorer. I also knew that the Chinese sources described Zheng He's career and activities reasonably well, but had little information regarding his thoughts or inner life. I eventually chose a subtitle to reflect the fact that the focus of the book was not just Zheng He the man, but also the period of Chinese maritime activity within which he was the central actor. After thoroughly reviewing the primary Chinese sources, I concluded that the purpose of the voyages was actually "power projection," to use the language of contemporary writers on international relations: rather than mere exploration, Zheng He's voyages were undertaken to force the states of Southeast Asia and the Indian Ocean to acknowledge the power and majesty of Ming China and its emperor. This objective required a much greater naval presence than any amount of exploration would have needed. Zheng He's armada was frightening enough that it seldom needed to fight, but being *able* to fight was its primary mission. This insight helps to explain why Zheng He's ships needed to have their great size and carrying capacity.

In telling this story, I have attempted to set Zheng He's career and achievements in the context of Chinese history during the early Ming period. Zheng He's life (1371–1433) corresponds closely to the reigns of the first five Ming emperors (collectively 1368–1435). This was a period of great change in China, and Zheng He's voyages are now the best remembered of several major initiatives undertaken by his patron, the third Ming emperor, Yongle (ruled 1402–1424). Yongle's grandson Xuande (ruled 1425–1435) ordered one last voyage, but later Ming emperors, all of whom were based in Beijing and oriented toward the north, had no interest in the oceans.

Zheng He rests squarely on the primary Chinese sources, and, while it is not footnoted in the traditional manner, it does include precise source references in the Note on Sources, the Glossary, and in the tables in Chapter VI. I hope that this compromise approach will make the book both accessible to students and useful to other researchers in Chinese history.

Acknowledgments

When Peter N. Stearns, series editor of the Longman Library of World Biography, approached me with the idea of writing a biography of "Cheng Ho" my first inclination was to decline politely. I had another project in mind, and I was aware of the limitations of the sources. Nevertheless, I consulted my wife, June Teufel Dreyer, a contemporary China specialist, and, somewhat to my surprise, she encouraged me to accept. Anyone who has been married as long, and as happily, as I have been will understand how mandatory such spousal encouragement can be. June is therefore to some extent responsible for the existence of *Zheng He*, and I hope that some day she will read it.

The Interlibrary Loan Department of the University of Miami library system is now a purely Internet operation, so I do not know personally the people who found the out-of-print books and articles, in Chinese and French as well as in English, that I needed to complete this project, but I am grateful for their assistance.

Earlier drafts of *Zheng He* were read by scholars chosen by Longman. Naturally I agreed with some more than with others, but overall the comments were very helpful. The reviewers who have allowed their names to be identified with this project are Leslie Heaphy, Kent State University (Stark); Kimberly J. Morse, Washburn University; Pamela G. Sayre, Henry Ford Community College; Kenneth R. Hall, Ball State University; William Wei, University of Colorado; Joseph Aieta III, Lasell College; Greg Rohlf, University of the Pacific; Linda Cooke Johnson, Michigan State University; and J. Michael Farmer, Brigham Young University. I am grateful to them all.

After Janet Lanphier took over as Senior Acquisitions Editor for World History and Western Civilization at Longman, she provided just the right mixture of patience and encouragement needed to complete this project. It has been a pleasure working with her and Kristina Witt, and Virginia Riker, also of Longman.

Finally, I want to give special thanks to Edward L. Farmer, Professor of History and East Asian Studies at the University of Minnesota, for his thoughtful and complimentary review of a late version of the manuscript. Ted and I met as graduate students at Harvard over forty years ago. His review arrived in the period after Hurricane Wilma hit South Florida, at a time when I had electrical power and Internet connections in my university office, but my wife and I were going home to a dark house every evening for nine days. Ted had not seen the manuscript before; his review was encouraging both because it showed that the central arguments in *Zheng He* were clear and convincing to an established authority in Ming history who was intimately familiar with the Chinese sources, and because it provided a blueprint for trimming the manuscript to make these arguments even more clear to the general reader.

Of course, any errors and deficiencies that may remain to be discovered by later readers are there only because of the author, who hereby assumes sole responsibility for them.

EDWARD L. DREYER

Zheng He

The Enigma of Zheng He

Soon after usurping the throne, the Ming Emperor **Yongle** (ruled 1402–24) decided to "display the wealth and power" of China to countries in Southeast Asia and around the Indian Ocean that could be reached only by sea. To that end, he ordered the construction of a fleet that included the largest wooden ships ever built, and in 1405 he sent them on the first of seven voyages across the South China Sea and the Indian Ocean. He entrusted the command of the fleet to **Zheng He** (1371–1433), a eunuch who had served him since 1381. Zheng He had had no previous naval experience, but he had been a loyal and resourceful military commander in the civil war that brought Yongle to power. Now commanding a fleet crewed by more than 27,000 men, most of whom were professional soldiers, Zheng He sailed as far as the Arabian peninsula and the eastern coast of Africa, spreading awe of China and bringing back ambassadors and tribute items from the countries he "visited." On Sumatra and Ceylon he fought and won major battles against recalcitrant elements who refused to be overawed. In contemporary strategic language, Zheng He's career represented Ming China's projection of its power by sea over a great distance, and it is a unique episode in Chinese history. In world history, there is no prior example of power projection by sea comparable in scale, distance, and duration to Zheng He and his fleet, and even afterward the overseas colonial empires created by the various European powers were sustained by smaller fleets composed of smaller ships. Zheng He's life is therefore worth examining, even though we can know little about him as a person, and even though the enigma at its center—why were the voyages undertaken?—is difficult to answer conclusively.

The Chinese Tributary System and the Purpose of Zheng He's Voyages

Emperor Yongle willed Zheng He's fleet into existence and sent it on its way early in his reign, yet after a final voyage in the reign of Yongle's grandson, China abandoned the sea almost as quickly as it had embraced it. Zheng He's life is of interest only because of his seven voyages; without them he would have been just another eunuch who served his emperor in various capacities. The Chinese sources tell us almost nothing about Zheng He as a person, and less than we would wish to know about the voyages, which were almost forgotten by the Chinese themselves until Western scholars began to study them early in the twentieth century.

Those scholars questioned the apparently fantastic dimensions attributed to Zheng He's largest ships and pondered the fundamental enigma of Zheng He's seven voyages: Why were they undertaken? And why, after huge ships had been constructed for the voyages at great expense, were the voyages abandoned so suddenly and permanently after 1433? Answers to these questions tended to draw on Western perceptions of how the oceans should figure in human affairs: either Zheng He was an explorer who intended to found colonies, or his fleet was exercising sea power under the cover of which Chinese commerce could be expected to grow. Zheng He and his emperor thus represented a "maritime party" in favor of contact with the outside world. Chinese officials who opposed the voyages must then have been xenophobes whose opposition arose largely from cultural causes, and the apparently exaggerated dimensions of Zheng He's ships could plausibly be explained by the carelessness with numbers that sometimes affects Chinese historical writing.

This book is based on a careful examination of the Chinese sources for Zheng He, and it attempts to set the man and his voyages in the context of Chinese history in the early Ming period. Looked at from that perspective, it soon becomes clear that Zheng He was not an explorer and that neither Zheng He nor the emperors he served ever had any theory of sea power of the sort made popular by the American admiral Alfred Thayer Mahan and other writers around the turn of the twentieth century. On the contrary, Emperor Yongle's father, the first Ming emperor **Hongwu** (born 1328, ruled 1368–98), had prohibited Chinese merchants from engaging in foreign trade, and Yongle and his successors maintained that prohibition even as they were sending Zheng He on his voyages. Despite the coercive power that Zheng He's armada wielded, there is no evidence to suggest that the Chinese fleets attempted to force trade into certain channels and bring it under control, as the later Portuguese and Dutch both did.

If interpretations derived from Western history are inadequate, why then were the expeditions sent and why did they end so abruptly? This book argues that the Chinese record is in fact reasonably clear on both points. Zheng He's biography in the *Mingshi*, the official history of the Ming Dynasty published in 1739 under the succeeding Qing or Manchu Dynasty (1644–1912), says that Yongle "wanted to display his soldiers in strange lands in order to make manifest the wealth and power" of Ming China. Zheng He's largest ships, which were in fact as large as they are reported in the sources, were not well suited for either exploration or for combat with other ships, but their sheer size was awe-inspiring, and they were intended to ferry Chinese troops around the Indian Ocean in order to impress, or if need be to overpower, the local authorities. The goal of this effort was neither conquest nor the promotion of trade, but the enforcement of the Chinese tributary system on the countries of the Indian Ocean.

Under the tributary system, foreign rulers or their ambassadors would come to China and present tribute in local products to the Chinese emperor, thus acknowledging his unique status as Son of Heaven and ruler of the Middle Kingdom of lands directly under Heaven. In return they would receive official recognition, imperial gifts—mostly paper money and silk in Zheng He's time—and a Chinese calendar, which they were required to use in their communications with China. Yongle's original decision to force states that could be reached only by sea into this system had something to do with the specific circumstances that existed at the beginning of his reign, but he made that decision without worrying about the cost of the voyages. Official opposition to the escalating costs of all the emperor's pet projects, including Zheng He's voyages, grew over the years. When the emperor announced a third Mongolian campaign in 1421, he triggered a political crisis that led to the suspension of Zheng He's voyages for the rest of the reign. Yet the voyages were only part of the overall cost problem, and Ming officials would have agreed with the Qing historians that the "goods and treasures without name" that Zheng He acquired "were too many to be accounted for, yet they did not make up for the wasteful expenditures" on his fleet. Yongle's grandson, Emperor **Xuande** (born 1399, ruled 1425–35), sent out the last voyage (1431–33) because the colorful tribute missions from the Indian Ocean countries, which he remembered seeing while growing up in Nanjing, had ceased to come. The subsequent Ming emperors all resided in Beijing and had no interest in the Indian Ocean countries.

Careful review of the Chinese sources thus suggests that Yongle's main motive in ordering the voyages was the very traditional Chinese goal of getting foreign countries to accept the Chinese tributary system. Yongle had recently become emperor by armed usurpation, and he must have had many private doubts about the legitimacy of his rule. Zheng He's voyages were not Yongle's only important initiative, and his reign would have been a very active one even if he had not ordered the voyages. But he did. Imperial interest thus explains why the voyages commenced, and the withdrawal of imperial interest explains why the voyages ended.

Traditional Chinese Interpretations of Zheng He's Career

Zheng He's biography in the *Mingshi* is translated in the Appendix. This biography is the most detailed outline of the events of Zheng He's life, but it requires some explanation because it either omits or alludes cryptically to matters known from other sources, and it assumes familiarity with the conventions of Chinese historical writing.

Zheng He was born in the province of Yunnan in southwestern China, into a family surnamed Ma, a surname that often though not always indicates Muslim faith. His father and grandfather both were named **Hajji**, suggesting that they were indeed Muslim and had made the pilgrimage to Mecca. While the Muslims of Yunnan are not as well known as the Muslims of Gansu and other areas in the northwestern part of China, they have been an important community down to the present, and Chinese Muslim tradition now claims Zheng He as an illustrious member of this community. Yet the biography refers to him as the Grand Director of the Three Treasures. Grand Director was the highest title a eunuch could hold; it carried the upper grade of the fourth rank (4a for short) in the system of nine ranks that defined status for Ming military officers and civil officials. Three Treasures is a standard term that refers to the Buddha, the Buddhist law *(dharma)*, and the community *(sangha)* of Buddhist monks. While many of Zheng He's associates were Muslims, Zheng He himself practiced Buddhism and eventually took a Buddhist name. He is today venerated as a god by the overseas Chinese community, whose religion combines Buddhist and native Chinese elements in a manner that is eclectic but certainly not Islamic.

In 1381 Ming armies conquered Yunnan. Eunuchs under the Ming and other dynasties often came from minority peoples and peripheral regions. After the conquest of Yunnan, the young Zheng He (then named **Ma He**) was selected for eunuch service, castrated, and given to Hongwu's fourth son, the later Emperor Yongle, who in 1380 had been given the title Prince of Yan and sent to his princely fief, located in the city (then called Beiping, now called Beijing) that he would make the capital of Ming China. Yongle "raised troops"—as the *Mingshi* puts it— in 1399 in rebellion against his nephew, the second Ming emperor **Jianwen** (born 1377, ruled 1398–1402), who was the grandson and successor of Hongwu. The reign name Jianwen means "establishing the civil," in contrast to the military overtones of Hongwu ("overflowing martial accomplishment").

Zheng He's biography refers to Jianwen as Emperor Hui ("gracious"), a posthumous title usually awarded to emperors who came to tragic ends, and in this case awarded only in 1736, well after the fall of the Ming. Yongle prevailed in his rebellion, conquered Nanjing in 1402, was acclaimed as emperor, and proclaimed the reign name Yongle ("perpetual happiness"), by which he is usually known. In 1538 Yongle's formal posthumous name was changed from Taizong ("grand ancestor"), traditional for second emperors of dynasties, to Chengzu ("perfect progenitor"). The name change suggests that later Ming rulers were uncomfortable with Yongle's effort to eradicate the memory of Jianwen, the actual second emperor of the Ming Dynasty. The achievements of Emperor Yongle included an effort to conquer Vietnam that turned into a nightmare for China, five large military expeditions into Mongolia which accomplished little, the permanent move of the Ming capital to Beijing, and the sponsorship of Zheng He's voyages. Beijing is still China's capital, and Yongle is now best remembered, at least outside of China, as Zheng He's emperor.

Zheng He's biography in the *Mingshi* begins the series of chapters on "eunuch officials," who are grouped with "flatterers and deceivers," "treacherous ministers," and "roving bandits," all intrinsically evil categories of people. For the generations of humanistically educated civil officials who actually ruled the Ming Dynasty and who compiled almost all the Chinese historical sources, the voyages led by Zheng He were departures from the proper path of government. If they were to be remembered at all, it was so their repetition should be avoided.

Yet many in Chinese society remembered the voyages in a positive light. Even though the biography of Zheng He is short, much of the information in the nine chapters of the *Mingshi* devoted to "foreign countries" was derived from the expeditions. Three accounts of the countries visited by the expeditions survive. These are the *Yingyai Shenglan* (Overall Survey of the Ocean's Shores, 1433) by **Ma Huan**, the *Xingcha Shenglan* (Overall Survey of the Star Raft, 1436) by **Fei Xin**, and the *Xiyang Fanguo Zhi* (Monograph on the Foreign Countries of the Western Ocean, 1434) by **Gong Zhen**. "Star Raft" is a literary expression for an ambassador's flagship. Ma Huan was a

Chinese Muslim from Shaoxing, near Hangzhou in the coastal province of Zhejiang; he was proficient in the Arabic that was the *lingua franca* of seafarers from South China to the African coast, and he accompanied Zheng He as an interpreter on the fourth, sixth, and seventh expeditions. Gong Zhen was a literate soldier who served as Zheng He's private secretary on the seventh expedition. Fei Xin, another literate soldier, served as a soldier in the fleet on the third, fifth, and seventh expeditions. The accounts of Gong Zhen and Fei Xin derive heavily from that of Ma Huan (often word for word), while the accounts in the *Mingshi* incorporate material from other official sources concerning the continuing diplomatic relationships of the various countries with China.

The locations and sailing directions given in these accounts are so detailed and accurate that it is possible to identify almost every place they mention with a place on a modern map. Until the Western impact of the mid-nineteenth century, Chinese geographical understanding of Southeast Asia and the lands washed by the Indian Ocean was largely informed by these accounts. Zheng He became the patron deity of the overseas Chinese communities of Southeast Asia. Zheng He is also the central character in **Luo Maodeng's** picaresque novel of 1597, *Sanbao Taijian Xia Xiyang Ji Tongsu Yanyi* (The Grand Director of the Three Treasures Goes Down to the Western Ocean), cited henceforth as *Xiyang Ji*, in which the basic plot of the fleets and their voyages is mixed with fantastic material, including an episode in which Zheng He visits the underworld. Zheng He's exploits might be remembered fondly by storytellers, but basically only as a source of marvels and wonders; in the considered opinion of elite culture, foreign countries produced only strange and useless things, which proper Chinese should avoid.

Zheng He's Voyages and Western Imperial Expansion

Modern interest in Zheng He's voyages, both inside and outside China, stems from more fundamental historical concerns. For good or ill, a new era began in Asia with the voyages of Vasco da Gama (1497–99) and Pedro Cabral (1500–01). By forceful means the Portuguese established a system of rule over the oceangoing trade in the Indian Ocean that lasted until they were ousted by the even stronger Dutch. The Spanish in the Philippines, and later the French and the British, also aimed to promote and protect their trade with naval power. While Western imperialism in Asia did not lead to such extensive displacement of the native populations as it did in the Americas, it did lead to colonial rule over much of maritime Asia that lasted until the mid-twentieth century, and to revolutionary transformation in every Asian state. And what drew the Western powers into the Indian Ocean and Southeast Asia in the first place was the wealth they could gain by controlling the seaborne trade of the region. Ming China easily established a powerful presence on the oceans from 1405 to 1433, and then it withdrew and never returned.

Had Ming China wished to continue exercising the maritime hegemony over Southeast Asia and the Indian Ocean that Zheng He's voyages seem to demonstrate, the empire certainly possessed the means. The census of 1393 recorded a population of 10,652,789 households and 60,545,812 individuals. The actual numbers were probably higher, but even the numbers that were recorded dwarf the million or so estimated for Portugal and the five million or so estimated for England in this period. Zheng He's fleet, composed of over two hundred ships crewed by more than 27,000 men (these numbers will be discussed later), was comparable in numbers to the fleets at major events in Western naval history, such as the Spanish Armada of 1588 and the combined British, French, and Spanish fleets at the battle of Trafalgar in 1805, rather than to the Spanish and Portuguese voyages of exploration that usually consisted of a few ships crewed by a few hundred men. The sizes reported for Zheng He's largest ships raised doubts when the Chinese histories were first read by Western scholars, but it is now believed that these descriptions are essentially accurate—that China built the largest wooden ships ever seen in the world. The underlying Chinese economy was also strong in the Ming period, so strong that much of the silver that flooded the world market as a consequence of the Spanish conquests in the Americas ended up in China, in payment for Chinese silk, tea, jade, "china," and other goods. Like Europe, China imported spices but not much else, and the balance of trade remained strongly in its favor. In strictly technical and quantitative terms, China was much better placed to exploit the wealth of the Eastern seas than the European powers that in the end did so. In the language of a later era of navalism, China had the ships, had the men, and had the money, too.

The contrast between China's exercise of sea power in the early Ming and the later history of China's extreme weakness at sea has strongly influenced modern scholarship on Zheng He. In the 1890s the historical studies of the American admiral and theorist Alfred Thayer Mahan created an extremely influential doctrine that related sea power to national prosperity and strength. Spain, Portugal, the Netherlands, France to a certain extent, and then Britain had sailed and fought their way to power, and Germany, Japan, and the United States were following in their wake—but on the correct course—when Mahan wrote. Zheng He's career, however it was understood, indicated that China not only had the capability to pursue a program of imperial and colonial expansion based on sea power, but it had done something like that in the early part of the Ming and had then suddenly abandoned the sea. Narratives of exploration and sea power taken from Western history thus made Zheng He's voyages more interesting, even to the Chinese, than they had ever been before.

Zheng He's Early Life and His Patron, Emperor Yongle

Zheng He was born in 1371 in Kunyang, in the central part of the southwestern province of Yunnan, across Lake Dian from the provincial capital at Kunming. His original name was Ma He, and he was one of many descendants of **Saiyid Ajall Shams al-Din** (1211–79)—"also named Umar"—a Central Asian Muslim descended from a distinguished family of Bukhara who had risen in the service of the Mongol emperors **Möngke** (born 1209, ruled 1251–59) and Khubilai. Khubilai appointed Saiyid Ajall Shams al-Din governor of Yunnan in 1274, and he served successfully as governor until his death, being followed by two of his sons, **Nasir-al-Din** and **Mas'ud**. Another son, **Bayan**, was the father of Hajji, whose son, also named Hajji, was Ma He's father. The Chinese surname Ma often indicates, as it does in this case, a Muslim family, and the name Hajji is usually added to a Muslim name after the required pilgrimage to Mecca has been accomplished. Whatever their full names were, it is reasonable to conclude that Zheng He's father and grandfather both made the pilgrimage. Zheng He came, in other words, from a devout Muslim family with a strong awareness of Islam's religious heritage, which included a religious law that prohibited castrating or enslaving Muslims. His immediate family included an older brother and four sisters.

Very little is known about Zheng He's emotions or inner life, but one thing that seems certain is the eclectic nature of his religious beliefs as an adult. His nickname Sanbao refers to the Buddhist "Three Treasures," or *Triratna*, and his inscriptions of 1431 at Liujiagang and Changle show the intensity of his devotion to the Sea Goddess **Tianfei**. This eclecticism is all the more remarkable in that he lived the first decade of his life in a probably pious Muslim environment, and he must have been aware of Islam's strict prohibition of apostasy.

Yunnan was still under Yuan Dynasty rule when Zheng He was born, and it was left alone for a decade longer as the Ming empire consolidated. Yunnan's ruler, **Basalawarmi**, Prince of Liang, was a Mongol prince descended from Khubilai, who had conquered Yunnan in the 1250s, before his own accession as emperor and his conquest of Song China. Yunnan's population consisted largely of non-Chinese ethnic groups that preferred the continuation of Mongol rule to Chinese conquest. Nevertheless, the Ming army that invaded Yunnan in the autumn of 1381 easily subdued Basalawarmi's government. Kunming fell in January 1382, Basalawarmi and his immediate retinue committed suicide, and Dali in the northwest fell in April.

Zheng He's father, Hajji, was killed (at age 39) resisting the Ming conquest, and Zheng He was taken prisoner and castrated for service as a eunuch. Soon afterward he was sent to join the household of the future Emperor Yongle, then governing Beiping, the future Beijing, with the title Prince of Yan.

Castration was often the fate of boys captured in war, and in this period of Ming history not only the immediate imperial family but also the households of princes and generals had staffs of eunuchs. In later Ming history only the emperor maintained an organization of eunuchs, by then swollen to tens of thousands, and large gangs of men who had castrated themselves in the hope of joining the eunuch household had become crime and security problems in Beijing. While it is hard to think of castration as other than traumatic, thousands of men in Ming history saw the eunuch career as a tempting route to wealth and power, and a handful of eunuchs rose to positions of such influence that officials saw them as dictators who were manipulating weak and pliant emperors. Thus Zheng He's castration made him a member of a recognized personnel category in Imperial China, rather than an outcast.

The theoretical justification of the eunuch organization was that it could wait on the empress and other palace women without the risk of its compromising the genealogical integrity of the ruling house. Most of these service functions could also be performed by the palace women themselves, who in the Ming as in other dynasties had an elaborately bureaucratized organization of their own. But eunuchs were useful because they could also serve as imperial agents outside the palace, in the empire at large. Emperors tended to trust the eunuchs who had been their childhood playmates, and sometimes their adult lovers, though in this and in every other matter that concerns eunuchs it needs to be remembered that civil officials wrote all the historical sources and were invariably hostile to eunuchs. Civil officials felt obliged to protest policies they did not approve; eunuchs were dependent on the emperor and obeyed him. Eunuchs often served as directors of important and expensive projects that civil officials opposed, and for Zheng He to command the seven great naval expeditions was a special case of this general practice.

Before the Ming conquest, Zheng He might have expected to lead the life of a member of the non-Chinese local elite of Yunnan during the Yuan Dynasty. Now, despite the injury inflicted on him, he had been transported to a position that turned out to be an intimate personal relationship with a man who would become a forceful Ming emperor. Yongle's wishes and commands turned Zheng He into the "admiral" who led seven voyages into the Indian Ocean. Understanding Zheng He's life thus requires understanding the new context in which the young eunuch grew to maturity and the nature of his patron, Emperor Yongle, in whose reign the adult eunuch spent the most productive years of his life.

The Fall of the Yuan and the Rise of the Ming to 1368

After long governing China without much regard for China's native Confucian political philosophy, the Mongol elite that ruled the Yuan Dynasty succumbed to the Confucian classics and their accompanying culture of political factionalism in the 1330s. Yuan rule in central China declined precipitously in the following decade as rebellious conspiracies proliferated.

The most important of the anti-Yuan conspiracies combined the idea of restoring the Song Dynasty (960–1276; the last native Chinese dynasty before the Mongols) with an apocalyptic form of Buddhism tinged with Manichaean beliefs. The leader of the White Lotus Society, the principal conspiratorial group, claimed descent from a Northern Song emperor whose reign (1100–25) was now remembered as a period of prosperity and culture before the barbarian invasions. The restored Song emperor would also be an earthly incarnation of Maitreya, the Buddha of the Future, whose advent would overturn the old order and bring his previously humble worshippers into positions of leadership. Maitreya was also seen as the greater King of Light *(da Ming Wang)*, the head of the forces of light in their eternal struggle with darkness. Manichaean doctrine held that the appearance of the greater King of Light would be preceded by the appearance of a lesser King of Light *(xiao Ming Wang)*. These doctrines may not have had much logical coherence, but they existed together in the interior of China in the mid-1300s, and their combination was emotionally compelling.

White Lotus adherents were numerous among the workers mobilized in 1351 for the Grand Canal project, which triggered their rebellion. The rebels wore red headbands, so they were called Red Turbans (*Hongjin* in Chinese; translating "headband" as "turban" is misleading but conventional). The scope of their rebellion took the Yuan authorities by surprise. The rebels overran most of the lower Yangtze region north of the river, conquered Sichuan province, and threatened much of North China, even holding Kaifeng, the old Song capital, for a time. The Red Turban movement was also the arena in which Hongwu, the first Ming emperor, fought his way to power. He appears in 1352 as the leader of a band recruited from his native village, joining a more important Red Turban leader who gave him an adopted daughter as his wife. (She became the mother of Yongle.) After a year of fighting that included the betrayal of the heir of his deceased patron, Hongwu had more than 10,000 men under his command.

In 1355 Hongwu and his followers crossed the Yangtze, and in the following year they captured the city now known as Nanjing. After more than a decade of warfare against rival contenders for rule, Hongwu proclaimed himself emperor early in 1368. Calling his dynasty Ming (meaning "light," as opposed to dark) was his sole concession to a Red Turban past that he was determined to put behind him.

The Reign of Emperor Hongwu, 1368–98

Neither the institutions nor the policies of the new Ming Dynasty were rigidly set in its early years, and what they became had a lot to do with the wishes of the first Ming emperor, an autocratic and suspicious personality who did not tolerate opposition. Ming China eventually came to be dominated by the educated Confucian literati or gentry class, with little challenge from any other social group, and it is tempting to see this development as inevitable in a Chinese-ruled dynasty. Yet the Red Turban movement from which the Ming had emerged had been viewed with hostility and suspicion by most of the educated Confucian class, and the actual creation of the empire was the work of an army whose expectations derived from the familiar Yuan Dynasty military model rather than from more distant Chinese examples. In foreign policy the Yuan emperors had ruled Mongolia and Xinjiang and had dominated Tibet, other parts of Central Asia, and Korea, and they had attempted conquests in other areas. Would the new Ming Dynasty try to rule all of these territories, and to continue the expansive policies of the Yuan?

With regard to Mongolia and Central Asia, at first the answer seemed to be yes. The last Yuan emperor fled from his capital, which the Ming renamed Beiping ("the North has been Pacified"), and he took the Yuan imperial seal into exile with him. But the Yuan Dynasty retained the loyalty of the army that had defeated the Red Turban rebels in North China, and in 1372 this army decisively defeated a Ming effort to conquer Outer Mongolia. This defeat caused Emperor Hongwu to shift to a defensive policy along the northern frontier until 1385. Limited offensives then resumed, only to be terminated abruptly by a new round of purges in the Ming leadership that began in 1393. Afterward a defensive stance resumed that lasted until Hongwu's death in 1398.

In 1378, as he began to create a permanent line of defense along the northern frontier, Hongwu placed his second and third sons in command of troops as the princes of Qin (Shensi) and Jin (Shanxi), respectively. In 1380 he sent his fourth son, the future Yongle, to Beiping as Prince of Yan, and the following year the newly castrated 10-year-old Ma He became part of Yongle's household. After a Muslim childhood under Mongol rule, the future Zheng He spent the next two decades on the northern frontier, growing up to be a large and powerful soldier and earning his prince's confidence and trust.

Hongwu decided to limit Ming ambitions in the north because of military defeat in 1372, but his decision not to expand overseas had occurred even before then and was not the result of a setback—indeed, he made this decision at a time when China was unchallengeable at sea. In 1371 the emperor stated that "foreign countries beyond the seas that are not harming China should not be attacked without cause," and in the guidance he provided to his successors (the "Imperial Ming Ancestral Injunctions," or *Huang Ming Zuxun*) he left a list of fifteen countries that future Ming emperors should not attempt to conquer. The first four of them were Korea (here called *Chaoxian* or Chosŏn, reflecting the establishment of the Yi Dynasty in 1392), Japan, and the Greater and Lesser Ryūkyū Islands, all of which were traditional tributary countries; the fifth was Vietnam (here called *Annan*, "the pacified south"), which Emperor Yongle later tried to conquer despite his father's injunction. Most of the remaining ten countries would be on Zheng He's itinerary: **Cambodia, Thailand,** Champa (the Hindu kingdom in present-day southern Vietnam), Semudera (*Sumendala*, on the north coast of Sumatra), the Indian Ocean (*Xiyang*, meaning the Western Ocean, not a country in the strict sense), **Java** (*Zhaowa*, the Empire of Majapahit in central and eastern Java), **Pahang** in Malaya, **Pajajaran** (*Baihua*, in western Java), *Sanfoqi* (the fallen Indonesian Empire of Shri Vijaya, centered at Palembang in southern Sumatra), and **Brunei** in Borneo. In the Confucian context of Ming politics, the first Ming emperor's injunction against attacking these countries had great force as an argument against Zheng He's expeditions.

Emperor Hongwu's rise to the throne had depended on his army. He had originally raised a small band from his native area and with it had joined a Red Turban warlord. By the time he crossed the Yangtze in 1355 he had taken over most of his original patron's followers and had been joined by others, including fishermen who formed the core of his navy. By 1360 Hongwu controlled perhaps 250,000 soldiers organized in "wings" whose commanders reported to him directly. Eight of these wings were located in Nanjing and included the forces Hongwu commanded when he took the field in person.

In 1364, to accommodate the influx of surrendered soldiers resulting from the victory over his principal rival, Hongwu reorganized his military system. Each wing became a guard (*wei*), theoretically of 5,600 soldiers, plus officers, divided into five battalions. There were also independent garrison battalions not belonging to any guard. All military ranks from guard commander down were hereditary. The common soldiers also had a hereditary military obligation, and for census purposes they were enrolled on a military register distinct from the civilian register on which most of the population was enrolled.

To command his major armies Hongwu relied on his nobility of merit. This was a group of about three dozen men who received the title duke or marquis in the early years (mostly in 1368–70) of the dynasty. The senior duke who headed the list was the first Ming chancellor or head of the civil administration. The other six dukes and all of the marquises were military commanders. Most of these nobles were Hongwu's childhood friends from his native area who had formed his original band.

In 1380 a political explosion affected Zheng He's later life and the course of the Ming Dynasty in many ways. The emperor executed his chief minister, Chancellor Hu Weiyong, and many others accused of involvement with him, along with their families. The list of the guilty continued to grow through the 1380s and 1390s, and posthumous conviction could exterminate a deceased offender's living heirs. Allegedly 30,000 people perished in the Hu Weiyong case, and 15,000 more in the second round of purges that began in 1393. Even though the general accusation against Hu Weiyong—organizing factions among the officials and conspiring with foreigners to assassinate the emperor—was stated in various ways, it is not clear what specifically Hu Weiyong was suspected of plotting, and there is no way of judging his guilt or innocence.

In response to the Hu Weiyong case, Hongwu abolished the office of chancellor and ordered the death penalty for anyone who proposed reestablishing it. He took direct control of the principal offices of the central government, he divided the army command among five headquarters of equal rank, and he established three coequal authorities in each province. In principle he was the only person in the empire who knew everything that was happening, as long as he could keep up the pace of reading the reports and memoranda.

Also in 1380 Hongwu sent his fourth son, the future Yongle, already Prince of Yan, to "go to his fief" (*zhiguo*, a standard rite of passage for the younger sons of emperors) and to take up residence in Beijing, at this time still Beiping, the name it had been given in 1368 after the Ming conquest. Yan was the classical name for what is now the province of Hebei; Yongle, as Prince of Yan, thus joined his elder brothers, the princes of Qin and Jin, on the northern border. Earlier in the 1370s Hongwu had indicated that he would follow the traditional practice of enfeoffing his younger sons as "hedges" (*fan*, also translated as "fief") for the main imperial line, leaving no doubt that these princes would be part of his system of rule as they grew up. But since he began in 1380 to eliminate the dukes and marquises who had constituted the nobility of merit, the princes ended up as the primary instruments through which the aging emperor commanded his armies.

Whatever trauma his castration may have induced, Zheng He recovered from it and grew up in the 1380s and 1390s as an increasingly favored member of Yongle's retinue. The prince was eleven years older than Zheng He, but both were then comparatively young. Yongle's position at Beiping involved him in conflicts with the often hostile Mongol tribes in the vicinity, and he grew to enjoy the hard life of campaigning on horseback on the Mongolian steppe. Zheng He participated in these campaigns, winning the confidence of his master as a brave soldier and a capable leader. He also grew up physically. "When he entered adulthood, he reportedly became seven feet tall and had a

明 成 祖 真 像

帝名棣太祖四子
國陵永樂在位二十年

This formal portrait of Yongle makes him look exactly
as a Chinese emperor should. © ChinaStock

waist about five feet in circumference. His cheeks and forehead
were high but his nose was small. He had glaring eyes and a
voice as loud as a huge bell (or gong). He knew a great deal
about warfare and was well accustomed to battle." The "foot,"
or *chi*, referred to here was probably between 10.5 and 12 inches
in length.

Hongwu's eldest son had died in 1392, leaving his own ado-
lescent son, the future emperor Jianwen, as the new crown
prince. The later deaths of the princes of Qin and Jin left Yongle
as the oldest surviving son when Hongwu finally succumbed
(24 June 1398). Meanwhile the extermination of the original
Ming leadership elite continued, gaining new momentum in 1393.
As only a handful of military nobles remained alive, Hongwu
assigned still more military authority to his enfeoffed sons, especially to Yongle and the others stationed on the northern

frontier. At the same time, in the last rendition (1395) of the
"Imperial Ming Ancestral Injunctions" that he had issued in
1380 as his first group of sons were going to their fiefs, he imposed new restrictions on the princes. They were now prohibited from visiting one another or appointing their own officials.
Having ruled China with great success since 1368, Emperor
Hongwu died leaving the basic structure of military command
in a state of uncertainty and instability, and leaving the succession to the throne open to manipulation.

Civil War, 1398–1402

After his seizure of the throne in 1402, Emperor Yongle ordered
the revision of the "Veritable Records," or *shilu* ("true record" is
a more literal translation), of the two preceding reigns, the basic
source material from which the official history of the dynasty
would eventually be written. Denying his nephew's legitimacy
as emperor, Yongle incorporated the events of the Jianwen reign
into the material that eventually became the *Taizong Shilu*, covering his own reign. Yongle's version of the *Taizu Shilu*, covering
his father's reign, the third rendition and the only one that survives, includes a number of suggestions that Hongwu intended
to name Yongle as his heir but somehow never got around to it.
In the summer of 1392, soon after his eldest brother's death,
Yongle came to Nanjing, and it is possible to imagine him lobbying his father for the succession. Nevertheless, at this stage in
the development of the Ming Dynasty it was highly unlikely
that the normal Chinese pattern of succession to the eldest son
or his heir would be set aside. Principled Confucian scholars
consistently argued strongly for the rights of the eldest son or
his heirs, and against any deviation from the natural order of
birth. Succession based firmly on primogeniture, after all, was
one way of distinguishing Chinese from the Mongols and other
barbarians, and in 1392 Yongle still had two living elder brothers. After four tense months, Emperor Hongwu designated his
grandson Jianwen as the new crown prince.

Now Jianwen was emperor, advised by a group of perhaps
overly theoretical Confucian scholar officials. The new emperor

ordered his uncles, the princes, many of whom were in command of troops, not to attend their father's funeral. When Yongle marched south with his princely guard, the emperor deployed an army to stop him. By the end of summer the emperor and his advisers had embarked on the policy of "wasting the feudatories" suggested by early Han history and probably inevitable in the circumstances of 1398. "Wasting the feudatories" meant depriving fiefholders of their territorial authority and rule. In 1398 the only fiefholders, apart from a single military noble in Yunnan, were the princes who were the new emperor's uncles and cousins. The principality of Yan was sealed off while the emperor took action against princes he considered weaker. In August 1399 Yongle moved into open rebellion, issuing a manifesto that quoted the "Ancestral Injunctions" as giving a prince the right to come to Nanjing to "suppress difficulties" caused by deceitful ministers.

The resulting civil war was long-lasting (until July 1402) and hard-fought. After the first imperial commander in chief suffered defeat, the second raised an even larger army and laid siege to Beiping. Defeated there in December 1399, in a battle in which Zheng He had a prominent part, he raised another army, only to lose it in an invasion of Shanxi. The imperial forces recovered under a third commander in chief, who inflicted defeats on Yongle's forces and forced them onto the defensive in Beiping and its vicinity during 1400 and 1401. Late in 1401 Yongle gave way to something like despair, lamenting that after years of fighting, he controlled only the three prefectures around Beiping. Nevertheless, disunity among the supporters of Emperor Jianwen meant that his armies were less strong than they appeared. In January 1402 Yongle moved swiftly southward and defeated the forces still loyal to his nephew. On 3 July he crossed the Yangtze near Zhenjiang, aided by the defection of the river fleet commander **Chen Xuan** (1365–1433), afterward a major naval figure as Earl of Pingjiang. Aided by other defectors, including one of the former imperial commanders in chief, the Prince of Yan entered Nanjing on 13 July and—with feigned reluctance—accepted the elevation to emperor four days later.

Yongle's Reign as Emperor, 1402–24

During the tumult of the rebel entry into Nanjing, fire broke out in the imperial palace compound, and Emperor Jianwen was never seen again. Eventually two charred corpses were identified as the late emperor and empress and buried, but rumors that Jianwen had somehow survived and escaped began immediately, and sightings were reported down to the 1440s. Yongle began his reign with a purge of the scholar officials who had supported Jianwen that led to more than a thousand executions. Despite this unpromising beginning, throughout his reign Yongle actively promoted the ascendancy of Confucian scholar officials within the Ming government, even as he carried out activities that those officials disapproved. His agents for carrying out these activities were military officers and eunuchs.

Hongwu ordered that eunuchs were to be kept few and illiterate, and prohibited from involvement in government affairs. In fact, throughout his reign he kept adding to the numbers of eunuchs and raising the ranks of their leaders. In 1384 he created the Directorate of Ceremonial, the most important of the eunuch offices called the "twelve directorates." A reorganization in 1395 created the last of these directorates, which endured until the end of the dynasty. One of the twelve was the Directorate of Palace Servants, which functioned as a kind of physical plant department for the inner palace and had more personnel than any other directorate. Immediately on becoming emperor, Yongle made Zheng He Grand Director (*taijian*) of this agency. He now wore a red robe, in contrast to the blue worn by lower ranking eunuchs, and while his rank was not high (4a, corresponding to a prefect or mid-level administrator in the civil service), it was the highest rank a eunuch could aspire to, and regular direct contact with the emperor gave Zheng He an importance beyond his formal rank.

During the siege of Beiping by the imperial forces in 1399, Zheng He, then still Ma He, had distinguished himself commanding the troops defending one of the city's reservoirs, the Zheng Village Dike. In the later popular tradition, at least, his successful defense was a major factor in the success of the rebel counterattack. This episode cannot be found in the account of

In contrast to the standard heroic image of Zheng He that emphasizes his height and girth, this representation makes him look like a conventional Chinese official; only his lack of a beard identifies him as a eunuch. Zheng He's actual appearance is unknown. © ChinaStock

the siege in the Veritable Records, but there is no doubt that the compilers of these records were hostile or indifferent to the memory of Zheng He. In any event, on New Year's Day, 11 February 1404, Emperor Yongle conferred the surname Zheng on Ma He in commemoration of his role in the battle.

Yongle's "relentless pursuit of power, prestige and glory are apparent throughout the story of his extraordinary life," according to his most recent biographer. In addition to the literary and cultural glory involved in the creation of the great encyclopedia *Yongle Dadian*, the sort of activity of which the educated class approved, Yongle promoted four major projects with the common theme of expansion, all of which the official class criticized. Two of them—Zheng He's voyages and the Vietnam war—took place in the south, and the other two—the transfer of the capital to Beijing and the five Mongolian campaigns—were in the north. The logistical needs of both the new capital and the Mongolian campaigns led to the revival of the Grand Canal. Civil officials opposed this agenda even while Yongle was alive, and after his death they made a general effort to reverse it: there were no more Mongolian campaigns, Vietnam was abandoned in 1427, and from 1424 to 1441 moving the capital back to Nanjing remained official policy under three emperors. Zheng He's last voyage, in 1431–33, took place only because of the personal interest of the then emperor, Yongle's grandson Xuande. Zheng He's expeditions thus took place as part of a broad pattern of activity initiated by Emperor Yongle and opposed by his civil officials.

Other than the Zheng He voyages, Yongle's major initiative in the south was the war in Vietnam, called Annam under the Trần Dynasty (1225–1400) that had successfully resisted the Mongol invasions. In 1400 a usurper seized the throne and killed most of the Trần princes. In 1403 he petitioned Yongle for recognition of his son as king, which the emperor granted. In 1404 a Trần pretender arrived in Nanjing, and Yongle reversed himself, ordering the usurper to step aside in favor of the Trần prince. Whether or not the pretender was genuine, his murder at Lang-s'on in early 1406 on his return to Vietnam was a clear defiance of imperial authority. Later that year Yongle sent a powerful army into Vietnam, which captured the usurper and his son on 16 June 1407. In the absence of a plausible Trần claimant, Yongle decided to annex Annam, making it a province under its old Han and Tang designation, Jiaozhi. Ming forces crushed local resistance during the next year.

The biography of Zheng He in the *Mingshi* notes the "agitation" of other foreign countries at the Ming invasion of Vietnam, and it is important that the first port of call for all of Zheng He's voyages was Qui Nhon, now in Vietnam but then the port city nearest to the capital of the kingdom of Champa, Vietnam's traditional rival to the south. After Zheng He's voyages were long over, and after the Ming acknowledged the failure of their attempt to conquer Vietnam, the most powerful of the Lê kings conquered and annexed Champa in 1471. Zheng He's voyages thus fit into a period of international relations in which China was hostile to, and often in occupation of, Vietnam and correspondingly friendly to Champa. "Brown water" naval operations along the coast were the key to the initial Ming success in the Vietnam war, but Zheng He's fleet was not directly involved.

During the years in which Zheng He led his first six voyages to the Western Ocean, Emperor Yongle spent increasing amounts of time in the north (1409–10, 1413–16, and from 1417 until his death in 1424). Yongle promoted the rebuilding and expansion of Beijing, designating it the primary imperial capital in 1421. To supply grain to the capital, and to support Yongle's military campaigns against the Mongols, the Grand Canal was reopened (partially in 1411, completely in 1415). Until the canal was reopened, oceangoing transport of grain to Beijing was badly disrupted by storms and piracy, even during this period when Zheng He's fleet was projecting Chinese power in the Indian Ocean.

Like the Zheng He voyages and the invasion of Vietnam, the rebuilding of Beijing, the reopening of the Grand Canal, and the emperor's five campaigns against the Mongols (1410, 1414, 1422, 1423, and 1424) were expensive projects that required the mobilization of enormous resources—and the Mongolian campaigns were fruitless. The defeat of a large Ming army in 1409 provoked the emperor to lead the 1410 campaign in person. The announcement (6 August 1421) of a third campaign led to protests directed at the costs of all the emperor's projects. Yongle responded by imprisoning Minister of Finance Xia Yuanji and others, and by suspending the Zheng He voyages—in principle, temporarily—while still insisting on the third Mongolian campaign. By the time of his death (12 August 1424) during the fifth campaign, Yongle seems to have decided that waging war in Mongolia was more important than further voyages by Zheng He's fleet.

Nonofficial accounts state that Yongle was in poor health in his final years, having had several strokes. Allegedly he was taking an elixir prescribed by Daoist practitioners; since such elixirs usually contained combinations of arsenic, lead, and mercury, the medication may have worsened his condition. He is now remembered as the emperor who sent Zheng He on his voyages, and if not for them he would be remembered as the emperor who built a new imperial capital at Beijing. These were expensive undertakings, as were the campaigns in Mongolia and the war in Vietnam. In Vietnam the rebel Lê leader took a royal title in 1418, and the military situation worsened with the death from disease of the Chinese commander in chief on 5 February 1422, but it is not clear how aware Yongle was of the situation in the extreme south of the empire. No one has been able to demonstrate a tangible benefit to the Ming empire resulting from the campaigns in Vietnam and Mongolia.

Evaluation of Zheng He's voyages must be similarly tentative. Zheng He's fleet was an armed incursion into a Southeast Asian and Indian Ocean world of relatively weak states long linked by established patterns of trade, yet Emperor Yongle ordered Zheng He's voyages merely to display his power and to force them to comply with the Chinese tributary system, goals that did not include either the promotion of trade or the establishment of Chinese colonies. It is difficult to discover any long-term benefit to China, or indeed any long-term consequences for China, deriving from the voyages.

III

China and the Asian Maritime World in the Time of Zheng He

The modern idea of Zheng He as an explorer is largely a creation of Western scholarship. Zheng He's fleet was actually an armada, in the sense that it carried a powerful army that could be disembarked, and its purpose was to awe the rulers of Southeast Asia and the Indian Ocean into sending tribute to China. Foreign tributary missions enhanced the legitimacy of the Chinese emperor and received rich gifts in return, yet most of the states visited by Zheng He's fleet sent tribute only under compulsion, and they ceased to do so after the voyages ended.

Zheng He's fleet operated within the equatorial and subtropical waters of the South China Sea and the Indian Ocean, sailing long-established trade routes that were themselves constrained by the annual cycle of alternating monsoon winds. In Java, Sumatra, and the Malay Peninsula the Chinese fleet became a new power factor in a Malay-Indonesian world whose previous evolution had disturbed Yongle's father, Emperor Hongwu. In Ceylon and Southern India Zheng He's fleet also changed the local balance of power, and by making the sea routes safe for trade it also made tributary embassies possible.

The Purpose of Zheng He's Voyages

Zheng He's fleet traveled as far west as the eastern coast of Africa on its last three voyages, bringing back giraffes and other African animals to present to the Chinese emperor. Most people who are only slightly familiar with Zheng He's voyages associate them with Africa. J. J. L. Duyvendak's books *Ma Huan Re-Examined* (1933) and especially *China's Discovery of Africa* (1949) reinforced that association and provided the implicit interpretation that Zheng He's voyages were primarily voyages of exploration.

Joseph Needham, in his influential multivolume *Science and Civilization in China*, forcefully expressed the idea that Zheng He's voyages were voyages not merely of exploration but of peaceful exploration. The Ming "was the greatest age of maritime exploration in Chinese history" due entirely to Zheng He's fleet, which "ranged far and wide in the South Seas and the Indian Ocean, greatly adding to Chinese geographical knowledge and bringing back all kinds of rarities to the imperial court." He goes on to say, emotionally, that much of this knowledge was "burnt and destroyed by administrative thugs in the service of the Confucian anti-maritime party," language that imposes an anachronistic interpretation on the sources. Needham then contrasts the allegedly peaceful nature of Zheng He's voyages with the excessively violent behavior of later Portuguese explorers, whose contrast with the Chinese "is an extraordinary one, for while the entire Chinese operations were those of a navy paying friendly visits to foreign ports, the Portuguese east of Suez engaged themselves in total war." Zheng He's fleets "could count on the co-operation of local rulers when they needed to careen, caulk, or even build, when far from home," Needham believes, though our discussion of Zheng He's ships (Chapter VI) will show that the largest ships could not be careened and could only be drydocked in Nanjing, where they had been built. He goes on to say that "on all their expeditions there were only three occasions when they got into difficulties and had to fight."

Two of those occasions on which the Chinese had to fight were on Sumatra, and in both cases the Chinese were the attackers. On the other occasion, in Ceylon, the Chinese were attacked after landing forces to coerce a ruler who had been difficult on a previous voyage. The emphasis given to these three conflicts (described in Chapters IV and V) in the sources indicates that the Chinese saw the three battles as major accomplishments of Zheng He's fleet, rather than as incidental exceptions to a career of peaceful exploration. In his inscriptions Zheng He brags that on each of his seven voyages he has commanded "several myriads of government troops and over a hundred big ships." Such an armada, appearing literally out of the blue before the capital of a small state in the Indian Ocean, must have been a terrifying apparition, one that in most cases allowed Zheng He to accomplish the traditional goal of Chinese military science, that of subduing the enemy without fighting.

The concept of the peaceful nature of Zheng He's voyages has become a useful tool for contemporary Chinese foreign policy. In the summer of 2004, as part of a general diplomatic theme of "China's peaceful rise," the government of the People's Republic of China publicized plans for the lavish commemoration of the six hundredth anniversary of the start of the first voyage in 2005. Since Zheng He's voyages were peaceful and did not result in the building of a Chinese colonial empire, China's neighbors have nothing to fear from the rise of contemporary China's economic and military power—or so the Chinese leadership argues.

Joseph Needham and the contemporary Chinese leadership certainly overstate the peaceful nature of Zheng He's voyages, but most of those who have written about the voyages have also assumed that they were voyages of exploration. In January 2003 a major press published *1421: The Year China Discovered America*, the researches of Commander Gavin Menzies, R.N., who believes he has found evidence showing that at least part of the fleet on the sixth voyage in 1421–22 (for which there is positive evidence that it divided into squadrons that went to different destinations) went southwest from Northern Sumatra, crossed the Indian Ocean, passed south of Madagascar, rounded the Cape of Good Hope, continued across the South Atlantic, and then, passing nearer to Antarctica than to Cape Horn, went up the western coast of South America before returning to China by sailing westward across the Pacific along the line of the Equator. These ideas will have to clear various hurdles before they are generally accepted; that they can be advanced at all is due to the general belief that exploration was the principal objective of the voyages.

J. V. G. Mills, in a section of his book in which he acknowledges his debt to Needham, nonetheless comes close to the truth when he states that "though an explorer, Cheng Ho [Zheng He] did not discover anything which had not been known to Indonesians, Indians, or Arabs for over a thousand years." Or to the Chinese, one might add, for several hundred years, since Chinese merchant ships had been sailing in the Indian Ocean for centuries, and after the Mongol conquest of China government fleets made expeditions to Java and Ceylon. Marco Polo's account of his voyage from China to Iran describes travel across the South China Sea, through the Straits of Malacca, across the Indian Ocean to Ceylon and the Malabar Coast of India, and then up the Arabian Sea and the Gulf of Oman to Hormuz. Zheng He's expeditions each followed all or some of this well-known and often traveled route.

The first (1405–07), second (1407–09), and third (1409–11) voyages each took essentially the same route. The fleet sailed from Fujian with the winter monsoon from the northeast, and it stopped first in Champa, now the southern part of Vietnam but then an independent Hindu kingdom. From Champa the fleet sailed across the South China Sea to Java and Sumatra. Palembang in Sumatra—meaningfully called the Old Harbor (*Jiugang*) in the Chinese sources—had been the seat of **Shri Vijaya**, the Indonesian island empire that had prospered through its trade with China. On the first voyage, Zheng He brought Palembang to order, creating a unique and exceptional, if temporary, form of Chinese colonial rule there. By then Palembang's previous ruling family had migrated to Malacca on the Malay Peninsula, and Malacca grew during the period of Zheng He's voyages into a trade center comparable to what Palembang had been.

After leaving Palembang, the fleet sailed up the Straits of Malacca to the northern end of Sumatra. Shipping assembled there before making the voyage to Ceylon. This voyage might involve two to four weeks of sailing out of sight of land. From Ceylon the fleet went up the Malabar Coast of India, where the major trading kingdom was Calicut. The fleet remained in the Indian Ocean, its doings unfortunately never documented, through the summer monsoon and the following winter monsoon, and then spread sail to return to China on the warm winds from the southwest of the next summer monsoon. This itinerary was identical for the first three voyages, and the two-year monsoon-dependent pattern of sailing was the rule for all of the voyages except the sixth (1421–22).

On the first voyage Zheng He's armada, with more than 27,000 mostly military personnel, destroyed the pirate fleet of **Chen Zuyi**, which had been preying on merchant shipping from its base in Palembang. More than five thousand pirates were killed and their chief was brought to China for execution. Zheng He's personnel received precisely graded rewards from the emperor for this success. On the third voyage Zheng He's forces were attacked by the possibly more numerous forces (said to be 50,000 men) of the King of Ceylon, who is said to have been committing piracy on ships of neighboring kingdoms that were carrying tribute goods to China. Zheng He was victorious at considerable cost, and the extensive scale of the rewards later conferred on his men confirms that this was the hardest-fought of the three campaigns that Zheng He commanded during the course of his voyages. Both the destruction of Chen Zuyi and the war in Ceylon had as implied objectives the control and protection of the sea lanes through which tributary missions came to China. This was also true of the brief campaign against the northern Sumatran pretender Sekandar during the fourth voyage (1413–15). This was the least difficult of the three campaigns, but again Zheng He's men received rewards from the emperor. The orders conferring the rewards provide valuable information about the personnel of the fleet.

In the fourth voyage the fleet traced the path to Calicut taken by the first three voyages and then went further, to Hormuz. This was hardly exploration, since Hormuz was the great trading center of its region, the place where the maritime trade of the Indian Ocean met the caravan trade from Central Asia and the Middle East. It is only on the fifth voyage (1417–19) that exploration seems to be taking place: the fleet sails as far as **Aden** on the southern coast of the Arabian peninsula and visits four locations in Africa. Three of them (Mogadishu, Brava, and *Zhubu* on the Juba River, all in present-day Somalia) have entries in the *Mingshi* that indicate their locations with precision. The fourth African location is Malindi in present-day Kenya, and Malindi was the country of origin of the giraffes that were identified with the mythical *qilin* beast when they were presented as tribute. Malindi's location is so vaguely stated in the *Mingshi* ("a long way from China") that one is left wondering if any of Zheng He's ships actually sailed that far, but Zheng He's biography does include it among the countries he visited. The hastily executed sixth voyage (1421–22) sailed under the shadow of the "temporary" suspension of the voyages ordered by Emperor Yongle in 1421. While detached squadrons went to more distant places (certainly to Aden), the main fleet may have gone no further than Calicut.

Yongle's successor, Emperor Hongxi, ordered in 1424 that the temporary suspension of the treasure voyages be made permanent, but his successor, Emperor Xuande, ordered one more voyage for old times' sake, regretting that the tribute-bearing ambassadors from the colorful countries of the Western Ocean were no longer coming to China. Xuande, like his grandfather Yongle, was fond of exotic luxuries and willing to rely on eunuchs to obtain them. Had he lived longer, there might have been more treasure voyages, even after Zheng He was no longer alive to lead them. But Xuande's premature death placed the control of the Ming court under his mother, the grand dowager empress, ruling on behalf of her grandson, the little boy who was the new Ming emperor. The grand dowager empress agreed with the Confucian civil official element that had always opposed the voyages on the grounds of their expense and their eunuch leadership. In any event Zheng He and his aging associates obviously saw the seventh voyage (1431–33) as their last, and the inscriptions they wrote on the stone steles erected at Changle and Liujiagang in 1431 have the strong sense of a career being summed up and an age passing. The main fleet on the seventh voyage did not explore but followed the familiar route of the fourth: Champa, Java, Palembang, Malacca, Semudera in northern Sumatra, Ceylon, Calicut, and Hormuz. Detached squadrons went to other locations, including Mogadishu and Brava in

Africa and Aden in Arabia. According to Ma Huan, seven men, possibly including Ma Huan himself, took passage to **Mecca**, most likely in a Calicut ship. The seventh voyage is the only occasion in which Chinese ships may have sailed to (the port of) Mecca, but even if the ship carrying the seven travelers was Chinese, this would hardly be exploration: the location of Mecca was familiar to Muslims everywhere, including those in China, and the travel by sea of Muslim pilgrims to Mecca had been going on for centuries. The names of both Zheng He's father and grandfather indicate that they made that pilgrimage, though there is no evidence for the route they took.

The voyages of Zheng He's treasure ships thus had very little connection with exploration, but there is an important caveat to that generalization. Just as Chinese shipbuilding techniques appear to have been passed from master to apprentice by word of mouth and by hands-on training, so also the long history of Chinese merchant shipping and trade with Southeast Asia and the countries of the Indian Ocean has left little trace in the Chinese written sources. While Zheng He's voyages were not approved of by the men who wrote the records, they were nonetheless noted in those records, as merchant voyages were not. Zheng He's inscriptions, and the accounts of his voyages and of the foreign countries visited by his fleet in the other Chinese sources, are thus also silent testimony to the extent and duration of the Chinese maritime activity in these waters before the time of Zheng He.

If the idea that exploration was the purpose of Zheng He's voyages is a modern Western myth, the actual goals of the voyages were stated clearly by the Qing Dynasty historians who compiled the *Mingshi* in a few sentences that deserve a closer reading. After mentioning Yongle's fear that his nephew, Emperor Jianwen, had "fled beyond the sea"—possibly a factor at the start of the voyages, but diminishing in importance as the Yongle reign progressed—Zheng He's biography states that Yongle "wanted to display his soldiers in strange lands in order to make manifest the wealth and power of the Middle Kingdom." In order to carry out this mission Zheng He's fleet "went in succession to the various foreign countries, proclaiming the edicts of the Son of Heaven and giving gifts to their rulers and chieftains. Those who did not submit were pacified by force." This is a concise statement of the

Chinese tributary system that was the theoretical basis for the conduct of foreign relations by Chinese imperial dynasties. Foreign rulers were to recognize the unique and superior status of the Chinese emperor as the Son of Heaven and the mediator between Heaven, earth, and mankind. They were to show this recognition by presenting tribute in the local products of their countries and by accepting and using the Chinese official calendar, at least in their communications with China. In return the emperor would give them presents—Chinese silk goods and paper money are the items most often mentioned in Zheng He's time— and would issue imperial edicts appointing them monarchs of the countries they already ruled. The sight of the "wealth and power" represented by Zheng He's armada helped foreign rulers to make up their minds. The Rasulids of Aden were a respectable regional power with their seven or eight thousand well-drilled soldiers, but this number was dwarfed by Zheng He's 27,000 men. But sometimes the recalcitrant had to be "pacified by force." Needham translates this passage as though only the threat of force is meant, but the prominence given to the military actions in both the biography and the two inscriptions refutes that interpretation.

The tributary system was often no more than a thin cover for trade, in that foreign merchants, especially the Muslim traders who were ubiquitous along both the Central Asian caravan routes and the southern sea lanes, often posed as envoys in order to engage in trade. Most Chinese officials trained in the Confucian tradition considered this practice an abuse and tried to stop it when they detected it. Personnel of Zheng He's fleet were also engaged in straightforward commercial operations, demonstrated by the cutting of the incense logs on the island of **Pulau Sembilan** in 1409. One Chinese naval historian argued that the voyages may have been profitable in the commercial sense. China had plenty of cheap silk and paper money, and it could afford to build the ships. The Qing historians, however, are unambiguous in their judgment. "The goods and treasures without name that he acquired were too many to be accounted for, yet they did not make up for the wasteful expenditures of the Middle Kingdom." That is as near as we will ever come to a balance sheet, and this conclusion is probably correct. Emperor Yongle seems to have initiated his grand projects without any consideration of their cost, and the opposition of responsible officials to these projects stemmed from their cost as well as from ideological factors.

Zheng He's voyages put into effect an imperial decision to extend the tributary system by naval means to the states of Southeast Asia and the Indian Ocean, regardless of cost. The voyages were not the product of lobbying by a maritime industry interested in promoting trade and colonization, as would be the case in certain Western European countries a century later. The sources permit speculation, but no firm conclusions, as to why Yongle decided on this course. But imperial support explains why the voyages commenced, and withdrawal of imperial support explains why they ended.

Patterns of Trade in the Indian Ocean and the South China Sea

Zheng He's seven voyages all took his fleet through the South China Sea and into the Indian Ocean to Ceylon and southern India, and the later voyages reached the Persian Gulf, the Red Sea, and the coast of Africa. All of the voyages were within waters dominated by the seasonal pattern of monsoon winds. From December to March, high pressure over Central Asia produces cold, dry winds that blow from the north and the northeast and give the winter monsoon the alternative name of northeast monsoon. This weather pattern reverses itself usually in April, when winds laden with water vapor arise in the subequatorial waters of the Indian Ocean. Blowing northward in a generally circular pattern, they approach India and Southeast Asia from the south or southwest, giving the April to August summer monsoon the alternative name of southwest monsoon.

The general predictability of the monsoons has been an important factor in human society in India and Southeast Asia for millennia. The wait for the summer monsoon is always a cause for anxiety. If the monsoon is on time and brings sufficient rain, the harvest will be adequate; if it is late or too dry, people will suffer. Predictable monsoon winds also aided navigation. With latitude calculated fairly easily from stellar observations, predictable monsoon winds gave navigators the confidence to sail

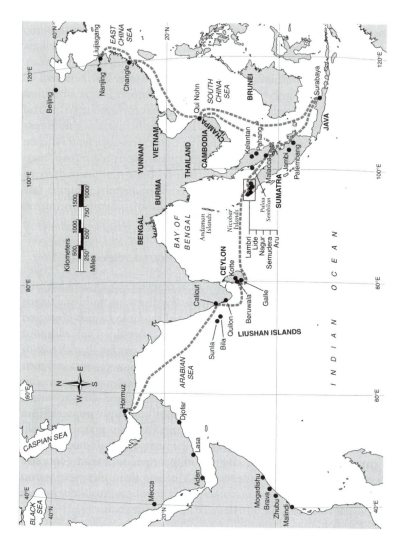

straight from the southern Arabian peninsula to the west coast of India, or from Ceylon and southern India to Sumatra and the Malay Peninsula, following a particular latitude line. Well before the rise of Islam, Arabs from the southern part of the peninsula had discovered this secret, and they were joined on the ocean by Tamils from southern India and Indonesians from

Sumatra and other islands. This trade contributed to the rise of Hindu and Buddhist kingdoms in Indonesia and Southeast Asia, and later to the spread of Islam to Malaya and Indonesia.

Trade goods distributed through this system at various times have included Chinese silks, teas, and porcelains for export, cloves from the Halmaheras, pepper from Java and Sumatra, cinnamon from Ceylon, cotton goods from India, gold, silver, pearls, coral, amber, ivory, and rhinoceros horns (the latter is still valued in Chinese medicines), camphor, frankincense, incense generally, sapan wood, and other scented woods. China was the sole source for silk goods in the earliest times, and silk goods of various kinds continued to be the most important items sent with Zheng He as gifts for the foreign rulers whose harbors his fleet visited. China was also an important destination for goods of all sorts, especially pepper and other spices, incense, and cotton goods. During the Tang (618–907) the kingdom or empire of Shri Vijaya derived its prosperity from its position as the entrepôt for Southeast Asian trade with China. Shri Vijaya's capital and commercial center was at Palembang in southern Sumatra, and its culture mixed Shaivite Hinduism with Buddhism. But many of the merchants who passed through Shri Vijaya's ports were Muslim, who sailed on to buy and sell in the autonomously governed and largely Muslim foreign merchant community in Canton (Guangzhou). Canton was sacked in 879 by the Chinese rebel Huang Chao, and the most vivid account of the ensuing massacre is in Arabic rather than Chinese. Shri Vijaya endured, but in 1025 it faced a devastating attack from the powerful Chola kingdom on the "Coromandel" (*Cholamandalam*) coast of India. Details are sparse and controversial, but the ability of King Rajendra Chola (ruled 1014–42) to send a fleet as far as Indonesia demonstrates both the long duration and the wide extent of the maritime activity across the waters on which Zheng He was to sail.

Despite the importance of China in this trade, Chinese ships and Chinese merchants and crews did not become important participants prior to the Song (960–1276). Well before then, voyages between China and India were made in large ships accompanied by tenders. The Chinese Buddhist pilgrim **Faxian** travelled in 413 aboard a large merchant ship (*dachuan*, literally "big ship") carrying more than two hundred men, accompanied by a smaller vessel (*bo*, a word that in modern usage usually means a seagoing merchant ship) as a tender in case of damage to the large ship. Zheng He's treasure ships are called "oceangoing *bo*," or *haibo*, by Fei Xin and "great *bo*," or *jubo*, by Zheng He himself in the Changle inscription; in the Liujiagang inscription the term "oceangoing ship(s)," or *haichuan*, is substituted. All of these terms refer to the large ships most commonly called treasure ships. Scholars who analyzed Faxian's journey concluded that vessels designated *bo* were some 200 feet long and could carry six hundred to seven hundred persons. The terms *chuan* and *bo* thus may be distinct in the usage of particular writers, but they are not in general technical terms. The largest ships of Faxian's day were therefore very large, and like the ships of Zheng He they sailed straight across the ocean accompanied by tenders. But they were Indonesian, not Chinese.

Shri Vijaya's prosperity during the Tang had depended on a unified and prosperous China that attracted foreign merchants in a period when China itself had little oceangoing shipping and little interest in overseas naval activity. Conditions changed in the Song, when Chinese merchants began trading as far west as India and did not need the central harbor that Shri Vijaya had provided. The Song, and the Southern Song (1127–1276) in particular, valued sea power as part of their defensive arsenal against the Jurchen and Mongols, and they actively promoted foreign trade. The accounts of Zhou Qufei (1178) and Zhao Rugua (1225) both date from this period, and both describe ships as large or larger than those that had transported Faxian, but this time Chinese built and crewed. Both also state that Shri Vijaya (still called *Sanfoqi*) had to use force to compel merchant ships to visit its harbors, of which the most important was now **Jambi**, north of Palembang on the southeast coast of Sumatra.

Zheng He's voyages thus took place at a time when trading patterns in Southeast Asia and the Indian Ocean were becoming less centralized, and major changes were taking place in the Malay-Indonesian world, both politically and in the sphere of religion and culture. The Chinese fleets withdrew abruptly after a comparatively brief presence, having had little effect on long-term developments in the regions where they had sailed.

The Malay-Indonesian World in the Hongwu Era

Before Zheng He's fleet arrived in Indonesian waters, rulers from the region had attempted to forge relations with the new Ming empire, and Emperor Hongwu had come to be frustrated at his inability to understand the complicated and evolving politics of the Malay-Indonesian world.

A major theme in Malay-Indonesian history is the interaction between the maritime Malays, whose major political creation had been the trade-dependent empire of Shri Vijaya, and the Javanese monarchies based on the rice surpluses that could best be grown on that smaller island. During the Southern Song, Yuan, and Ming, the realm of **Singosari and Majapahit** (1222–1451) flourished on Java. The reign of its fifth ruler had ended in rebellion in 1292; the arrival of a Mongol fleet sent by Khubilai Khan enabled that ruler's successor to use the Mongols to overthrow the usurper and then ambush the Mongols and drive them out. The kingdom prospered afterward, and the chief minister who dominated its affairs during most of the next three reigns swore a famous oath in 1331 not to rest until "the land below the wind" (*Nusantara*, referring to the maritime Malay world) was subdued. The narrative poem *Nagarakertagama* (1365), a major source for Majapahit history, claims Brunei in Borneo, Palembang in Sumatra, Pahang and other places on the Malay peninsula, Makassar on Sulawesi, and the Bandas and Moluccas in the eastern archipelago as subject to Majapahit. While the true nature of whatever thalassocracy Majapahit wielded has been much debated, under **Rajasanagara** (Hayam Wuruk, ruled 1350–89), during whose reign the Ming Dynasty came to power, the Javanese kingdom was certainly able to exert military power at least in southern Sumatra.

The proclamation of the Ming Dynasty in early 1368 coincided with an impressive display of Chinese naval power, since troops transported by sea established Ming authority over the southern coast of China at the same time as the Ming main army marched overland to capture the Yuan capital. A new dynasty reigning at Nanjing might well be expected to revive traditional maritime connections between a regime based in south China and southeast Asia. In reality Emperor Hongwu from the beginning based his revival of the tribute system on his understanding of ancient precedents, and he considered the more recent precedents of the Yuan and Southern Song undesirable. He maintained a public posture of indifference to wealth derived from overseas trade, and he was very suspicious of the political and social consequences that might accompany oceangoing commerce. He welcomed tribute missions, but only from truly independent states. He allowed trade to take place only under official auspices and only when tribute was presented. He prohibited private trading between Chinese and "barbarians" and prohibited Chinese from sailing overseas. He repeated his prohibitions against foreign trade and overseas travel frequently, and in an edict of 1394 he admitted that, because he had prohibited even tribute missions from most countries, Chinese merchants were sailing overseas to buy spices and aromatics. His solution was that they should use Chinese substitutes. These prohibitions had the effect of turning the already numerous (even if the numbers are difficult to estimate) Chinese maritime population into pirates and smugglers, since they could not be expected to give up their livelihood. Hence Zheng He found Palembang under the control of a Chinese pirate fleet on his first voyage, and the Chinese sources describe "pirates"—certainly Chinese pirates—preying heavily on shipping in other areas.

Since Hongwu had prohibited overseas commerce, he was also concerned that tribute missions not become a mere cover for trade, and therefore he looked for proof that entities sending tribute missions were in fact independent countries. By 1082 Jambi rather than Palembang had become the capital of the state the Chinese still called Shri Vijaya (*Sanfoqi*), even though trade was conducted in both harbors and a dynasty still ruled Palembang in a subordinate status. The founding of the Ming raised great hopes for the revival of trade with China, and from 1371 to 1377 both harbors sent missions to China. In 1374 a mission came from Palembang, whose ruler called himself both king of *Sanfoqi* and maharaja (transcribed as *manada* in Chinese) of Palembang (here called *Baolinbang*); Hongwu formally invested this unnamed person as king and granted him a calendar and other gifts. In 1377 Hongwu approved the request of the ruler of Jambi (also called Malayu or Malayu-Jambi) for investiture as ruler of *Sanfoqi*. Java protested that *Sanfoqi* was a dependency of Java and waylaid and murdered the Chinese embassy sent to confer this investiture. The events of 1377, sometimes described as a Javanese conquest of southern Sumatra, seem in fact to have been more like a firm reassertion of a suzerainty established earlier.

Hongwu, furious that he had been deceived, cut off relations with *Sanfoqi* for twenty years. In 1380, when he executed his chancellor Hu Weiyong and massacred hundreds of high officers and their families whom he accused of involvement in Hu's crimes, intrigues with foreigners and illicit trade in connection with the tribute missions were a major element in the accusations. Foreign rulers, he felt, often conspired with merchants to turn tribute missions into occasions for trade, and for that reason tribute missions from foreign countries were often rejected. Chinese missions to Southeast Asia during 1377–97 went only to countries that could be reached by land.

Sometime between 1377 and 1397, probably in 1391–92, Java expelled the now subordinate but still hereditary ruler of Palembang from his capital, compelling him to begin the journey that transformed him into the founder of Malacca. Trade unauthorized by Ming China continued to sail to and from Palembang, and in 1397 the old emperor sent an angry letter by way of Thailand to Java, ordering the Majapahit king to order the Palembang ruler to mend his ways. Instead, Java appointed a "small chief" to manage affairs in Palembang, where things were rapidly slipping out of Javanese control partly because of the influx of Chinese merchants. "At this time"—the *Mingshi* says—"Java had already overthrown Shri Vijaya (*Sanfoqi*) and annexed the country, changing its name to Old Harbor (*Jiugang*). But after the demise of Shri Vijaya, there was great disorder in the country, and Java also was not able to hold on to all of this territory. Chinese people residing there temporarily more and more often came to live there permanently. There was **Liang Daoming**, originally of Nanhai District in Guangdong, who had lived in this country for a long time. Several thousand families of soldiers and people from Fujian and Guangdong, who had sailed across the sea and joined him, selected Liang Daoming as their leader." This was taking place while China was distracted with the civil war that followed Hongwu's death. By the beginning of the Yongle reign, Palembang had become a southeast Asian city ruled by an overseas Chinese community drawn from the Chinese maritime population whose oceangoing trade Yongle's father had tried to prohibit.

In 1405 Yongle sent an official, a native of the same county as Liang Daoming, to summon the latter to court. Liang Daoming came to court, presented tribute in local products, received imperial gifts, and returned. In 1406 Chen Zuyi, described as a "headman" (*toumu*) of the Old Harbor and "also" (like Liang Daoming) originally a native of Guangdong, sent his son to court with tribute; Liang Daoming sent a nephew. "Even though Chen Zuyi had sent tribute to court, he committed piracy on the high seas, and tribute missions going to and fro suffered from this." Returning from his first voyage in 1407, Zheng He defeated and captured Chen Zuyi. Zheng He had been warned about Chen Zuyi's piracy by Shi Jinqing, another member of the Chinese community at Palembang, whom the Ming court then appointed as its chief. Liang Daoming's fate is unknown. (These events are described in Chapter IV.)

Palembang's previous hereditary ruler **Paramesvara**, alias **Iskandar Shah**, by then had ended his wanderings and had established himself as ruler at Malacca. His career consisted of three years in Palembang (1388–91), six years in Singapore (1391–97), two years en route to Malacca (1397–99), and fourteen years as ruler in Malacca (1399–1413), making up the full twenty-five years of rule ascribed to him by the Malay sources. Originally at Malacca he was subject to Thailand, with an annual tribute of 40 Chinese ounces, or *liang*, of gold, an item confirmed by both the *Mingshi* and Ma Huan. In 1404 the eunuch **Yin Qing** was sent as envoy to his land, and Paramesvara (*Bailimisula*), "very happy" at this, promptly sent back an embassy with tribute in local products. His reward the following year, in which Zheng He commenced his first voyage, was Ming investiture as king of Malacca. Malacca collaborated enthusiastically with the treasure voyages: Ming China, after all, had recognized their royal status; that, plus Zheng He's fleet, protected Malacca against any reassertion of Thai overlordship. Paramesvara's death in 1413 was reported to the Ming emperor in 1414 by his son, whom the Ming recognized as the second king of Malacca (1413–23). In 1424 Paramesvara's grandson received Ming confirmation as the third king of Malacca (1423–44). He was stranded in China from 1433 to 1435 with the other foreign rulers and ambassadors who had traveled to China on the final voyage. Soon after his return to Malacca in 1436 he embraced Islam and took the name **Sultan Muhammad Shah**, and Malacca prospered in his reign and those of his successors until the Portuguese conquest in 1511.

Southern India and Ceylon in the Time of Zheng He

The list of "over thirty" countries that Zheng He is said in his *Mingshi* biography to have visited has 36 names for 35 countries (Lambri on Sumatra is duplicated in the list, as *Nanwuli* and *Nanpoli*). Four of them were substantial mainland kingdoms: Champa, Cambodia, Thailand, and **Bengal**. Eleven others were in the insular or peninsular Malay-Indonesian region, including Brunei on Borneo, Java, and Pahang, **Kelantan** and Malacca on the Malay Peninsula, and six locations on Sumatra: Palembang, Aru, Semudera, **Nagur, Lide,** and Lambri. Seven others are in Arabia or Africa: Hormuz, **Djofar,** *Lasa,* and Mecca (called *Tianfang* or "Heavenly Square") in Arabia, and Mogadishu, *Zhubu* (Giumbo or Jumbo near present-day Kismayu in Somalia), and Malindi on the African coast. Aden in Arabia and Brava in Africa are both omitted from this list, though both ports were visited by Zheng He's ships. (The Arabian and African locations are discussed in Chapter V.) It is unlikely that any Chinese ship traveled to Mecca's port of Jidda, and there is reason to doubt that the Chinese got as far as Malindi, but at least there is no problem locating those places. The location of *Lasa* has been debated in the past, but the reasoning of J. V. G. Mills has been followed here (see Chapter V). The location of the other places (including Aden and Brava) mentioned so far is not in doubt.

The thirteen remaining locations all seem to be either in the southern part of the Indian peninsula (nine) or in the islands that are relatively nearby (four), but the location of some is debated, and the debate is relevant to our conception of Zheng

He's voyages. To get to the debate, we must follow Zheng He's fleet across the Indian Ocean.

If the straits now guarded by Malacca are the door to the Indian Ocean from the east, northern Sumatra is the parking lot. Ma Huan called Semudera, the most significant of the five little countries in this area, the "main route" (*zonglu*) to the Western Ocean, a phrase that appears in the *Mingshi* as the "main assembly [area]" (*yaohui*), where shipping would prepare for the long voyage out of sight of land to Ceylon. Aru to the south of Semudera, and Nagur, Lide, and Lambri to the north, along with Semudera, all came to be included in the territory of the later sultanate and now Indonesian province of Aceh. Ma Huan described all five countries as having the same pure, simple, and honest customs as their fellow Muslims in Malacca, except that in Nagur the people tattooed their faces. Except for Semudera, these countries were relatively poor and not heavily populated: three thousand households in Lide, slightly over a thousand in Lambri, and Aru and Nagur were "merely small countries."

From Sumatra ships would sail for Ceylon, sometimes making a landfall at the Nicobar Islands to establish the correct latitude. The Andaman and Nicobar Islands, with their naked people in dugout canoes, are never referred to as a tributary country in the Chinese sources. The internal problems in Ceylon that led to unpleasantness on Zheng He's first voyage and hostilities on the third are discussed in Chapter IV. From southern India ships could sail to *Liushan*, a term often used for the Maldives and Laccadives collectively, but *Bila* and *Sunla* have been tentatively identified as Bitra and Chetlat atolls, respectively, both in the Laccadives. Whether or not *Liushan* included the Maldives, it was also "merely a small country" and "one or two treasure ships from the Middle Kingdom went there and purchased ambergris, coconuts, and other such things," according to Ma Huan, whose use of the term "purchased" here is another indication of the private trading that went on on Zheng He's expeditions.

Of the remaining nine countries, all on the Indian mainland, three are certainly identified and have substantial chapters in Ma Huan's account. They are Calicut, **Cochin**, and **Quilon**, which Ma Huan calls *Xiao Gelan*, or "Lesser" Quilon. Calicut was then the most important trading center in southern India, and Ma

Huan calls it the "Great Country of the Western Ocean." (His comments on its social structure are reserved for Chapter IV.) Calicut was the most distant destination reached by Zheng He's fleet on its first three voyages. To get there the fleet, having sighted the mountains of Ceylon from far at sea, would either pass south of the island or make a port call there, then sail up the west coast of India from Cape Comorin at the southern tip of the subcontinent.

On the mainland of India, the fleet would first reach Quilon, whose people Ma Huan, and the *Mingshi* following him, calls "Chola" or *Suoli*, which normally refers to speakers of Malayalam, but Ma Huan did not distinguish between Malayalis and Tamils. Ma Huan misidentifies the people of Quilon as Buddhists; since they "venerate the cow" they are clearly Hindu.

Quilon was only a small country, but Cochin further up the coast was Calicut's closest commercial competitor. Cochin's people are also "Chola" and Hindu. The class structure was identical to Calicut's, headed by an elite (*Nankun* or *Nanpi*) of Brahmans, including the king, followed by Muslims; Chettys (*Zhedi*), or members of the trading castes, "who are all rich people" according to the *Mingshi*; Kling (*Geling*), "who are all brokers and middlemen," according to the *Mingshi*; and *Mugua*. "Kling" is still a Malay-Indonesian word for Tamils from southern India. *Mugua* transcribes the Malayalam word *mukkuvan* (a diver), and the *Mugua* were very poor and earned their livings as fishermen and coolies; they lived by the sea in huts that by law were no more than three feet high. In contrast to the variety of goods produced in Calicut, Cochin's only product was pepper. Both Calicut and Cochin had a matrilineal system of succession to their thrones, each king being normally followed by a sister's son; this tradition was maintained in the princely states of Travancore and Cochin under the later British Raj.

The other six states that are tentatively located on the mainland of India are "Greater" Quilon (*Da Gelan*), **Chola** (*Suoli*), **Chola of the Western Ocean** (*Xiyang Suoli*), *Abobadan*, *Shaliwanni*, and *Ganbali*; to them must be added *Jiayile*, which is not in the list given in Zheng He's biography but which his fleet nevertheless visited on its fourth and sixth voyages. None of these states is noticed by Ma Huan, but five have brief notices in the *Mingshi* and the other two each have a few lines appended to another entry. "Greater" Quilon, Chola, Chola of the Western Ocean, and *Jiayile* were all in the general area of southern India usually referred to as the Malabar and Coromandel coasts. While their exact locations are uncertain, they were on the general itinerary of a fleet whose main destination was Calicut and whose other known stopping points included Ceylon, Quilon, and Cochin.

This leaves *Ganbali*, on whose location the location of *Abobadan* depends. Some writers have seen *Ganbali* as Cambay in Gujarat, "the Kambayat of the Arabs." The *Zhufan Zhi* of the Song writer Zhao Rugua has a chapter on Gujarat, a commercially important region on the northwestern coast of India that both Ma Huan and Fei Xin ignore. The port city of Cambay sits at the head of a long, funnel-shaped bay that concentrates the daily tides into a wavelike bore that is a considerable hazard to navigation. Zheng He's largest ships were most comfortable in smooth tropical seas and brown waters like the river leading to Palembang; they would have been at risk in a tidal bore or other rough waters.

Ganbali has also been identified as Coimbatore in southern India. This city is not only inland but, unlike Nanjing and Palembang, both of which are inland yet very important in Zheng He's story, it cannot be reached by water. If *Ganbali* was Coimbatore and Zheng He visited it, he had to do so by going overland. This is not an insurmountable objection; Zheng He was certainly on land when he fought his battles in Ceylon and against Sekandar in Sumatra, but it is nonetheless unusual that Coimbatore should be the only one of Zheng He's destinations that could not be reached by sea. Cape Comorin, at the southern tip of India, is another possibility for the location of *Ganbali* and nearby *Abobadan*. Cape Comorin is transcribed on the Mao Kun map included in the *Wubei Zhi* as *Ganbali* Headland (*tou*). This problem cannot be resolved conclusively, but a location in southern India for both places would be most consistent with the general pattern of Zheng He's voyages.

In the Malay-Indonesian world the voyages of Zheng He had an impact by contributing to the rise of Malacca. Elsewhere Zheng He's voyages had a less lasting influence. Major continental monarchies like Thailand and Bengal were not trade-dependent and would have sought or avoided diplomatic relations with China for their own reasons, regardless of the presence or absence of Zheng He's fleet. For the smaller, weaker, and more trade-dependent coastal states of India, Arabia, and Africa, and the islands of the Indian Ocean the presence of Zheng He's huge ships and the powerful army they transported was overwhelming but ephemeral. Zheng He's mission was to enforce outward compliance with the norms of China's by now ancient tributary system of foreign relations. Most rulers were wise enough to comply, and they benefited both from outright Chinese gifts and from the opportunities for illicit trade that Zheng He's large-capacity ships no doubt provided. When Zheng He's fleets stopped sailing, China's diplomatic relations with these countries ceased.

IV

Sailing to India

Zheng He's First, Second, and Third Voyages

Zheng He's first three voyages kept his ships and men in continuous overseas deployment from 1405 to 1411, broken by two brief periods of turnaround in China in 1407 and 1409. Each of the three voyages took the same basic route: to Champa, up the Straits of Malacca to northern Sumatra, then straight across the Indian Ocean to Ceylon and on to Calicut and other destinations on India's southwest coast. The outward voyage coincided with the winter monsoon, and the return voyage with the summer monsoon of the following year.

Emperor Yongle had ordered the voyages to take place and took an active personal interest in their outcome. This interest was probably greatest during the period of the first three voyages, as the emperor was resident in Nanjing while the original treasure ships were being built, at the departures of the first and third voyages, and at the return of the fleet on all three voyages. Afterward, the building of the new capital at Beijing and his campaigns in Mongolia increasingly dominated the emperor's attention.

The First Voyage, 1405–07

Yongle appointed Zheng He to command the expeditions to the Indian Ocean, despite his lack of previous naval experience, because he had proved his courage, loyalty, and ability in battle, and (presumably; no record survives) because the emperor knew him to be a capable organizer of large-scale construction projects. He had previously appointed Zheng He as Grand Director of the eunuch Directorate of Palace Servants, which was responsible for the construction and physical maintenance of the palace buildings. That appointment is evidence of his trust in Zheng He for work of this kind.

Zheng He's work as head of the Directorate of Palace Servants may have been the major factor in his appointment to command the expeditions. From an essentially land-bound Chinese perspective, construction projects and naval expeditions appeared to be related activities. In China, palaces and temples, like ships, were made of wood. Cutting timber for either shipbuilding or construction projects was an assignment that eunuchs supervised and soldiers carried out, and the expeditionary fleets were similarly commanded by Zheng He and his fellow high-ranking eunuchs and crewed by military personnel. Civil officials usually criticized both palace construction and the timber cutting associated with it as creating opportunities for graft, extortion, and oppression, and they criticized Zheng He's fleets for their expense. Emperor Yongle insisted on having his own way with regard to Zheng He's voyages and other initiatives, and his eunuchs and military officers obeyed, even when civil officials were critical. But the hostility of the civil officials to any project that could be characterized as imperial extravagance was a consistent theme in later generations of Ming history.

The ships of Zheng He's first expedition were built hastily, in response to imperial orders issued on several occasions during 1403. These orders commanded first the government of Fujian Province and later the military units in Nanjing and in Suzhou and other cities directly administered from the capital, as well as the provincial governments of Jiangxi, Zhejiang, and Huguang, to build large numbers of ships. Because there was not enough timber to build all the ships ordered, timber-cutting expeditions were ordered along the Min River in Fujian and in the upper reaches of the Yangtze.

Many of the ships, and all of the large "treasure ships," were built at the so-called Treasure Ship Yard, or *baochuanchang*, on the Qinhuai River that flowed around the southern and western reach of the recently enhanced walls of Nanjing. During the wars preceding the Ming founding, the Ming naval forces had been called the Qinhuai Wing of the army, and long after the Zheng He voyages were over the same establishment, under the name Longjiang Shipyard, continued to construct the smaller vessels that the Ming empire continued to need in quantity. Both the name of the yard and the size of the largest docks within it indicate that the treasure ships, the largest ships in Zheng He's fleet, were built there, and that in turn means that their draught was shallow enough that they could reach the sea via the Yangtze estuary. This fact has important implications for determining the dimensions and overall seaworthiness of Zheng He's largest ships.

The entry dated 11 July 1405 in *Taizong Shilu* treating the dispatch of the first expedition states simply that the "palace official Zheng He and others were sent bearing imperial letters to the countries of the Western Ocean and with gifts to their kings of gold brocade, patterned silks, and colored silk gauze, according to their status." The fleet consisted of up to 255 ships carrying 27,800 men, most of whom were military personnel. The *Mingshi* says of this voyage that "62 great ships had been built, 44 *zhang* long and 18 *zhang* wide." These 62 "treasure ships" were the heart of Zheng He's fleet and had most of its carrying capacity; they are included in the 255 ships that the *Taizong Shilu* indicates were constructed in time for the first voyage. Despite the *Mingshi* account, it is unlikely that the treasure ships were all of the same size, but they would still have had plenty of room for the crews stipulated, and the large ships were probably all referred to informally as treasure ships. The normal organization of the fleet had several smaller ships assigned to each of the large ships, in the manner made familiar by the accounts of the earlier voyages of Faxian, **Marco Polo** and **Ibn Battūtah**.

The first voyage established the pattern for Zheng He's expeditions. The fleet assembled at Nanjing. From Nanjing the fleet proceeded to Liujiagang (literally, "Liu Family Harbor"), upstream from Wusong and northeast of Taicang on the south bank of the Yangtze. In 1431 Zheng He set up one of his two commemorative inscriptions at this harbor. Now called Liuhe and silted up as a consequence of the natural expansion of the Yangtze delta region, Liujiagang was the Shanghai of its day. There Zheng He organized the fleet into squadrons, and the crews would pray and sacrifice continuously to the goddess called Tianfei (Heavenly Princess) or Tianhou (Heavenly Empress), then as now the goddess of sailors. The commemorative inscriptions (see Appendix 11) of Zheng He and his associates at Liujiagang and at Changle in Fujian both honor this goddess.

The fleet then took four to eight weeks to sail down the convoluted and island-rich coast of Zhejiang and Fujian provinces to the mouth of the Min River, downstream from Fuzhou, the capital of Fujian. There it assembled at Taiping Anchorage in Changle District, where Zheng He set up the second of his two commemorative inscriptions in 1431. More prayer and sacrifice accompanied the wait for the northeast monsoon, which usually began in December or January. The fleet then sailed out from the anchorage by way of the Wuhumen (Five Tiger Passage) and headed for Champa. With sails spread day and night, and with navigators skilled enough to avoid the Paracel and Spratly Islands in the South China Sea, the voyage to Champa might be made in ten days, though Zheng He took fifteen in 1432.

The first port of call on all of the voyages was in Champa, at the site of the modern Vietnamese city of Qui Nhon. This city in Champa—called Xinzhou, or "New Department," by the Chinese—was about fifteen miles from the (now ruined) inland capital of Vijaya. The ancient kingdom of Champa (Zhancheng, or "Cham City" in Chinese) was then ruled by King **Jaya Sinhavarman V** (ruled 1400–41) of its thirteenth recorded dynasty. Champa had been losing its wars with Vietnam ever since Vietnam gained independence in 939, but it was about to have an intermission from these troubles; the ultimately unsuccessful Ming effort to conquer and annex Vietnam began during Zheng He's first expedition, and while the wars in Vietnam lasted (until 1427–28), Vietnam's enemy was China's friend. This state of affairs covered the entire period in which Zheng He's first six voyages took place. Even after China recognized Vietnam's independence in 1427, China continued to support Champa, and Vietnam, exhausted by the war with China, did not resume its wars with Champa until the death of Jaya Sinhavarman V led to internal discord in the southern kingdom. Ma Huan describes a Cham society whose domestic economy resembles that of Vietnam (palm thatched houses, water buffalo) even as their religious practices are clearly Hindu. Since "most of the men take up fishing for a livelihood" the society is oriented toward the sea, and the fishermen may turn into pirates and smugglers who were difficult for the institutionally weak Cham state to control.

Leaving Champa, Zheng He's fleet sailed to the island of Java, where successive kings of Majapahit had caused trouble for both Yuan and Ming emperors. The current king was the successor of Hayam Wuruk, whose murder of the Chinese envoys sent in 1377 to recognize the independence of Palembang on Sumatra had provoked the anger of Emperor Hongwu. Ma Huan noted the strong presence of Chinese in the coastal trading cities of Java, Sumatra, and the Malayan peninsula. Chinese traders had founded Gresik in Java, and at Palembang a committee of Chinese merchants contended with a Chinese pirate fleet after the withdrawal of the former royal dynasty.

Zheng He would deal with the pirate fleet of Chen Zuyi on his return, but he bore a commission as ambassador to the countries of the Western (Indian) Ocean, and therefore he headed up the Straits of Malacca to Aru and Semudera, both on the northeast coast of Sumatra, and Lambri at the tip of the island. Ma Huan describes the three countries as Muslim states, with customs identical to those of Malacca; the people were "very honest and genuine." From there familiar and often traveled monsoon routes led to Ceylon and southern India.

From Lambri, three days of a fair wind would bring a ship to the Andaman and Nicobar Islands, whose inhabitants went naked and had a primitive fishing and gathering economy. Six more days with a fair wind would yield the first sighting of the mountains of Ceylon, though two more days were needed to make port on the island's west coast. It cannot be known whether the winds were fair on Zheng He's first voyage, but he clearly sailed straight across the Indian Ocean rather than follow the coast around the Bay of Bengal. Zheng He was showing the flag to overawe, rather than exploring in any sense; fleets of Chinese official ships like Zheng He's armada had not been seen in these waters since the period of Mongol rule (though

Chinese merchant ships had), and they had navigators who knew the way. When Zheng He reached Ceylon he "realized" that the king was hostile and intended to do him harm, so he "left and went to other countries," according to the *Mingshi*. Rounding Cape Comorin at the southern tip of the Indian peninsula, Zheng He probably stopped at Quilon, either on the outward or the return voyage, for the king of Quilon returned to China with him in 1407. It would have been on the way to stop at Cochin, north of Quilon, but there is no evidence that he did so on this voyage. Both south Indian trading port cities had Malayalam (*Suoli*, "Chola" in Chinese) speaking Hindu populations, and both were overshadowed by Calicut to the north.

Calicut was truly "the Great Country of the Western Ocean" in the opinion of Ma Huan, the Muslim author of the *Yingyai Shenglan*, who took part in Zheng He's voyages. Its port was a free trade emporium and point of exchange for the trans-Indian Ocean seaborne trade. The royal title of Calicut's rulers was *Samutiri*, a Malayalam word for "Sea King" that was transcribed *Shamidixi* in Chinese and later transformed by the Portuguese into the familiar "Zamorin" of later accounts. Succession to the throne was matrilineal, the king being succeeded by his sister's son, as in later south Indian states. Because of both the geography of the Indian Ocean and the seasonal nature of the monsoon winds, this trade tended to be segmented into western (from and to the Red Sea and the Persian Gulf) and eastern (from and to Sumatra and Malaya) halves, and Calicut had outperformed its rivals on the west coast of India in the competition to be the port where the two halves met.

Ma Huan praises the scrupulous attention of the Calicut authorities to weights and measures and the regulation of trade. He describes the class systems of Calicut and Cochin in almost identical terms: the king belongs to an upper class called *Nankun* in Chinese, which is believed to refer to Brahman priests and Kshatriya warriors in combination; the latter were very rare in southern India. Muslims are the second class listed, followed by the Chetty class of moneyed property owners, and the ordinary Malayalam speaking population, called *Geling* in Chinese, from Kling, which usually refers to Tamils, but Ma Huan did not distinguish the Tamil and Malayali peoples. The bottom caste or class, called the *Mugua* in Chinese (Mucoa or Mukuva, from Malayalam, "diver"), were fishermen and divers. Muslims are prominent in the administration of the kingdom, reflecting the fact that the kingdom lived by trade and that (despite a Chinese presence that was to prove temporary) Muslim sailors controlled the Indian Ocean trade. Indeed, this trade was the major vehicle for the propagation of the Islamic faith in the Indonesian archipelago.

Returning, Zheng He's fleet no doubt called again at Malacca, since an envoy from Malacca's founding king accompanied Zheng He back to China in 1407. But the major event on the return voyage was the showdown with Chen Zuyi, the Chinese pirate leader who had occupied Palembang with his fleet in the turmoil following the Javanese invasion of Sumatra. The *Taizong Shilu* describes this action in the entry that reports the return of Zheng He's fleet to Nanjing on 2 October 1407:

> Grand Director Zheng He, who had gone as envoy to the countries of the Western Ocean, returned holding in fetters the pirate Chen Zuyi and others. Originally Zheng He had arrived at the Old Harbor [of Palembang] and had encountered Chen Zuyi and the others, to whom he sent a messenger summoning them to submit. Chen Zuyi came down and pretended to submit, but kept his plans secret and actually intended to escape from the imperial fleet. Zheng He and his associates realized this and deployed their forces, preparing to stop him. Chen Zuyi, leading his forces, came out to plunder, and Zheng He sent forth his troops and did battle with him. Chen Zuyi was heavily defeated. Over five thousand of the pirate gang were killed, ten pirate ships were destroyed by burning and seven ships were captured, along with two forged seals made of copper. Chen Zuyi and two others were taken prisoner and delivered to the imperial capital, where all were ordered to be beheaded.

Here Chen Zuyi is secretly planning to "escape" or "withdraw" from Zheng He's fleet, but Zheng He catches him. The much later account in the *Mingshi*, though based on the above passage, changes critical words and has Chen Zuyi secretly planning to "intercept and ambush" or "intercept and plunder" Zheng He's fleet—describing Chen Zuyi as bent on active attack, in other words, rather than evasive action. These later embellish-ments, which are not based on additional evidence, serve to de-fine Chen Zuyi as an evil pirate in contrast to the peaceful Chinese merchants at Palembang who had submitted to Ming authority.

Some modern scholars see Zheng He's fight with Chen Zuyi as a sea battle fought in the Strait of Malacca, and they speculate on the use of cannon or other weapons using gunpowder as a flame-inducing agent. The burned pirate ships might be seen as evidence that such weapons had been used. Cannon and smaller firearms had already emerged on the Chinese military scene, but there is little evidence for firearms at sea and none for the broadside firing and line ahead tactics that only began in Euro-pean waters almost two centuries after Zheng He. There is also little evidence that Zheng He's ships were warships, in the sense of their being specialized for a naval combat role. The large treasure ships, each accompanied by a flotilla of smaller vessels, were a powerful military force only because of the army they could land, or conceivably because of the swarm of small craft Zheng He could send into the brown waters of a river estuary.

Palembang was called the Old Harbor because for centuries it had been the center of the Indonesian maritime empire of Shri Vijaya. But it was not a seaport in the strict sense. Both Palem-bang and its rival Malayu/Jambi further north were connected to the Java Sea through river delta systems extending through swamplands in their eastern reaches, whose exits and channels were easily confused. Yet Palembang was the dry land nearest to the sea for the export of Sumatra's pepper, and the wealth generated by pepper exports had enabled the rulers of Shri Vijaya to attract the seagoing trade of the archipelago into his port, as long as this trade was in the hands of Arab and Indonesian shippers. The rise of a carrying trade in Chinese bottoms during the Song had made the role of Palembang as an entrepôt less relevant, yet it remained an important commercial center, and ironically the vanished Maharajah had been replaced by a com-mittee of Chinese merchants as the local authority. Chen Zuyi and his fleet seem to have been part of this scene.

The battle with Chen Zuyi, whom the *Mingshi* account de-scribes categorically as the "chief" of the Old Harbor of Palem-bang, was more likely fought among twisting river channels and mangrove swamps. In all probability, Zheng He's larger ships blocked all exits to the sea while smaller craft obstructed the channels through which Chen Zuyi's ships sought to escape, so that the pirate ships were burned and captured and the pirates killed in the estuary. This was the pattern in the later and better documented British and Dutch wars with the Malays, Dyaks, and other pirates in these waters. (Fei Xin's brief and confused account—which wrongly dates this event in 1415— offers this interpretation: Chen Zuyi and his gang are already plundering the "foreign merchants" in "Shri Vijaya" and "they intended to plunder our ships, but Zheng He and his colleagues placed troops in ambush and defeated them.")

Zheng He and company are said to have "realized" that Chen Zuyi "actually intended to escape from the imperial fleet." Ma Huan says that Shi Jinqing, "a man of Guangdong" then residing in Palembang, came out to Zheng He's fleet and informed him of Chen Zuyi's depredations. Shi Jinqing may also have helped Zheng He "realize" what Chen Zuyi's intentions were. More to the point, Shi Jinqing was presumably a merchant who could give Zheng He detailed information on the watercourses leading from the Java Sea to Palembang, enabling Zheng He to place his "troops"—certainly aboard boats of some sort—in ambush. Ma Huan states that Shi Jinqing was awarded a cap and belt by Emperor Yongle and returned to the Old Harbor as "grand chieftain ruling over the native people of that place." Grand chieftain *(da toumu)* was not a Ming official title, but the cap and belt indicate official Ming recognition. After Shi Jinqing's death, Ma Huan continues, "his son did not succeed him, but his daughter Shi Erjie became king, and all rewards and punishments and promotions and demotions were decided according to her will." Calling Shi Erjie a king is unusual: the word *wang* can mean king or prince according to context, but the title is not held by women, and it was never conferred on the men of the Shi family. Unsettling as this state of affairs was to patriarchal Chinese or equally patriarchal Muslims, the rule of the Shi family at Palembang continued. On 27 February 1424, *Taizong Shilu* reports that Zheng He was sent on a diplomatic mission to Palembang to confer "a gauze cap, a ceremonial robe with floral gold woven into gold patterns in the silk, and a silver seal" on Shi Jinqing's son Shi Jisun, whose succession to his deceased father's office of Pacification Commissioner Emperor Yongle had approved. "Pacification Commissioner" was one of a number of similar-sounding but differently ranked titles conferred by the Ming government, typically on the chieftains of aboriginal peoples in southwestern China. Calling a local potentate a Pacification Commissioner implied a higher degree of Chinese rule than would be exercised over a ruler recognized as the king of a tributary state.

While this seems to be a straightforward narrative of bad pirates destroyed and peaceful merchants relieved, the matter is complicated by an entry in *Taizong Shilu* dated 12 August 1406, at a time when Zheng He's fleet may have been in Indonesian waters, but was on the outward leg of its voyage to Calicut: "The chieftain of the Old Harbor Chen Zuyi sent his son **Chen Shiliang,** and Liang Daoming sent his nephew **Liang Guanzheng** as well as *Xigandaliye*"—a name that sounds as though it is compounded with the Muslim name Sekandar—"and the Muslim Hajji Muhammad and others to come to court. They were given paper currency according to their deserts." This is the last mention of Liang Daoming, whom the Ming court understood in 1405 to be the leader of the Chinese community in Palembang, and Chen Zuyi is now listed ahead of him as the "chieftain" *(toumu).* This was not an official Ming title, but Chen Zuyi's action indicates that he had hoped for official Ming recognition rather than merely being tipped in paper money. Instead Zheng He listened to Shi Jinqing, and Chen Zuyi was classified as a pirate and eventually executed. We may wonder whether Chen Zuyi and his rivals Liang Daoming and Shi Jinqing were all that different: all belonged to a floating world in which the roles of pirate and merchant frequently changed.

On 29 October 1407 the emperor ordered rewards for the officers and men of Zheng He's forces "who had gained merit capturing bandits at the Old Harbor" of Palembang, wording that suggests the battles were fought on the rivers rather than at sea. These rewards, to be discussed later, provide important information about the personnel of Zheng He's fleet, and their scale suggests that the emperor regarded the destruction of Chen Zuyi as an important military event.

Following the executions of Chen Zuyi and his lieutenants on 2 October 1407, the envoys from Calicut and Quilon in India, Semudera and Aru on Sumatra, and Malacca, as well as unspecified "other countries," who had accompanied Zheng He on his return voyage, presented "tribute in local products" according to the ancient customs of Chinese tributary relations. In turn, these envoys received paper money and copper coins. On the following day the envoys previously sent by King Jaya Sinhavarman V of Champa had a parting audience with the emperor; they were presented with "robes lined with patterned silk, and paper money." The emperor ordered the Ministry of Rites, the central government agency whose duties included the protocol concerning foreign ambassadors, to prepare gifts of "silk brocade, silk gauze, horses with saddles, and other items" for the kings who had sent envoys with Zheng He. In 1405 Zheng He carried "gold brocaded silk, patterned silk, and colored silk gauze" to present to the kings he visited.

Emperor Yongle probably issued the order for the second voyage, whose main charge was to confer formal investiture on the king of Calicut, on 23 October 1407. On 30 October 1407 another eunuch Grand Director was sent with an imperial letter to the king of Champa, along with 300 Chinese ounces of silver and twenty robes and linings of colored thin silk. The same eunuch's name accompanies Zheng He's name in the trilingual inscription dated 15 February 1409 at Galle in Ceylon. Since Champa was one of the destinations on the second voyage, the despatch of a Chinese envoy to that kingdom probably marks the start of that expedition. Possibly the subsequent confusion regarding Zheng He's presence or absence on the second voyage was caused by the other envoy's going on ahead, while Zheng He and the main body followed later. In any event, the Ming envoys could be sure of a welcome in Champa, and the Ming emperor was happy that Champa had sent troops to help the Ming in their conquest of Vietnam, Champa's old enemy.

Zheng He's first expedition was in one sense his most important: the fleet built to undertake it was then available for the later voyages. The decision to send the first expedition seems to require an independent assessment, but some of what follows applies to the other voyages as well.

It is unlikely that the first voyage was a search for Yongle's nephew, the presumably deceased Emperor Jianwen. The idea that this was the motive first occurs in the *Mingshi* biography of Zheng He, which was published only in 1739 though it had been in preparation for decades. Elsewhere the *Mingshi* says this of Jianwen: "But some said the emperor had gone out through a tunnel and escaped. In the 5th Year of Zhengtong (1440) there was a Buddhist monk who went from Yunnan to Guangxi falsely claiming to be Emperor Jianwen. . . . After this . . . traditions arose intermittently that there had been an emperor who had become a monk." These passages no doubt reflect the growth of a widely believed legend, but no Ming material hints at the search for the deceased emperor as a motive for the voyage, and other factors explain it better.

The Tamerlane factor, sparsely mentioned in the Chinese sources, was probably important. By 1403, Tamerlane (Timur, 1336–1405; nominally vizier and actually *güregen* or son-in-law of the figurehead khan of the Chaghatai Horde in the western part of Central Asia) had defeated his former vassal Tokhtamysh, Khan of the Golden Horde (1391), taken Bagdad (1393), invaded India (1398–99), and defeated and captured the Ottoman Sultan Bayazid I (1402). Having insulted and imprisoned an embassy from Hongwu, he was even more enraged by an embassy sent by Yongle in 1403 to announce his accession: The usual Chinese claims to preeminence were in conflict with Tamerlane's own idea of his place in the world. And 1403 was the year that Yongle ordered Zheng He to begin building the fleet.

Historically minded Chinese, like Yongle, remembered that emperors of the Former Han Dynasty (206 BC to 9 AD) had sent ambassadors to the west to seek distant allies against the Xiongnu, who then ruled the Mongolian steppes and against whom the Han were waging war. Western enemies of Tamerlane, potential allies of China, could only be reached by sea because Tamerlane himself blocked the land routes to the west. In 1404 Tamerlane mobilized a large army, intending to conquer China and convert its surviving people to Islam. He died at Utrar, still within his own territory, early in 1405. His son and successor Shāhrukh (ruled 1405–47) had all he could do to hold his inheritance together, and he established friendly relations with China.

The foregoing is totally speculative, and it needs to be, considering the nature of the sources. Up until the moment of his death Tamerlane was a threatening presence throughout Asia, and his hostility to China was known to the Chinese authorities. Yet the threat vanished immediately on his death. Yongle and Zheng He had a close personal relationship, and one may imagine their discussing the threat posed by Tamerlane, but none of their private conversations have entered the sparse historical record.

By the time Zheng He set sail, the goal of spreading awe of China's wealth and power seems to have dominated Yongle's motivations. Zheng He's first stop was Champa, which China had been supporting, and whose alliance became even more important because of the war in Vietnam that began, coincidentally, during the first voyage. In the area of the Straits of Malacca, China also had a perceived enemy in the Javanese kingdom that had ignored Hongwu's admonitions and murdered his envoys, and an ally in the form of the new Sultan of Malacca, formerly ruler of Palembang. Malacca in time replaced Palembang as the regional trade hub, Chinese merchant ships (sailing without authorization) helped to fill up her harbors, and Malacca's alliance with the Ming helped to ensure regional stability even after China withdrew from the seas. The three Sumatran states (Lambri, Semudera, Aru) visited on the first voyage were way stations on the route to southern India, whose prize was Calicut, and friendly relations with Calicut would be valuable as long as China was trying to extend the tribute system into the Indian Ocean. Here too China had a potential enemy in sullen Ceylon, whose rulers became actively hostile during the third expedition.

The countries visited, the routes traveled, and some of the activities undertaken during the first expedition might give the impression that Yongle and Zheng He had some idea of a foreign policy based on expanded foreign trade, much of it carried in Chinese ships, being supported by a Chinese military-naval presence and the cultivation of local allies with shared interests. Even if it had been present, this idea was unlikely to appear in writing, given the antimercantile bias of China's official culture.

But in fact Yongle shared his father's suspicions about trade by privately owned Chinese ships, and he never relaxed his father's ban on foreign trade by Chinese merchants. His primary purpose was to show off the wealth and power of China, and the cost and the other economic consequences of the voyages were secondary considerations.

The Second Voyage, 1407–09

The order for the second voyage occurs in *Taizong Shilu* under the entry for 17 October 1408. Zheng He's inscriptions, however, clearly indicate that the expedition was ordered in 1407, and this year is confirmed by a passage in Ma Huan's entry on Calicut, which says that in 1407 the court ordered "Grand Director Zheng He and others to bear imperial letters conferring a patent of investiture and a silver seal to the king, and to reward his leading men with promotion in rank and grade, with the appropriate caps and belts."

Changing the present *Taizong Shilu* entry from the sixth year (1408) to the fifth year (1407) of Yongle, and leaving the month and day unchanged, makes the specific date 23 October 1407, some six days before the announcement of the rewards to the troops engaged in the suppression of Chen Zuyi (29 October) and seven days before the despatch of the eunuch ambassador to Champa (30 October), which was most likely the opening voyage of the second voyage. The relocated *Taizong Shilu* entry reads: "Grand Director Zheng He and others, bearing imperial letters, went as envoys to the countries of Calicut, Malacca, Semudera, Aru, *Jiayile*, Java, Thailand, Champa, Cochin, *Abobadan*, Quilon, Lambri, and *Ganbali*, and conferred silk brocade and silk gauze upon their kings." *Jiayile*, *Abobadan*, and *Ganbali* were minor states in southern India whose uncertain locations were discussed in Chapter III. The other countries were all major players in the Zheng He story, and their being named here indicates that the mission of the second voyage was to repeat the achievements of the first by sailing as far as the southwestern coast of India.

The fleet consisted of the 249 "sea transport ships" that the high-ranking military officer **Wang Hao** was ordered on 5 October 1407 to "convert" or "refit" (*gaizao*, "reconstruct") in "preparation for embassies to the countries of the Western Ocean." This number includes all the treasure ships that sailed on the second voyage plus the smaller ships that accompanied them, as on the first voyage. The number of the treasure ships in the second expedition is therefore not certainly known. The number of troops is also not given, but the scale of the second expedition was comparable to that of the first, and, given the brief turnaround time that the sources indicate, the specific ships and personnel of the second voyage must have largely overlapped with those of the first.

The visit of the second expedition to Java was the occasion for settling the relations between Ming China and the declining Javanese empire of Majapahit. In 1377 Emperor Hongwu had become angry with the Majapahit king Hayam Wuruk (ruled 1350–89), who had conquered Palembang and killed the envoys China had sent to recognize its independence. Hayam Wuruk's nephew, also his son-in-law and successor, was challenged by a natural son by a lesser wife, who was given a large appanage in eastern Java. The Chinese recognized both kings and referred to them impartially as the East King and the West King. Civil war between them broke out in 1401 and ended in 1406 with the East King's head in his cousin's possession, but in the course of the war the West King's troops had attacked the personnel of a Chinese embassy, who had "come ashore and were trading in the marketplace" of the former East King's capital. Either 170 or (less probably) 710 Chinese were killed. In an entry in *Taizong Shilu* dated 23 October 1407, soon after the second expedition had been ordered but probably before it had set out, Yongle summoned the Javanese ambassadors and accused Java of begging forgiveness only because they knew China was about to raise an army to punish them. He demanded 60,000 ounces of gold as restitution, and most revealingly ordered them to "reflect upon the situation in Annan" (Vietnam), where the Chinese war of conquest had recently begun. Javanese sources suggest that the Javanese settled for one-sixth of the amount demanded.

The order of listing of the various destination countries in the *Taizong Shilu* entry quoted above obscures both the order in which they were probably visited and the purpose of the expedition. Like the first, the second expedition created a powerful and visible Chinese military presence throughout the South China Sea and among the trading cities in southern India. Ceylon, where Zheng He had discovered hostility during the first voyage, was bypassed on the second, but it remained important as a landfall. As the most important destination, Calicut is mentioned first. However, the voyage probably had the following sequence: (1) the usual outward voyage, from Nanjing to Liujiagang to Changle and then across the South China Sea to Qui Nhon (Xinzhou) in Champa; (2) either Thailand and Java in that order, or perhaps visits by detached squadrons to those countries; (3) regrouping at Malacca; (4) up the straits, visiting the Sumatran Muslim states of Semudera, Aru, and Lambri; (5) straight across the Indian Ocean until the mountains and headlands of Ceylon were sighted, then around the southern tip of India, where *Jiayile*, *Abobadan*, *Ganbali*, Quilon, and Cochin could be visited in succession before the fleet arrived at Calicut. Calicut, still the "Great Country of the Western Ocean," was now under a new king, whom Ma Huan calls a fervent Buddhist even as he provides evidence that he was a Hindu. Nevertheless "the great chiefs are all Muslim people," and Hindus and Muslims had sworn to respect each other's religion and customs.

The fleet returned to China in the late summer of 1409. On their return they stopped at the island of Pulau Sembilan in the Strait of Malacca (called *Jiuzhoushan* or "nine province island" in Chinese, *sembilan* being Malay for "nine"). Fei Xin's brief paragraph about this island dates the visit to 1409 without giving a month or day, but accepting the chronology of the Liujiagang and Changle inscriptions means placing this visit on the return leg of the second expedition because the third expedition, ordered in 1409, did not leave the China coast until early 1410. Earlier literature on Zheng He has used Fei Xin's notice merely to name another place that the fleet "visited," but Fei Xin's words deserve to be quoted at greater length. "In the seventh year of Yongle" (1409), he writes, "Zheng He and his associates sent government troops onto the island to cut incense. They obtained six logs, each eight or nine *chi* in diameter and six or seven *zhang* in length, whose aroma was pure and far-ranging. The pattern [of the wood] was black, with fine lines. The people of the island opened their eyes wide and stuck out their tongues in astonishment, and were told that 'We are the soldiers of the Heavenly Court, and our awe-inspiring power is like that of the gods.'" The wood in question is the aromatic wood the Chinese call *chenxiang* or "heavy incense," also called *garu* or *gaharu* in Malay, or "eagle wood" from the pattern described. (A *zhang* is ten *chi* and a *chi* is 10.5 to 12 inches.) Fei Xin's choice of words strongly suggests that Zheng He, since he is mentioned by name, accompanied the second expedition, as both of the inscriptions imply. The fleet has landed troops to cut the incense logs not for repairs but purely for their commercial value. And the words quoted surely suggest that the personnel of the expeditions behaved in an overbearing manner, as soldiers of great powers typically do.

The mission of the second expedition followed from the success of the first. The new king of Calicut and his recently promoted officials, and the rulers in Malacca and Champa who had made it a matter of policy to cooperate with China, gave Zheng He's fleets a series of bases from which they could roam the already well explored and established sea routes of the South China Sea and the Indian Ocean at will. In 1409 the threat from Tamerlane had vanished, Vietnam seemed to be essentially pacified, and Yongle had yet to begin the Mongolian campaigns and the creation of the new capital at Beijing that would occupy the last half of his reign. Zheng He's fleets so far had not traveled to out-of-the-way places. Wherever he sailed, Zheng He arrived with a military force stronger than that of any local power, yet there is no evidence, either from Zheng He's activities or from Chinese written sources, of any attempt to control the trade of the Indian Ocean and the South China Sea through the exercise of sea power. The official mission of the fleet continued to be power projection rather than exploration or trade promotion. Yet the visit to Pulau Sembilan, which is not described in any of the official sources, demonstrates that profits were to be made on the side.

The Third Voyage, 1409–11

Zheng He's inscriptions record an imperial order, dated Yongle seventh year, first month (16 January to 14 February 1409), and directed to himself and other senior eunuchs, to lead a third voyage to the Western Ocean. The fleet sailed from Liujiagang in the ninth month (9 October to 6 November 1409), arrived at Changle in the following month (7 November to 6 December 1409), and departed in the twelfth month (5 January to 3 February 1410). The voyage to Champa took ten days, with a fair wind from the northeast or winter monsoon. The voyage made the usual itinerary after Champa: first Java, then Malacca, then up the straits to Semudera in Sumatra, then across the Indian Ocean to Ceylon. The fleet landed at Galle in Ceylon, rather than the more usual Beruwala, in 1410, and there Zheng He set up the trilingual inscription dated 15 February 1409 (see below). The confrontation with and capture of the Sinhalese king that was the main event of the third voyage is more likely to have taken place on the outward voyage in 1410 rather than on the return in 1411. After the conflict in Ceylon, the fleet went up the south Indian coast to Quilon and Cochin, ending up at Calicut. Except for the military action in Ceylon, China's main fleet was making its by now customary voyage to Calicut and back.

The second expedition was still in the Indian Ocean when the imperial order for the third was issued. Either Zheng He was with his fleet, and the order was issued in his absence, or Zheng He did not accompany the second expedition. The trilingual inscription at Galle in Ceylon, dated 15 February 1409, poses an analogous problem: either its date is the date on which it was erected, in which case it was put up on the return voyage of the second expedition, or it was prepared well in advance and erected in Ceylon in 1410 at the earliest. The evidence is inconclusive, and the problem shows how elusive Zheng He remains as a subject for biography. The emperor himself was absent from Nanjing from 23 February 1409 to 7 December 1410, during which time he was either in Beijing or in Mongolia conducting his first Mongolian campaign, so whatever communication passed between the emperor and the admiral had to be through documents or messengers. The most likely explanation is that Zheng He did indeed lead the second expedition in person, and that the previously composed Galle inscription was erected in 1410.

Fei Xin's book says that Zheng He commanded 48 ships on the third voyage, and he refers to the ships as *haibo* ("ocean traders") rather than as treasure ships. But since Zheng He commanded "over 27,000" men according to the same author, the fleet cannot have had any less carrying capacity than the fleet of the first two voyages. The ships that Fei Xin calls "ocean traders" were probably all of the large treasure ships that were available, and they were probably accompanied once again by as many as two hundred smaller ships. The similar numbers of personnel for the different voyages suggests that Zheng He's fleet had a more or less fixed "table of organization" or "establishment" strength of over 27,000 men that was related to the estimated carrying capacity of the ships constructed for the expeditions in 1403–05. And indeed, the short turnaround time between the second and third voyages, like that between the first and second voyages, is evidence that most of the same ships and men continued to be involved.

Zheng He's adventures on his third voyage are described in *Taizong Shilu* in an entry dated 6 July 1411 that records the return of the fleet:

> Palace official Zheng He and the others, who had gone as envoys to the barbarian countries of the Western Ocean, returned and presented as captives the King of Ceylon, **Alagakkonara**, together with his family and dependents.
>
> Zheng He and the others, in the course of their first embassy to the barbarians, had arrived at Ceylon, and Alagakkonara had been rude and disrespectful and intended to kill Zheng He. Zheng He realized this and left. Moreover, Alagakkonara was not on friendly terms with the neighboring countries, and he had often intercepted and plundered their embassies *en route* to and from China. Since the other barbarians all had suffered from this, when Zheng He returned they once more treated Ceylon with contempt. Because of this provocation, Alagakkonara lured Zheng He into the interior of the country and sent his son **Nayanar** to demand gold, silver, and other precious goods. If these goods were not turned over, then over 50,000 barbarian troops were to rise from concealment and plunder Zheng He's ships. Moreover, trees had been felled to block the narrow passages and cut off Zheng He's path of retreat, so that the separate Chinese contingents could not reinforce one another.
>
> When Zheng He and the others realized they were in danger of becoming separated from the fleet, they pressed their troops

to return to the ships quickly. When they reached the road-blocks, Zheng He said to his subordinates, "The main body of the bandits has already come out, so the interior of the country must be empty. Moreover, they are saying that we are only an invading army that is isolated and afraid and incapable of doing anything. But if we go forth and attack them, then contrary to their expectations we may gain our objective." Then he secretly ordered messengers to go by other unblocked roads back to the Chinese ships, to order their petty officers and soldiers to hold out to the death with all their strength. Meanwhile he personally led the over two thousand troops under his immediate command by indirect routes. They assaulted the earthen walls of the capital by surprise and broke through, capturing Alagakkonara and his family, dependents, and principal chieftains. The barbarian army then returned and surrounded the city. Zheng He engaged them in battle several times and heavily defeated them.

Afterward, when Zheng He returned, the assembled Ming ministers requested that Alagakkonara and the other captives be executed. But the emperor pitied them as ignorant people who were without knowledge of the Mandate of Heaven; he treated them leniently and released them, giving them food and clothing, and ordering the Ministry of Rites to advise on selecting a worthy one from among Alagakkonara's family to be set up as king, in order to continue the sacrifices of the kingdom of Ceylon.

This campaign has been treated in the literature on Zheng He as an exceptional event in a basically peaceful narrative of exploration and diplomacy. But because this passage is the sole account of the third voyage in the official sources (the description of the third voyage in the *Mingshi* is based on it), it requires a closer reading. First, however, the red herring that Zheng He's real purpose was to steal the Sinhalese tooth relic (*daladā*) needs mention.

Ceylon had been the religious center, and the center for expansion through missionary activity, of Buddhism throughout Southeast Asia. Relics of the historical Buddha, including his begging bowl, a lock of his hair, and—most important—a tooth, were preserved on the island. In 1284 the Mongol ruler Khubilai sent a naval expedition to Ceylon to demand these relics. According to the Sinhalese accounts, the demands for the principal relics were politely rejected, but the Sinhalese gave something else to the Yuan envoys, who went away happy. While Khubilai was always supportive of Buddhism, Chinese sources indicate that all of the naval expeditions during his reign had conquest and/or commerce as primary motivating factors.

Given the centrality of the tooth relic in Sinhalese culture, it is understandable that the Sinhalese accounts of Zheng He's third voyage contain a story of the Sinhalese tricking the Chinese into capturing the wrong king and saving the tooth in the process. In contrast, the later Chinese imaginary accounts of Zheng He's exploits have him taking the tooth, which then guided his voyage back to Nanjing. To judge from his inscriptions and his later reputation, Zheng He, despite his Muslim youth and his close interaction with Muslim traders on his voyages, was a pious Buddhist in his adult life, and he was no doubt personally interested in the relic. Emperor Yongle had Buddhist monks among his informal advisers, and he undertook important measures to promote Buddhism, including the building of the Great Baoen Temple at Nanjing, which Zheng He supervised from 1428 on, but the main emphasis of his cultural and literary policies was the promotion of the orthodox Confucian canon and the values associated with it. There is no mention of the tooth relic in the *Taizong Shilu* passage quoted above, and here the argument from silence speaks loudly. The civil officials who opposed the voyages from the beginning also opposed spending on Buddhism and Buddhist relics. Had the search for the tooth relic been part of the common understanding of what the voyages were about, this would have been mentioned negatively in the historical record.

On all seven voyages, after departing Sumatra and sailing westward across the Indian Ocean, Zheng He's ships first sighted Namanakuli, or Parrot's Beak mountain, 6,680 feet in elevation and about 45 miles from the eastern coast of Ceylon, the easternmost of the mountains of Ceylon and the first part of the island to be visible from the sea. They then corrected their course to pass south of Dondra Head, or Buddha Hall mountain, the southernmost tip of the island, after two or three days. By then the ships would have been at sea for some time (26 days on the seventh voyage), and it would have been natural for them to make a port call, possibly at Galle, where Zheng He set up the

trilingual inscription dated 15 February 1409, or more often at
Beruwala further up the coast. The *Taizong Shilu* entry of 6 July
1411, referring to the third expedition, is the source of the information that Zheng He was badly treated on the first expedition, but he did not make an issue of it then, since he was hurrying
on to Calicut. Spreading awe of China was his mission, not
searching for Buddhist relics.

At the time of Zheng He's third voyage, the Hindu Tamil
kingdom of the Āryachakravartis, based at Jaffna, was the most
powerful state on Ceylon. The ancient Buddhist Sinhalese state
had been driven from its former capital at Polonnaruva in the
northeast into the southwest, where the Sinhalese had built the
fort of Jayavardhanapura, or Kotte, a few miles inland from
modern Colombo. Kotte was the seat of a revived Sinhalese
coastal kingdom from the time of Zheng He's withdrawal until
the Portuguese conquest of 1597. The Alagakkonara family,
traders of Tamil origin, had moved to Ceylon, converted to
Buddhism, and intermarried with the royal family. Alakeshvara,
the "Alagakkonara" mentioned in the Chinese account, had become the *de facto* ruler under a puppet king from the previous
royal dynasty. He gained prestige by military success in the
wars against the Jaffna kingdom, and he was king by usurpation when Zheng He returned to Ceylon in 1409. The Buddhist
Sinhalese were well located to prey on ships sailing between
southern India and the Straits of Malacca. Already waging war
against a Tamil state in the northern part of "their" island, they
were disposed to be hostile to the Tamil and Malayalam states
of southern India, which had Muslim trading classes that were
interested in promoting the volume and safety of oceanic trade.
The Chinese had asserted their power in this area during the
first voyage, despite Alakeshvara's hostile intentions, and they
now suppressed Alakeshvara forcefully.

Here, in contrast to the battle against Chen Zuyi, which was
certainly naval and probably fought in the rivers and channels
between Palembang and the sea, there is no doubt that Zheng
He and the two thousand men under his immediate command
had disembarked and were fighting on land. Alakeshvara's goal
was to make a surprise attack on the fleet while Zheng He was
cut off from direct communication with his ships, anchored at

Colombo. Probably Alakeshvara had intended to do the same, or had tried something similar, during the first voyage. The Chinese sources present Zheng He as a smart commander who thinks and moves quickly; unexpectedly breaking into Kotte, he captures the king and the leadership group. The Sinhalese army is presented as being large enough to overwhelm Zheng He's entire armada, though as usual the number given (50,000) is too vague to be certain. Emperor Yongle, for reasons that remain unclear, freed Alakeshvara but asked the Ministry of Rites to recommend a new king. Meanwhile, back in Ceylon, a ruler from the legitimate dynasty had begun a long reign at Kotte, and when the next Chinese embassy arrived, the new king was strong enough to disregard both Alakeshvara and the candidate recommended by the Chinese Ministry of Rites. All subsequent Chinese fleets stopped at Ceylon, and there is no further mention of Sinhalese piracy or attacks on the Chinese fleets.

The inscription dated 15 February 1409 and erected at Galle is evidence that Zheng He called at that port, but Beruwala near Colombo, 52 miles up the coast from Galle, was the preferred port of call; Ma Huan calls Beruwala "the wharf of the country of Ceylon." The inscription at Galle is in three languages: Chinese, Tamil, and Persian. The Chinese version praises Buddha for protecting the Chinese fleet in its voyages; the Tamil version gives similar praise to a local god who is an incarnation of Vishnu; and the Persian version gives the same thanks to Allah. The list of presents offered to the divine is identical in all three languages: 1,000 pieces of gold, 5,000 pieces of silver, 100 rolls of silk, 2,500 catties of perfumed oil, and lists of bronze ornaments. On the same date in China, the God of the South China Sea *(Nanhai Shen)* was awarded the title "Earl who Calms the Sea," and earlier, on 21 January 1409, the goddess Tianfei had been offered a new and longer title at a ceremony so important that, in J. J. L. Duyvendak's opinion, it required Zheng He's personal presence, thus precluding his presence on the second voyage.

These ceremonies were a coordinated imperial offensive to persuade the heavens and their diverse deities to smile on Chinese maritime activities, but the voyages most threatened by storms and piracy were not those of Zheng He but the transports of grain to Beijing, where the sea route was so insecure that the

Zheng He never saw the church and lighthouse shown here, but this photograph of Galle in Ceylon hints at both the navigational hazards of the harbor and its exposure to the southwest monsoon. © Courtesy Sri Lanka Ministry of Tourism.

emperor opted for the Grand Canal route to supply his enlarged capital. This fact should make us think further about how seaworthy Chinese ships actually were, and how much control of the seas China actually exercised, even during this period of considerable maritime activity. Zheng He's presence with the fleet in 1409, and thus on all of the second voyage, seems to be indicated by Fei Xin's account of the wood cutting expedition on Pulau Sembilan. The Galle inscription must therefore have been prepared in advance in China and erected at Galle during the third voyage, either on the way out in 1410 or on the return voyage in 1411.

Galle harbor itself argues for the erection of the inscription in 1410. In the words of an authority on the later Portuguese period, it "possessed the strongest natural defenses of any site on the island and lay at the edge of Ceylon's prime cinnamon lands. It sat wholly on a stalklike promontory that might almost have been created with the military engineers of the black powder era in mind. Except for the neck of land that joined it to Ceylon, the site sheered abruptly down cliffs to the water on all sides and further confounded would-be landing parties with rocks, surf, and treacherous currents at its base. These also made access to Galle's self-contained harbor tricky, but the Portuguese had long since mastered the art of entering it and mooring their vessels with storm anchors against the current." The harbor itself had reefs and uncharted rocks that caused grief to the Dutch after they took it from the Portuguese. It provided good shelter during the winter monsoon, when the winds blew from the northeast, but it was largely open to the winds of the summer monsoon that blew from the west and southwest.

Since Zheng He landed at Galle, rather than the preferred anchorage at Beruwala, he probably did so on the way out, when the winds were best for the use of this dangerous harbor. Zheng He may have landed at Galle because he knew from his reception in 1405 that a confrontation with Alakeshwara was likely, and Beruwala was uncomfortably close to Alakeshwara's inland capital at Kotte. This suggests that the confrontation with, and capture of, Alakeshwara took place in 1410 rather than 1411, which is contrary to the position that most authorities have taken. Yet the Chinese sources, which tell of the confrontation with Alakeshwara in the *Taizong Shilu* entry that reports Zheng He's return, take no position on this issue. Placing the conflict in 1410 keeps Alakeshwara away from Ceylon for all of 1411, the year in which the next king of Ceylon established his rule.

Zheng He's first three voyages kept his ships under way and his men in action almost continuously from 1405 to 1411. On these three voyages the fleet sailed to the same group of countries, of which Calicut on the southwest coast of India was the most distant. Zheng He's armada engaged in two important military campaigns, first at Palembang in Sumatra in 1406, and then in Ceylon, probably in 1410. In both campaigns, their hard fighting and loss of life earned his troops special rewards from their emperor. Afterward the fleet would sail further and encounter less opposition, even as the transfer of the capital to Beijing led inevitably to declining imperial interest in the voyages.

Sailing to Africa
Zheng He's Fourth, Fifth, and Sixth Voyages

Emperor Yongle had been resident in Nanjing from 1402 until shortly after ordering the third voyage in 1409, when he returned to Beijing to supervise the building of the new capital. At Nanjing he had been physically close to the construction of the treasure ships and the departure and return of the fleet. For the rest of his reign, Yongle's eyes were on the north, on the new capital and on his campaigns in Mongolia, and the three remaining voyages that Zheng He's fleet undertook during the Yongle reign had to compete with those projects for imperial attention.

The Fourth Voyage, 1412/14–15

Zheng He and his fleet had been back from their third major voyage for a year and a half before Emperor Yongle ordered a fourth expedition. On 18 December 1412 he commanded Grand Director Zheng He and others to go "bearing imperial letters to confer gifts of silk floss, thin silk gauze, colored thin silk, and other goods, each according to his deserts" on the kings of several countries. *Taizong Shilu* lists the destinations in no apparent order, and other sources indicate that the fleet also visited Palembang (here called *Sanfoqi*, or Shri Vijaya) and Ceylon.

Yongle issued his order for the fourth voyage about three months before his departure (16 March 1413) for North China to command his second military expedition into Mongolia. He was still in the north when the fourth expedition returned in 1415. In the following year Yongle proclaimed Beijing an imperial capital, thus setting in motion the project of making it the primary capital. Yongle ordered the fifth expedition on 28 December 1416, six weeks after his temporary return to Nanjing on 14 November. He spent a season in Nanjing, then on 12 April 1417 left Nanjing "for a tour of the north," leaving his eldest son, the crown prince (afterward Emperor Hongxi), in charge. He spent the rest of his life in the north, presiding over the reconstruction and expansion of Beijing and commanding in person three more military expeditions into Mongolia, on the last of which he died.

The military expeditions proved abortive, and the transfer of the capital (Nanjing retained its formal status as an imperial capital and was briefly the seat of Ming pretenders after 1644, but no Ming emperor from 1418 to 1644 resided there) required not only outlays for construction but also long-term operating expenses. Beijing remained close to a vulnerable frontier, in view of the Mongol hostility to China that prevailed throughout the Ming. An army had to be stationed there, and grain supplies brought up from the south. In the long run the mere location of the imperial court and government in the north on the edge of the steppe took the minds of emperors and officials away from the south and the sea.

Zheng He probably left Nanjing in autumn 1413, and he set sail from Fujian in Yongle eleventh year, twelfth month (23 December 1413 to 21 January 1414), in accordance with the usual pattern of monsoon winds. While *Taizong Shilu* again lists the countries visited in random order, the voyage began by following the usual pattern. First the fleet, said to be 63 ships (probably the number of large ships only) carrying 28,560 men, sailed across the South China Sea to Champa and from Champa to the Malayan Peninsula. There Malacca was the main port of call, but Pahang and Kelantan could easily have been visited on the way. (These states on the Malayan peninsula still exist as members of the Federation of Malaysia.) Palembang was another traditional stop, even if its Chinese Pacification Commissioner did not rate the title of king. Previous difficulties with Java had been smoothed over, and a Javanese envoy arrived in China on 29 April 1415, presenting "western horses" and local products as tribute and expressing thanks for the gifts and favors bestowed by the emperor and delivered by Zheng He's fleet as it traversed the Java Sea on its way west.

Once through the Straits of Malacca, the fleet stopped at the north end of Sumatra, where once again the scanty sources mention the usual small states of Lambri (*Nanpoli*), Lide, Aru, and Semudera. Lambri had only a thousand families according to Ma Huan, who accompanied Zheng He for the first time on the fourth voyage, while Lide to the east had three thousand. Slightly further to the east, on the north coast of Sumatra, was Semudera, which Ma Huan calls "the most important port of assembly for the Western Ocean" in a phrase that recalls his description of Calicut as "the great country of the Western Ocean." Unlike Calicut, where Muslim merchants had an honored and influential position in a Hindu society ruled by a Hindu king, the north Sumatran states were Muslim and their customs the same as those of China's ally Malacca. Northern Sumatra is important not so much as a source of trade goods, but as the anchorage where the fleet assembles itself before undertaking the long voyage across the Indian Ocean to Ceylon and southern India.

After making landfall on Ceylon, the fleet sailed around the southwestern coast of India, from *Jiayile* opposite Ceylon, past Cochin, to Calicut. Calicut had been the westernmost destination of the first three voyages, all of which demonstrated a Chinese naval presence on an established trading route that went from Fujian to southern India by way of Champa, the Straits of Malacca, northern Sumatra, and Ceylon. This time, however, the fleet sailed north and west from Calicut, and *Taizong Shilu* records four new destinations. *Liushan* refers to the Maldive and Laccadive Islands in general, while *Bila* and *Sunla* have been identified with Bitra Atoll and Chetlat Atoll respectively, which are close to one another in the more northerly Laccadives. *Bila* and *Sunla* are both included under *Liushan* in the *Mingshi*. Ma Huan gives sailing directions to *Liushan* of ten days from Semudera, which makes more sense for the Maldives;

the sailing directions are not credible because they require what J. V. G. Mills calls "a very fast voyage of about 170 miles a day" or an average sustained speed of over six knots. Fei Xin gives sailing directions of seven days from Ceylon, which would take a treasure ship at least as far as the Maldives at a more reasonable 70 miles per day. The *Mingshi* wisely or perhaps accidentally follows Fei Xin here. Land-poor islands, *Liushan* nevertheless produced ambergris, whose applications were already known, and cowrie shells that circulated as currency in Thailand, Bengal, and other countries. This time Zheng He's fleet probably stopped only at the Laccadives, since its primary destination was Hormuz.

Hormuz, the island city in the strait between the Gulf of Oman and the Persian Gulf, could be reached by ordinary merchant ships, given a fair wind, on a twenty-five-day voyage to the northwest from Calicut. This works out to 61 nautical miles per day, or 2.4 knots. In 1432–33 Zheng He's fleet took thirty-four days for the same voyage, equaling 45 nautical miles per day, or 1.8 knots. Neither is an impressive speed for well-handled sailing ships under dependable monsoon winds. We cannot say if Zheng He had less favorable winds than average, or if his large ships were as lubberly as their calculated dimensions indicate (see Chapter VI) and were therefore slower than smaller ships would have been. If Semudera was where the ships gathered and Calicut was the great country of the Western Ocean, Ma Huan was even more expansive about Hormuz: "Foreign ships from every place, together with foreign merchants traveling by land, all come to this territory in order to gather together and buy and sell, and therefore the people of this country are all rich"—an explicit association of trade and wealth that would not be made in Chinese texts of the usual Confucian cast. Hormuz was the shipping point for many trade goods shipped across the Arabian Sea to southern India as the first stage in a voyage that might take them as far as China. The sources seem to indicate that Zheng He's fleet went there straight from Calicut, visiting only locations in the Laccadive Islands and stopping at no other mainland location before Hormuz, a port well known to traders. As with Calicut on the first three voyages, the choice of Hormuz as ultimate destination on the fourth indicates again that the purpose of the voyages was not primarily exploration but showing the flag and establishing a Chinese armed naval presence on familiar trade routes and trade entrepôts. The choice of Hormuz as principal destination illustrates the fundamental enigma of the Zheng He voyages: while prohibiting foreign trade by his own subjects, the emperor nonetheless wished to display Chinese power to foreign countries whose own wealth was gained from such trade.

On the return voyage in 1415, when the fleet stopped in northern Sumatra, Zheng He captured Sekandar, a rebel against **Zain al-'Abidin,** the king of Semudera recognized by the Chinese. This is the third important military operation recorded in the accounts of the voyages, after Palembang on the first voyage and Ceylon on the third. As in the first two operations, Zheng He's fleet and its embarked military personnel possessed strength enough to win, but as in Ceylon Zheng He fought a land campaign against an enemy fighting on his home turf, and it is unlikely that a smaller force would have prevailed. All three operations had the purpose of demonstrating Chinese power along the routes from China to the Western Ocean. Where Chen Zuyi of Palembang was described as a pirate and Alakeshvara of Ceylon had been committing piracy against his neighbors' embassies to China, Sekandar was similarly seen as a threat to order in Semudera, the great "place of assembly" for the east end of the trans-Indian Ocean trade.

Zheng He's biography describes the Sekandar episode briefly: "Before this Sekandar, who pretended to be the son of a king, was just then plotting to kill his lord and set himself up as king. He was angry that Zheng He did not give him any presents, and he led his troops in person to intercept and attack the Imperial Army. Zheng He battled him forcefully, pursued him to Lambri, and took him prisoner, also capturing his wives and children." The words "before this" refer in this account to Yongle tenth year, eleventh month (4 December 1412 to 2 January 1413), but both Ma Huan and the account of Semudera in the *Mingshi* set the battle with Sekandar in 1415, which would place it on the return voyage from Hormuz. Had Sekandar received gifts from the Chinese emperor, it would have symbolized his status as a recognized ruler, so his annoyance was not mere pettiness.

The *Mingshi* account of Semudera is based on Ma Huan but includes additional material. Referring to Zheng He's first three expeditions, it continues:

> Before this, the king's father had done battle with the tattooed faced king of the neighboring kingdom and had been killed by an arrow. The king's son was still young, and the king's wife said to her people, "Whoever can avenge my husband's death I will make my new husband and share with him the rule of the kingdom." There was a fisherman who led the men of the kingdom to attack and behead the tattooed faced king; when he returned, the former king's wife then joined him in marriage, and he was called the Old King. When the son of the former king grew up he plotted secretly with the tribal chiefs and killed the Old King and succeeded to his position. The Old King's younger brother Sekandar then fled into the mountains, and year after year he led his followers to invade and disrupt. In the thirteenth year (1415) Zheng He came once again to this country (Semudera), and Sekandar became angry because he was not included among those receiving gifts. Leading several myriads of men, he engaged and attacked the Imperial Army. Zheng He kept tight control of his own forces and the native troops and withstood the attackers. Zheng He heavily defeated the bandit forces and pursued them to Lambri, where he captured [Sekandar] and returned with him to China.

Ma Huan makes Sekandar the son, rather than the younger brother, of the Old King, has him erect a single stockade or fort in the mountains, does not mention how many troops he had—even with a figure as vague as "several myriads"—and does not accuse him of attacking Zheng He's forces. Zheng He, on the other hand, is credited with a "great fleet of treasure ships," which he certainly had, and he is said to have simply "dispatched troops" to capture Sekandar, implying that it was some kind of police action. The true king of Semudera was grateful and sent a tribute mission to express his thanks.

Earlier Western scholars who dealt with this material came to varying conclusions. Zain al-'Abidin was king of Semudera from at least 1405 to 1433, so if he was the young son of the "former king" who murdered the Old King, this event must have taken place in 1405 at the latest, but this is consistent with the statement in the *Mingshi* that Sekandar's invasions had taken place "year after year." The "tattooed faced king" was the ruler of Nagur, a name that transcribes the Sanskrit word *nagara* (city), but it was a poor and primitive country west of Semudera on the Sumatran coast, whose population was only "something over a thousand families," the same population Ma Huan assigns to Lambri. West of Nagur was Lide, another small country, with three thousand families. No population estimate is given for Semudera, but it clearly is an order of magnitude greater and is the most important of the northern Sumatra states. Even so, it seems unlikely that Sekandar could muster an army of "several myriads." However, in its general thrust the *Mingshi* account is clear and consistent. Whatever his true origins, Sekandar was an autonomous ruler; when he was not recognized as such, he attacked. Zheng He fought him on land, with Chinese soldiers disembarked from his ships who cooperated with native troops from Semudera. By capturing Sekandar, Zheng He protected the existing pattern of political authority and the trade it sheltered, once again affirming the power of the Chinese emperor over the foreign states and the ocean routes connecting them.

Like the capture of Chen Zuyi and the war with Alakeshvara, the action against Sekandar was no exception to a pattern of peaceful exploration. Rather, it was a clear demonstration of the purpose of Zheng He's voyages: to bring the Western Ocean into the Chinese tributary system by overawing, or if need be by overpowering, opposition. Zheng He's fleet, in other words, was an armada, in the sense of the Spanish Armada of 1588: its primary purpose was not to fight other fleets but to transport Chinese troops who could be disembarked to overcome resistance on land.

Taizong Shilu notes the return to Nanjing of Zheng He's fourth voyage in an entry dated 12 August 1415. On the following day, one of Zheng He's eunuch colleagues was sent on a mission to Bengal with gifts lovingly catalogued as velvet brocade, gold woven cloth, patterned silk, silk gauze, and "other goods." According to Ma Huan, the pretender Sekandar, whom Zheng He had captured in Sumatra, was publicly executed in the capital, but it is not clear how long after Zheng He's return this occurred.

The Fifth Voyage, 1417–19

Emperor Yongle arrived in Nanjing from the north on 14 November 1416, beginning his last period of residence in his father's capital. His first act, the histories tell us, was to visit his father's tomb, the Xiaoling ("Mausoleum of Filial Piety"), on the Purple Mountain or Bell Mountain east of the city, next to where the Nationalist government later built the tomb of Sun Yat-sen.

Five days later, on the first day of the eleventh lunar month, at a grand ceremony in which the Directorate of Astronomy presented the calendar for the following year and the emperor gave gifts to the assembled princes, civil officials, and military officers, the ambassadors of seventeen countries (represented by eighteen names) and one Pacification Office (*xuanweisi*, the self-governing Chinese community at Palembang), which was carefully separated from the "countries" in the text, offered their tributes of horses, rhinoceroses, elephants, and other "local products." On 28 December the ambassadors of the same eighteen entities came to court to take their leave. "All of them were given robes with linings of patterned silk."

Zheng He and unnamed "others" were ordered to take the ambassadors home. In addition to letters from the emperor, he carried silk brocade, silk gauze, colored thin silk, and other items as presents for the several kings. The king of Cochin, whose kingdom Zheng He had visited on every voyage, received special treatment. He had sent tribute beginning in 1411, and later he had sent ambassadors requesting a patent of investiture and a seal. He now received both, along with a long inscription, allegedly composed by Emperor Yongle himself, conferring the title State Protecting Mountain on a hill in his kingdom. These orders authorized Zheng He's fifth voyage.

Twelve of the eighteen entities listed (in slightly different orders, with the Pacification Office at Palembang coming last in both entries) in the *Taizong Shilu* entries for 19 November and 28 December 1416 are familiar places. In the logical order of sailing, they were: Champa, Pahang on the eastern shore of the Malay Peninsula, Java (as usual, both *Guawa* and *Zhaowa* are written), the Pacification Office of the "Old Harbor" at Palembang in Sumatra, Malacca, and then Semudera and Lambri (the two names for which, *Nanwuli* and *Nanpoli*, appear nonconsecutively on both lists) in northern Sumatra. From northern Sumatra the fleet made its usual trip across the Indian Ocean to Ceylon, then sailed around the Indian coast to Cochin and Calicut. The fleet visited *Shaliwanni* on this voyage for the first and only time; if the identification of this country with Cannanore in India is correct, it would have been next after Calicut (the brief notice of *Shaliwanni* in the *Mingshi* gives no hint of its location). *Liushan*, visited on the previous voyage, denotes both the Maldive and the Laccadive Islands, and as on the previous voyage, it would have made sense for the fleet to swing through the Laccadives, but not the Maldives, on its voyage to Hormuz.

The five remaining countries had never before been visited by the Chinese fleet. Two (*Lasa* and Aden) are on the southern coast of the Arabian Peninsula, and three (Mogadishu, Brava, and Malindi) are on the coast of Africa. All but *Lasa* are still current names, with Aden, Mogadishu, and Malindi remaining important port towns. Brava (also written Braawe) is south of Mogadishu on the Somali coast; its people remain conscious of their town's historical role in the trade of the Indian Ocean, and they speak a distinct dialect of Swahili (not Somali). All of these places except Malindi have sailing directions in the *Mingshi* that are referenced to Calicut (*Lasa* and Aden), Ceylon (Brava), and Quilon (Mogadishu), indicating that voyages out of sight of land from the western, as well as the eastern, coast of India were normal for the Chinese navigators of Zheng He's day. On this occasion it is more likely that the route from Hormuz went first to *Lasa* (at or near present-day Mukalla in Yemen) and then Aden before going down the African coast to Mogadishu, Brava, and Malindi in succession.

The fifth voyage is the only one of the seven for which there is no specific information at all regarding the numbers of ships and personnel, but the evidence for the other voyages suggests strongly that Zheng He was operating with a fleet of a set composition, and it is unlikely that this composition differed greatly on the fifth voyage. Duyvendak concluded, in his reconstruction of the dates, that Zheng He's fleet left the China coast sometime in the autumn of 1417. Before leaving Fujian, Zheng He and the fleet made port at Quanzhou and remained there a long while, taking on a cargo of Chinese porcelains and other goods. A Ming tablet at Quanzhou dated 31 May 1417 commemorates Zheng He's burning incense to invoke divine protection for his upcoming voyage. Chinese porcelain from this period has turned up in archaeological excavations in the east African locales visited by Zheng He's fleet, whose carrying capacity ensured that by itself it could add significantly to the volume of trade, even though the sources dwell on the diplomatic aspects (and, to a lesser extent, the "power projection" aspects) of the voyages. Quanzhou, Marco Polo's Zayton, had a large Muslim community, a result of its long history as a port of entry into China during the centuries when much of this trade was conducted by Muslim shippers. The return of the fleet is noted in a *Taizong Shilu* entry dated 8 August 1419.

As far as Calicut, Zheng He and his fleet followed the path they had sailed in the first three expeditions, and from Calicut to Hormuz (perhaps by way of the Laccadives) they went where they had gone on the fourth voyage. South and west of Hormuz, on the Arabian and African coasts, the fleet was sailing where it had not gone before and may not have been entirely welcome. Luo Maodeng's novel of 1597 has Zheng He using gunpowder weapons against the walled town of *Lasa*, and it has the ruler of Mogadishu imagining that the Ming emperor would not have sent soldiers so far from his own country unless he intended conquest. Duyvendak believed that Luo Maodeng's account had historical value, and, since resistance is implied at only those locations, one recent authority has put *Lasa* "near Mogadishu." Another has identified it with Zeila, also in Somalia, following an earlier suggestion that the characters had become inverted from an original *Sala*.

Whether *Lasa* is in Africa or Arabia is obviously important. J. V. G. Mills, analyzing the Mao Kun map found in the *Wubeizhi* and based on the Zheng He voyages, noted the names *Shilier* (Ash-Shihr in the Hadramaut region of present-day Yemen), *Lasa*, Aden (instantly recognizable in the form *Adan*), and *Luofa* (Luhaiya on the Red Sea coast of Yemen) lined up in that order on the coast of the Arabian peninsula. Since the other three are current place names, and *Lasa* suggests Arabic forms such as Al-Ahsa or El-Hasa, Mills' suggestion that *Lasa* was at most a few miles from Mukalla "and lost its importance with the rise of the latter" is likely to be correct. Mills goes on to say that the description of *Lasa* in the *Mingshi* "does not help to establish its situation." This is that description:

> *Lasa*: sailing with the wind from Calicut for twenty days and nights one may get there. In 1416 it sent an ambassador with tribute. Zheng He was ordered to return him. Afterward there were three tribute missions in all, always along with such countries as Aden and Brava. In 1430 Zheng He was again ordered to go as ambassador bearing imperial letters. From then on there were no tribute missions. The country is located where the climate is always hot, and the fields are barren and yield little. The customs are simple, funerals are conducted with ceremony, and for every occasion they pray to their gods. Grass and trees do not grow, and there are long droughts without rain. All of their houses are like those of such countries as *Zhubu*. Such things as frankincense (*ruxiang*), ambergris (*longxianxiang*), and "thousand *li* camels" are produced there.

The "thousand *li* camels" were presumably named for their endurance; the *li* was a unit of measurement of about one-third of a mile. In *Zhubu*—definitely in Africa and discussed below—a similar lack of vegetation caused people to "pile up stones to live in," and both *Zhubu* and Brava also produced frankincense and ambergris. Lest this clinch the matter, both *Zhubu* and Brava reportedly have territories adjoining Mogadishu's, as *Lasa* does not, and both are reached by sailing from locations south of Calicut, the indicated port of departure for both Aden and *Lasa*. East of Hadramaut, in the southernmost reaches of present-day Oman, the region of Djofar (variously Dhafar, Dhufar, Zafar, and other forms in works in English) corresponds to the *Zufaer* of the *Mingshi* and Ma Huan. Frankincense was Djofar's most important product, and Djofar would have been a near neighbor of *Lasa* if *Lasa* was near Mukalla in Hadramaut. Like Aden and *Lasa*, Djofar is reached by sailing from Calicut, but with a voyage of only ten days and nights (according to Ma Huan, whom the compilers of the *Mingshi* followed here), as opposed to the twenty required for *Lasa* and the twenty-two required to reach Aden. This makes the trip from Calicut to Djofar "a fast voyage of 134 miles a day," according to Mills. But Fei Xin places Djofar (here *Zuofaer*) directly after *Lasa* in his text, and repeats "twenty days and nights from Calicut" as the sailing directions to both countries. This reduces the voyage to 67 miles per day, or about 2.5 knots average sustained speed, surely the upper limit of the probable for the stately treasure ships. This is consistent with the duration of certain other voyages whose sailing directions are given by Ma Huan (62 miles per day to Aden, 61 miles per day to both Bengal and Hormuz, in each case from the designated port of departure). All of these considerations support the location of *Lasa* near Mukalla in Hadramaut. Duyvendak's discussion of the same point at least got *Lasa* out of the Persian Gulf and out of Africa; he finally settled on Oman, but Mills' argument is preferable.

Luo Maodeng's novel has *Lasa* resisting the Chinese, who retaliate by using siege engines called Xiangyang *dapao* to batter down the city's walls. Siege engines built by Muslim engineers and called *Huihuipao*, or "Muslim catapults" (also *Xiyupao*, or "Western-style catapults," and *Jushipao*, or "huge stone catapults"), had indeed figured prominently in the Mongol siege of Xiangyang in 1268–73, which was the opening stage in the final Yuan conquest of the Southern Song Dynasty. Engines of the same type were called *Xiangyangpao*, or "Xiangyang catapults," from then on (the *da* in *dapao* means "large"). They were counterweighted stone-throwers of the kind usually called "trebuchet" in the west. In the 1200s they were comparatively new in the west, and they could throw heavier stones than the traditional catapults of the torsion type. In Luo Maodeng's narrative the Xiangyang *dapao* are mounted on what appear to be mobile siege towers called "cloud ladders" (*yunti*, a compound usually meaning scaling ladders). Twelve shots (three at each of the city's four gates) shatter the walls and terrify the natives. Since the Chinese historical sources state clearly that both *Lasa* and Mogadishu produced no wood, there was no way to fabricate the cloud ladders unless the Chinese were willing to cannibalize some of their ships.

Luo Maodeng, and Duyvendak interpreting him, consider the Xiangyang *dapao* to be "bombards," or cannon of some sort. But only small firearms, rather than siege artillery, could have been mounted on the cloud ladders because of the recoil factor. Cannon were certainly used in the wars of the Ming founding, and Emperor Yongle's organization of his army in Beijing included a major headquarters devoted to firearms training. It is certainly possible that Zheng He's fleet carried firearms as part of its armament, but Luo Maodeng's novel does not add to the evidence on that point. In fact, his use of the term Xiangyang *dapao* suggests that he wove his narrative of the fight at *Lasa* from the history of the historical siege of Xiangyang plus some awareness of the firearms in existence in the 1590s, which had contributed to Ming China's victory over the Japanese in Korea in that decade.

Aden at the time of Zheng He's fifth voyage was enjoying a final period of stability under al-Malik an-Nasir Salah-ad-Din Ahmad (ruled 1400–24), the eighth ruler of the Rasulid dynasty that had wrested control of Yemen from Egypt in 1229. Ma Huan describes a prosperous Muslim country whose "people are of an overbearing disposition" and whose ruler had "seven or eight thousand well-drilled horsemen and foot soldiers; therefore the country is very powerful, and neighboring states fear it." The *Mingshi* repeats this information and adds that Aden sent tribute missions on four occasions, their last ambassadors leaving China to return in 1436. King Ahmad "welcomed the imperial edict and bestowal of gifts" and saluted the Chinese envoys "with great reverence and humility." At this time Egypt's Mamluk Sultanate was expanding southward and threatening Yemen, and Ahmad may have hoped for Chinese assistance against the Mamluks, who were powerful militarily both on land and at sea. Ahmad was still ruling when Chinese ships returned to the Arabian Sea during the sixth voyage of 1421–22, but Yemen fell apart under his two sons 'Abdallah (ruled 1424–27) and Isma'il II (ruled 1427–28) and Isma'il's son Yahya (ruled 1428–39), when the slave soldiers who were the core of the army that Ma Huan admired rebelled repeatedly. Since Yemen under the Rasulids could be a significant regional power with its "seven or eight thousand" soldiers, Zheng He with his 27,000 men was clearly strong enough to spread awe even though the Chinese armada was far from home.

Rounding the Horn of Africa and heading south, the fleet came first to Mogadishu. The *Mingshi* has an account derived from Fei Xin, indicating normal sailing directions to Mogadishu as twenty days and nights across the Arabian Sea from Quilon in southern India. The country is between the mountains and the sea; the land is a stony desert whose fields do not yield much; it is hot year-round and sometimes it does not rain for several years. The customs of the people are bigoted and insincere (*wanyin*; these words can both mean "stupid," making this the most pejorative description of any foreign country on the Zheng He circuit), and they spend their time drilling their soldiers and practicing archery. Since "the land produces no wood, they also, as in Hormuz, pile up stones to make their dwellings," up to four or five storys, Fei Xin adds, telling us that the rich people depend on ships that conduct long-distance trade, while the poor people fish. Dried fish meal is fed to cattle, sheep, horses, and camels. In addition to the ubiquitous frankincense and ambergris, leopards (*jinqianbao*) are mentioned as a local product. Both of Zheng He's inscriptions say that on the fifth voyage Mogadishu presented zebras (*huafulu*) and lions as tribute. Mogadishu later resisted the Portuguese more stubbornly than any other African city. Luo Maodeng's novel has Mogadishu resisting the Chinese, who win as at *Lasa* with their Xiangyang *dapao* mounted on cloud ladders—in another country that, like *Lasa*, produced no wood.

Further down the coast is Brava (or Braawe; *Bulawa* in Chinese transcription). Here again the *Mingshi* follows Fei Xin closely. Brava, too, is between the mountains and the sea, and its territory borders on that of Mogadishu, but its customs are "pure" or "honest." Here also stones are piled up to make walls and buildings since there is no grass or wood. Much of the land is salt wastes, the fields cannot be cultivated, and except for garlic and onions, there are no crops, so the people eat fish. In compensation, salt is produced. Other local products include ambergris, frankincense, and myrrh, as well as cattle, camels, rhinoceroses, and elephant ivory. Brava sent four tribute missions between 1416 and 1423, always in conjunction with Mogadishu. Both of Zheng He's inscriptions say that on the fifth voyage Brava presented "thousand *li* camels" and ostriches, called "camel birds" (*tuoji*), as tribute.

Proceeding down the present-day Somali coast, the fleet would have come to the mouth of the Juba (Giuba) River, and its mariners would not necessarily have known that its outflow included that of its tributary the Shebeli (Scebeli), which flowed behind the "mountains" that pressed both Mogadishu and Brava against the Indian Ocean. Here the modern town of Kismayu is now the major port, but either the town of Jumbo (Giumbo; the Italian-style spellings are a legacy of the colonial period still found on many modern maps) or the Juba River itself is the origin of the *Zhubu* found in both Fei Xin and the *Mingshi*. Zheng He stopped there, according to the latter, which does not say when. The population of *Zhubu* was small, but their customs are "somewhat" honest (Fei Xin says "also" honest, like those of Brava). Once he had mentioned the lack of wood, the stone buildings, and the constant heat, the *Mingshi* compiler got fed up, noting that it was "all the same as Mogadishu." Mogadishu is also said to border on *Zhubu*, which seems unlikely because Brava was in between them. Local products included lions, leopards, ostriches, black pepper, and "golden amber" as well as the ambergris and frankincense which we have come to expect.

After *Zhubu*, if indeed the fleet stopped there on this voyage, Zheng He led his fleet perhaps as far as, and certainly no further than, Malindi in present-day Kenya. Rhinoceroses and elephants had been presented in tribute as local products by some of the ambassadors whom Zheng He was returning on this voyage. There is a Sumatran variety of rhinoceros, which may have been less rare then than it is now, and elephants were so associated with India in the Chinese mind that *Xiangzhu* ("elephant lord") was a recognized term for India. But it is more likely that the elephants and rhinoceroses mentioned as tribute from the African countries were of the African variety, and elephant ivory and rhinoceroses were mentioned as part of Brava's local produce. Malindi, however, had something even more exotic: it was the ultimate source of the *qilin*.

Malindi does not have a chapter in either Ma Huan or Fei Xin. It does have an entry in the *Mingshi*, which begins by describing its location as "a long way from China." A modern map indicates a voyage of a few days from Brava and *Zhubu*, but the *Mingshi* compilers, apparently working from documents that made no reference to its location, did not know this.

The *Mingshi* entry is devoted entirely to the presentation of the *qilin* in 1415, the efforts of courtiers to flatter the emperor to the effect that his good government has caused the creature to appear, the emperor's virtuous rejection of this flattery, and his ultimate acceptance of the idea that the virtues of his father Emperor Hongwu, reaching distant Malindi, had caused the authorities there to send the creature. A *qilin* from Bengal, by report originally from Malindi, had been received in 1414 and had caused a similar reaction. There is no description of Malindi as a country or as a society, in contrast to the other African and Arabian coast locations discussed in the sources. Malindi sent a final tribute mission with unspecified local products in 1416, and the return of this embassy, announced in the *Taizong Shilu* entry for 28 December 1416, is the only reason for believing that Zheng He's fleet sailed that far south. Malindi is not mentioned as a destination for either the sixth or the seventh voyage.

The beasts presented were giraffes, even though the giraffe does not look much like either the beast portrayed on the Kirin Beer label (*kirin* is the Japanese pronunciation of *qilin*) or the representations of the *qilin* found in various Chinese sources. Like them, however, it is exotic and spotted, and two realistic Chinese paintings (reproduced in Duyvendak's *True Dates*) indicate that Emperor Yongle confronted real giraffes. Fei Xin and both of Zheng He's inscriptions state that the native name of the *qilin* is *zulafa*, from the Arabic *zarafa* (giraffe). Aden sent giraffes as tribute on the fifth (that one apparently never arrived in China) and sixth voyages, and Mecca on the seventh. The *qilin* episode symbolizes Zheng He's voyages in the minds of many who have only a passing familiarity with them, but in reality the Chinese never found a primary destination in Africa of comparable importance to either Calicut or Hormuz.

The various reports of giraffes presented as tribute collectively say something interesting. The giraffe from Bengal is said to be a re-export originally from Malindi, and those submitted from Aden and Mecca are unlikely to have been native products. Duyvendak believed that many of the "ambassadors" referred to in the Zheng He sources were actually merchants, and it is tempting to speculate that news of Chinese susceptibility to the giraffe, and its positive message about imperial virtue transforming the world, was spreading by word of mouth among the (mainly Muslim) merchants of the Indian Ocean.

The return of the fleet is noted in a *Taizong Shilu* entry dated 8 August 1419. The emperor, then in Beijing, ordered the Ministry of Rites to give monetary rewards to the personnel of the fleet. As with the rewards given after the first and third voyages, the rewards given on this occasion give important information regarding the personnel of Zheng He's fleet (discussed in Chapter VI).

The Sixth Voyage, 1421–22

The first mention of the sixth voyage appears in an entry in *Taizong Shilu* dated 3 March 1421, which says that "the envoys of sixteen countries including Hormuz, returning to their countries, were given gifts of paper money and coin and ceremonial robes and linings. Grand Director Zheng He and his associates were despatched once again, bearing imperial letters along with silk brocade, silk floss, silk gauze, and other goods as gifts for the rulers of these countries, and they went along with the envoys." Another entry, dated 14 May 1421, states that "the treasure boats"—the term *baoxiang*, using a character for a small boat, is used here instead of the more usual *baochuan*—"going to foreign countries and the buying of horses and other items in the north and in the west were to be temporarily suspended."

The temporary suspension turned out to be permanent. Yongle spent the rest of his reign on his last three Mongolian campaigns and never ordered another voyage. When his son ordered the permanent end of the voyages in his first official act as emperor, he was, despite a reputed personal hostility to the enterprise, merely continuing a suspension that had been in force for more than three years and that had originally been ordered as part of a larger array of cost-cutting measures. The ongoing war in Vietnam and the reconstruction of Beijing as the capital, just completed in early 1421, had both consumed large amounts of revenue, and the voyages, despite the exchange of goods that was always an unacknowledged aspect of the Chinese tribute system, were unlikely to have been profitable, given the uneconomical size of Zheng He's largest ships. Now the emperor was insisting on another expensive expedition into Mongolia. On 11 December 1421, Minister of Finance Xia Yuanji was disgraced and sent to prison, along with the Minister of Justice, and the Minister of War committed suicide. All three men were civil officials of many years' service who had long been favored by Yongle, but all had advised strenuously against the third Mongolian campaign. Xia Yuanji in particular, famous for his detailed knowledge of the empire's current financial situation, had always found the means for Yongle's projects, but now he had been pushed to the breaking point.

It could be argued that the fleet left Chinese waters before 14 May 1421; otherwise its departure might have been stopped by the temporary suspension ordered on that date. Yet each of the previous voyages had taken time to organize, and early winter when the northeast monsoon begins was the normal time for the fleets to leave China, following their assembly at Nanjing and Liujiagang and a final outfitting at Changle while they waited for the monsoon. The most likely solution to this problem is to interpret the temporary suspension as meaning that no more voyages were to be planned after the sixth, which had been specifically authorized before the temporary suspension was ordered.

J. J. L. Duyvendak argued that Zheng He was still in China on 10 November 1421, citing Gong Zhen's *Xiyang Fanguo Zhi* for an imperial edict of that date instructing Zheng He and three other leading eunuchs that other eunuchs had received orders to conduct the barbarian envoys home. Even though Zheng He could have departed shortly afterward, the voyage would then have taken place entirely in 1422, and that would not allow enough time for Zheng He to personally visit all of the countries that he allegedly traveled to on the sixth voyage. Under this interpretation, he assigned squadron commanders to finish the business of the voyage, and it is explicitly stated for this voyage that the fleet was divided into squadrons. But the question is difficult to decide; *Taizong Shilu* records, under the date 3 September 1422, that "the palace official Zheng He and the others, who had been sent as envoys to the foreign nations, returned. Thailand, Semudera, Aden (here *Hadan* rather than the more often encountered *Adan*) and other countries all sent envoys accompanying Zheng He with tribute in local products."

On 2 October 1419 the construction of 41 new treasure ships was ordered, and previous study of Zheng He has assumed that these ships constituted the fleet that made the sixth voyage. The fleet may have included some of this new construction, but this assumption is unnecessary: 110 or 111 treasure ships had been built before 1419, none was older than sixteen years, and nothing in the sources suggests that large numbers of them had been lost. As in the earlier voyages, the fleet probably consisted of several dozen ships of the large classes collectively called treasure ships, each attended by up to half a dozen smaller ships serving as tenders or performing other support functions. There is no reason to believe that numbers or types of ships or numbers of personnel differed significantly from the remarkably similar totals reported for the other voyages.

It is most probable that Thailand was visited on the return voyage and that the first four of the sixteen countries whose envoys were returned on the outward voyage were Malacca and the three northern Sumatran states of Lambri, Aru, and Semudera. The fleet was divided into squadrons (*fenzong*) at Semudera, the great port of assembly for ships sailing to Ceylon and southern India. Even if they had sailed separately, the squadrons would all have made the westward voyage to Ceylon and thence to one or more of the four closely spaced southern Indian countries of *Jiayile*, Cochin, *Ganbali*, and Calicut. This accounts for nine of the sixteen countries. The others are *Liushan* (the term that includes both the Maldive and the Laccadive Islands), Hormuz at the entrance to the Persian Gulf, three locations on the Arabian Peninsula—Djofar, *Lasa*, and Aden—and two locations in Africa, Mogadishu and Brava. Two traditional stopping points, Java and the Old Harbor of Palembang, are not included in this list. The *Mingshi* states explicitly that in 1421 Zheng He was sent as envoy to *Ganbali* to reciprocate that country's "again" sending tribute (the first time was in 1414). This is the only one of the twelve countries west of Sumatra in which Zheng He is named as having been present in 1421.

The *Mingshi* rather desperately locates *Ganbali* as "another little country in the Western Ocean," which suggests that it had some coastal territory. The traditional identification of *Ganbali* with Coimbatore raises the problem (discussed in Chapter III) that, because Coimbatore is well inland, it would have taken Zheng He considerable time, both in 1421 and on his previous visit in 1408, to make the overland trip. One imagines the physically massive commander proceeding inland by elephant while some of his ships wait in Calicut. Unfortunately, the sources provide no colorful detail. While the main body stopped at Calicut before going on to Hormuz, the rest of the fleet sailed by squadrons to locations further west, all of which had been visited on the previous voyage.

One squadron under the eunuch Zhou—assumed to be **Zhou Man** by Duyvendak and Mills—contained "several" treasure ships (Gong Zhen and one text of Ma Huan say three) and went to Aden. According to the *Mingshi*, Aden, *Lasa*, and Djofar were all reached from Calicut by voyages of 22, 20, and 10 days and nights, respectively, but Fei Xin (as mentioned previously) corrects the voyage to Djofar to a more realistic 20 days and nights. The sailing directions found in the sources may reflect the experience of the different squadrons during the sixth voyage, which went only to previously visited places. Zhou Man's squadron probably visited Djofar and *Lasa* on the way to Aden.

According to the *Mingshi*, a ship can reach Brava after a 21-day voyage from the port of Beruwala in Ceylon. Mogadishu, on the other hand, requires a 20-day voyage from Quilon, one of the south India locations not named as having been visited on the sixth voyage, though it may still have served as a navigation point where the Mogadishu-bound squadron separated from the main fleet, which certainly continued on to Calicut. Some ships may have remained at Calicut, but a large squadron sailed to Hormuz, perhaps by way of the Laccadives. The detached squadrons then regrouped, certainly at Semudera if not previously at Calicut, and the combined fleet returned to China by way of Thailand.

Taizong Shilu dates their return on 3 September 1422. "The palace official Zheng He and others, who had been sent as envoys to the barbarian nations, returned. Thailand, Semudera, and Aden (here *Hadan* rather than *Adan*) all sent envoys accompanying Zheng He with tribute in local products." On 23 September Emperor Yongle returned to Beijing from his third unsuccessful foray into Mongolia. Within days he had imprisoned one of the

Grand Secretaries and the ministers of Personnel and Rites for their criticism; they joined their colleague, the former Minister of Finance Xia Yuanji, in disgrace. Resisted by his long-serving and long-suffering civil officials, Yongle on 24 October 1422 sent out eunuchs to scour the empire for grain and money to support the next Mongolian campaign.

The Last Years of the Yongle Reign, 1422–24

There is no information about Zheng He's activities for the rest of 1422 and all of 1423. During the latter year Yongle conducted his fourth Mongolian campaign, returning to Beijing on 10 December. In the relatively brief period between the end of the fourth and the beginning of the fifth and final Mongolian campaigns, Yongle ordered Zheng He on another diplomatic expedition. The relevant entry in *Taizong Shilu*, dated 27 February 1424, reads: "Shi Jisun, son of former Palembang Pacification Commissioner Shi Jinqing, sent his envoy **Qiu Yancheng** to petition for the succession to his father's official appointment. He also said that his old seal had been totally destroyed by fire. The emperor ordered that Shi Jisun should inherit the office of Pacification Commissioner, and gave him a gauze cap, a ceremonial robe with floral gold woven into gold patterns in the silk, and a silver seal. The palace eunuch Zheng He was ordered to deliver these items." Zheng He's biography in the *Mingshi* adds that by the time he returned from this trip, Emperor Yongle no longer ruled; he died on 12 August 1424 while returning from his fifth Mongolian campaign.

Zheng He's biography in the *Mingshi* allows the reader to assume that this short trip to Palembang is the sixth voyage; *Taizong Shilu* and, following it in confusion, the *Mingshi* merged the second and third voyages and therefore needed to find another voyage to make up the total of seven. In the basic annals section of the *Mingshi*, the section that gives a dated account of each emperor's reign, an entry dated 16 February 1424 makes the implicit explicit: "Zheng He was again sent as envoy to the Western Ocean." Based on his translation of the Liujiagang and Changle inscriptions, which clearly separate the second and third voyages, Duyvendak concluded that the voyage to Palembang in 1424 never took place. The matter is complicated by an entry in *Xuanzong Shilu* dated 17 September 1425, in the reign of Yongle's grandson, Emperor Xuande, stating that "the seal of the Old Harbor Pacification Office in Java was given to their envoy **Zhang Funama** on his return, because the old seal had been destroyed by fire." Old Harbor is the standard reference for Palembang, but the association with Java is new. Elsewhere the *Mingshi* (in the entry "Shri Vijaya") explains that "even though Shi Jinqing obeyed the commands of the Imperial Court, he was still a dependent subject of Java; his territory was small and constricted, and could not be compared with that of Shri Vijaya in former times." The *Mingshi* compilers made their choice among the evidence, having Shi Jisun's succession approved in 1424 and the new seal given in 1425, so that only one seal is destroyed by fire, even though the *shilu* of the two emperors repeat those words in both years. Shi Jisun disappears from history at this point, and the various *shilu* shed no light on his sister Shi Erjie, who according to Ma Huan was Shi Jinqing's immediate successor.

Duyvendak is undoubtedly correct that the voyage of 1424 is not a voyage to the Western Ocean in the manner of the earlier expeditions. This does not prove that the voyage never took place, and a careful look at *Taizong Shilu* and *Xuanzong Shilu* finds that it is not represented as being in any way comparable to the seven expeditions described in those sources. The *Taizong Shilu* entries of 11 July 1405 and 2 October 1407, describing the sending and return of the first expedition, refer to "the countries of the Western Ocean" (*Xiyang zhuguo*); the entry for 17 October 1408, which refers to the sending of the second expedition in 1407, has a list of named "countries" (*zhuguo*); the entry of 6 July 1411 recording the return of the third expedition refers to "the foreign countries of the Western Ocean" (*Xiyang zhufanguo*); and for the fourth expedition Zheng He is sent (entry dated 18 December 1412) to a list of named countries and returns on 12 August 1415 from the "foreign countries of the Western Ocean." For the fifth expedition Zheng He is sent (28 December 1416) to a list of named "countries" from which Palembang is carefully separated, and he returns from "the Western Ocean." The sixth expedition sends

Zheng He (3 March 1421) to "sixteen countries including Hormuz." The countries can be identified, and they do not include Palembang. Zheng He returns (3 September 1422) from "foreign countries" (*zhufanguo*). In other words, for all six of the expeditions launched in the Yongle reign, *Taizong Shilu* uses the plural "countries" or "foreign countries" and does so in a manner that explicitly excludes describing Palembang as a country. For all the expeditions but the sixth, *Taizong Shilu* uses the term "Western Ocean," and even on the sixth Zheng He's fleet went to the Western Ocean, since its specific destinations are listed. In the seventh expedition, the order in *Xuanzong Shilu* dated 29 June 1430 talks about "foreign countries, distantly located beyond the sea" (*zhufanguo yuanchu haiwai*), and the destinations again include Calicut and Hormuz in the Indian Ocean. Zheng He's seven expeditions, then, all visited multiple countries and always included Calicut and other destinations in the Indian Ocean.

When this is understood, the objections to the historical reality of Zheng He's trip to Palembang in 1424 disappear. This was a short trip in comparison to the treasure ship voyages to the Western Ocean, and it went no further than a Southeast Asian destination where a friendly reception was assured. Instead of mobilizing the entire treasure fleet, a squadron could be made up from the ships and men standing idle since the return of the sixth expedition in 1422. Zheng He's return from Palembang is not recorded, but by then the Chinese world had changed because of the death of Emperor Yongle.

VI

The Ships and Men of Zheng He's Fleets

By the time of Yongle's death in 1424, Zheng He's fleet had had two decades of operating together as an organization. The Chinese texts call it the **Xiafan Guanjun**, or the Foreign Expeditionary Armada, and it consisted of about 250 ships of various sizes crewed by more than 27,000 men, the vast majority of whom were regular Ming military personnel. The fleet's great days were then behind it, yet it remained together as an organization for the entire period between the sixth (1422) and last (1431–33) voyages, serving as part of the garrison of Nanjing, which Emperor Hongxi intended to make the capital again.

Zheng He's voyages have long served as a metaphor for the wealth, power, and technical sophistication of China on the eve of the age of Western exploration and expansion. The great size of Zheng He's ships and fleets contrasted with the small ships, few in number, of the expeditions led by Columbus and his contemporaries. This chapter takes a fresh look at Zheng He's ships as described in the best contemporary sources (Zheng He's inscriptions and the *Taizong Shilu*) and the physical principles that underlie all naval architecture. Zheng He's largest ships were certainly very large, but much that has been believed about them needs to be revised.

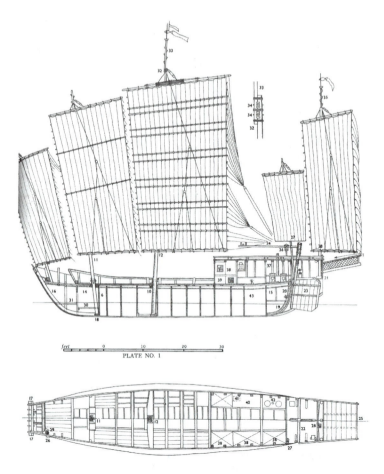

PLATE NO. 1

Drawing of Chinese Junque. Courtesy of the Picture Collection/New York Public Library.

This elevation of a Jiangsu trader, a much smaller ship than Zheng He's treasure ships, illustrates the transverse bulkheads into which the masts are stepped, and the lug and batten sails. While the rudder well cannot be seen, it is obvious that there is no sternpost. © Worcester Book

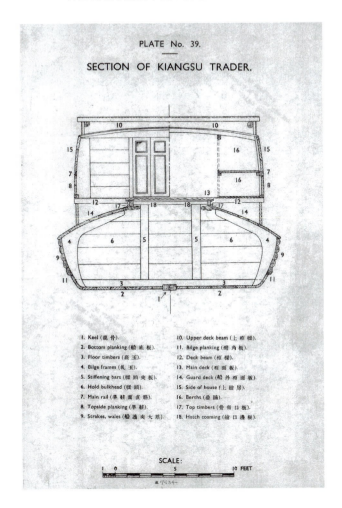

PLATE No. 39.
—
SECTION OF KIANGSU TRADER.

1. Keel (龍 骨).
2. Bottom planking (船 底 板).
3. Floor timbers (底 玉).
4. Bilge frames (乾 玉).
5. Stiffening bars (檔 頭 夾 板).
6. Hold bulkhead (樸 頭).
7. Main rail (舉 蘇 面 直 鬆).
8. Topside planking (舉 蘇).
9. Strakes, wales (船 過 夾 大 熙).
10. Upper deck beam (上 桓 樑).
11. Bilge planking (櫚 角 板).
12. Deck beam (桓 樑).
13. Main deck (桓 面 板).
14. Guard deck (船 外 桓 面 板).
15. Side of house (上 艙 房).
16. Berths (臺 舖).
17. Top timbers (骨 骨 口 板).
18. Hatch coaming (艙 口 邊 板).

SCALE:
1 0   5   10 FEET

Elevation of Chinese Junque. Courtesy of the Picture Collection/New York Public Library.

This section of the same Jiangsu trader shows the flat bottom and the external strakes or wales. While the longgu is labeled as a keel, it is clear from the drawing that there are no frames, so it is not a keel in the Western shipbuilding sense. © Worcester Book; Courtesy of the New York Public Library Picture Collection.

While Zheng He and his highest ranking associates were eunuchs, his crews were mostly members of the regular Ming military establishment, and the Chinese sources emphasize their military role by recording the rewards and promotions given to them for their hard fighting in these expeditions.

Dimensions and Displacements of the Treasure Ships

Zheng He's largest ships, the "treasure ships" or *baochuan*, were 44 *zhang* in length and had a beam of 18 *zhang*, according to his biography in the *Mingshi*. The *Mingshi* elsewhere calls this the "large" size and reports a "middle" or "next" size of treasure ship with dimensions of 37 by 15 *zhang*. In Luo Maodeng's novel *Xiyang Ji* only the "large" size is called a treasure ship, and its length is given as 44 *zhang* and 4 *chi* (44.4 *zhang*), the repetition of "4" having numerological significance. (One *zhang* contained ten *chi*, translated as feet, or "Chinese feet" when it is necessary to distinguish Chinese from English measurements.)

All Chinese weights and measures have varied in size from time to time and from place to place. The *zhang* was fixed at 141 inches for tariff purposes in the nineteenth century, making the *chi* 14.1 inches. The commonly stated value of the *chi* in the Ming was 12.2 inches (31.1 centimeters), but variations abound. The Ming Ministry of Works used a *chi* of 12.1 inches, and the Jiangsu builders of the widely used "sand boats" *(shachuan)* used a Huai River *chi* of 13.3 inches. Since some of the ships of Zheng He's fleets (but not the treasure ships, which were built at Nanjing) were built in Fujian, and since the fleets regularly left for Southeast Asia from the Changle Anchorage near Fujian's capital at Fuzhou, current opinion favors the *chi* used by Fujian shipbuilders. This was 10.5 to 11 inches, based on measuring rods found in excavations in that province. The estimates given below are in terms of *chi* of 12 inches and 10.5 inches. The length and beam (width) of the treasure ships then become either 440 by 180 feet or 385 by 157.5 feet.

The recorded dimensions of the treasure ships are so large that there is a natural tendency to prefer the smallest possible length for the *chi*, but the physical evidence does not contradict

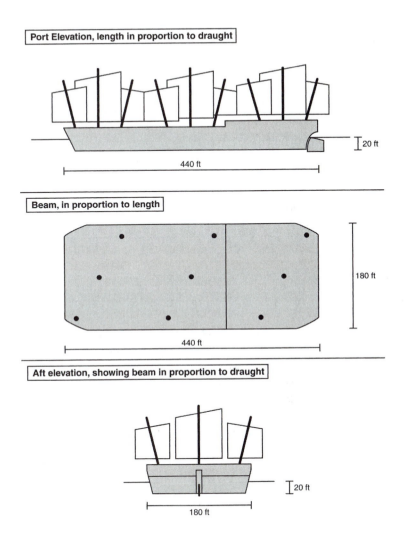

the higher figure. In 1962 a rudderpost of a large ship, presumed to be one of Zheng He's treasure ships, was unearthed in excavations of the Longjiang Shipyard at Nanjing (informally, the Treasure Ship Yard or *baochuanchang*). The length of the rudderpost indicated a rudder area of at least 452 square feet; by comparison with known Chinese ships and rudders, this indicated a ship of between 538 and 600 (English) feet in length, "depending on different assumptions about draught," as Joseph Needham explains. Two of the drydocks at the Longjiang Shipyard were 210 feet wide, certainly enough space to accommodate ships even as wide as 180 feet. The physical evidence for the treasure ships may not be conclusive, but it is important that it is all from Nanjing, where the treasure ships were built and from where they embarked on the first leg of their voyages.

Relying on Luo Maodeng's fantastic novel, earlier scholars imagined that there was evidence for the construction of five distinct classes of large vessels, with specific numbers of each type. Luo Maodeng gave these figures: 36 nine-masted treasure ships of 44.4 by 18 *zhang*; 700 eight-masted horse ships *(machuan)* of 37 by 15 *zhang*; 240 seven-masted grain ships or supply ships *(liangchuan)* of 28 by 12 *zhang*; 300 six-masted billet ships or troop transports *(zuochuan)* of 24 by 9.4 *zhang*; and 180 five-masted combat ships or warships proper *(zhanchuan)* of 18 by 6.8 *zhang*. All might be called treasure ships even though Luo Maodeng applies the term specifically only to the largest, nine-masted variety. The five categories add up to 1,476 ships that are very large by wooden ship standards. But Luo Maodeng's type names, dimensions, and numbers cannot be used to supplement the historical sources; his novel has no value as evidence.

Taizong Shilu provides the most reliable contemporary evidence for the numbers and types of ships constructed; it has twenty-four notices dated from 1403 to 1419 for the building or refitting of ships and or boats at various locations. In some cases the shipbuilding is explicitly connected to the voyages, as in the case of the 249 vessels ordered "to be prepared for embassies to the several countries of the Western Ocean" in 1407, three days after Zheng He's return from the first expedition. Two of the *Taizong Shilu* notices refer specifically to treasure ships: 48 were ordered from the Ministry of Works in Nanjing on 14 February 1408, and 41 were ordered from undisclosed builders on 2 October 1419. The original 62 or 63 treasure ships employed on the first voyage have to be included in the 200 "seagoing transport ships" *(haiyunchuan)* ordered from "the Capital Guards"—the military garrison of Nanjing—and other places on 4 September 1403, and the 50 "seagoing ships" *(haichuan)* ordered from the Capital Guards on 1 March 1404. The 14 February 1408 entry is the sole *Taizong Shilu* notice that both specifically mentions "treasure ships" and gives a building location. Since the physical evidence for the existence of treasure ships comes only from Nanjing, and the only literary evidence also indicates that they were built at Nanjing, it is reasonable to conclude that ships built at other places than Nanjing cannot be treasure ships.

Ming China in Zheng He's time was the wealthiest and most populous economy on earth, and it was capable of feats of shipbuilding that would have challenged the major Western naval powers (Britain, France, and Spain) during the eighteenth-century heyday of the sailing ship in the North Atlantic. In Chapters IV and V it was suggested that Zheng He's fleets were all of about the same size and composition: approximately 40 to 60 or more large ships that could all be called treasure ships if that term is understood to apply to all the very large ships, even if they were not all the same size, and about 200 smaller ships comparable in size to normal Chinese shipping. Each fleet was manned by about 27,000 personnel, who could have fitted very comfortably into the treasure ships alone. The sizes reported for the treasure ships, and supported by physical evidence, raise questions that are not resolved by reducing the *chi* from 12.0 to 10.5 inches. To appreciate these questions, it is necessary to look at the construction of large wooden ships in the better documented Western tradition.

Wooden ships in Western Europe in the Medieval and early modern periods were built up from a long and straight keel, to which a stem and a sternpost were attached at either end, with pairs of frames attached at right angles at intervals throughout its length. Planking would be attached to the frames, either edge to edge ("carvel built") or overlapping ("clinker built"), and caulked to form the watertight hull. The nonretractable rudder, standard as this system of building evolved, would be attached to the sternpost so that its bottom edge formed a straight line with the line of the keel. Under normal conditions of loading, the waterline would be at the maximum beam, and the underwater cross-section of the ship would be semicircular, so that the actual draught (as opposed to the depth of the hold, measured from the lowest deck to the keel) would be about half the beam. The deep draught improved seaworthiness in two respects. First, it lowered the center of gravity of the ship, thus increasing its metacentric height, an important measure of stability. (A ship with a high metacentric height will roll quickly upright when struck by a wave; if the metacentric height is too low, the ship will roll slowly and may still be at a dangerous angle when the next wave strikes.) Second, deep draught gives a ship a grip on the water and reduces leeway (the tendency of a ship to be blown in the direction of the wind) when tacking. This is often a matter of some importance, as when trying to beat off a lee shore in a storm.

By the mid-eighteenth century elaborately organized and administered navies existed in many European countries. In Britain, France, Spain, the Netherlands, Sweden, and Venice in particular, detailed records have survived, and it is possible to describe with some precision many ships that no longer exist. The three-deck, 100-gun ship of the line had by then become the largest warship, valued for its flag accommodations even though considered less handy than the two-deck, 74-gun ships that formed the majority of the battle line. Representative Spanish three-deckers had dimensions (212 feet long by 58 feet broad by 29 feet deep; about 2,200 to 2,300 tons) that were were nearly identical to those of the nineteenth-century USS *Pennsylvania*, the largest wooden warship ever built for the United States Navy. Lord Nelson's flagship, the famous *Victory*, was smaller at 186 by 51 feet and 2,142 tons. These dimensions may be compared with those of the *smallest* class (the "combat ships") of Zheng He's large ships, as reported by Luo Maodeng: 18 by 6.8 *zhang* would be 180 by 68 feet or 157.5 by 59.5 feet, depending on which length of *chi* is chosen. But more typical European warships were two-deckers (a representative example was 165 by 57 by 27 feet and 1,889 tons) and frigates (a representative example was 141 by 37 by 18 feet and 832 tons), and even these ships dwarfed the majority of sloops, brigs, and ordinary merchant and fishing craft.

The tonnage figures given above are measurement tons, which state a ship's internal volume; they were determined by physically measuring ("surveying") the interior of the completed ship. Tonnage continues to be calculated in measurement tons for merchant ships, for which cargo capacity remains the most important consideration. To float, a ship must displace a weight of water exactly equal to the weight of the ship and whatever it is carrying. In the nineteenth century it was discovered that this weight, the "displacement," could be calculated by "inclining" (tipping) the ship in harbor and measuring the force exerted by the ship's effort to right itself. Unlike measurement tons, displacement tons are an exact measure of weight, and so are preferred for warships. Measurement tonnage may vary for ships of the same general dimensions, but it is typically about five-eighths of the displacement tonnage: the still surviving *Victory*, of 2,142 measurement tons, actually displaces 3,500 tons. Displacement can also be estimated, since it is proportional to the product of length, beam (breadth), and draught (also spelled and always pronounced *draft*: the depth of the hull below the waterline): hence lbd/k, where k is a "constant" that must itself vary according to underwater hull shape and the system of weights and measures used. Zheng He's large ships were broad-beamed and flat-bottomed; for contemporary broad-beamed and flat-bottomed ships like contemporary United States aircraft carriers (ships displacing 60,000 to 90,000 tons or more) and World War I and II battleships (ships ranging from about 20,000 to more than 70,000 tons), k ranges between 60 and 70, for dimensions in feet and displacements in tons. We have already seen reasons for believing that the lengths and beams reported for Zheng He's ships are credible; estimating the draught will come later.

By the end of the eighteenth century the forests of the Americas had been opened to timber harvesting, but even so the large oak pieces needed for keels, stems, sternposts, and other major structural members had become scarce and were commanding premium prices. Shipwrights believed that it was not possible to build a wooden ship over 300 feet long, and the largest wooden ships actually in service were about 210 feet long at most. Even they were expensive and uneconomical to operate; the *Pennsylvania* made only one operational voyage, then spent most of her career hulked at Norfolk Navy Yard.

Chinese ships were constructed on radically different principles. They were keelless, though ships sometimes had a large bottom timber called a *longgu* ("dragon bone") to minimize the damage caused by grounding; it looked like a keel but did not perform the same structural function. Instead, structural strength was provided by external longitudinal timbering at or above the waterline ("wales"), and, most importantly, by transverse (side to side) bulkheads spaced at regular intervals, which had the effect of dividing the hold into a sequence of watertight compartments. In the Western shipbuilding style, the masts had to be stepped into the keel, so they were always in the center of the hull, which meant that in a multimasted ship the sails of one mast might mask those of another. In Chinese ships the base of each mast is secured to an adjoining bulkhead; this permits off-center (and off-vertical) mounting, and on a multimasted ship, the masts will spread out fanwise, so that the sails may catch the wind more effectively. The sails themselves are hoist by raising the upper yard by lines attached to pulleys high in the mast and pulled by crews on deck. Lowering the sails partially (the lower sections of the sail fold accordionwise along the lower yard) when the wind rises is the functional equivalent of reefing in a Western ship, and it can be done without sending men aloft. The yards are hinged to the mast in a manner that, to facilitate tacking, permits them to revolve around the mast with the sails raised.

The structural features described, and the fact that Chinese ships developed in often-shallow inland and coastal waters, encouraged the building of ships that were broad in proportion to their length and shallow in proportion to their breadth, "built squarely like rectangular wooden grain measures *(hu)*" as a Song period source puts it. Since such a ship lacked a sternpost, the rudderpost was put in a well and the rudder made retractable: it could be hauled entirely out of the water when the ship was at anchor, or it could be lowered even with the ship's bottom in shallow water. In deep water the rudder could be lowered below the level of the ship's bottom, where it would not only function more efficiently as a rudder but also serve as a drag on leeway. Leeway must always be a problem in a shallow-draught sailing ship, and, in addition to the retractable rudder, ships were often equipped with retractable leeboards and/or centerboards.

Even in earlier centuries, Chinese regimes had built massive "tower ships" *(louchuan)* to fight their wars on inland lakes and rivers. By the Song, much of the carrying trade in the South China Sea was done by Chinese seagoing ships built on the principles described above. Zhou Qufei in 1178 describes ships "like houses" with sails "like great clouds in the sky" when spread; each carried several hundred men and a year's supply of grain as well as pigs and wine. Marco Polo, escorting Princess Kököčin to Iran in 1292, was equipped with 14 great ships, each with four masts and 600 men, and provisions for two years. He also noticed and described carefully the system of bulkhead construction for the hull. Ibn Battūtah in 1347 described sails made of bamboo matting that could be revolved around the mast. Each large ship had 12 sails and was worked by 1,000 men, of whom 600 were sailors and 400 were marines; the latter included both archers and crossbowmen as well as men who threw pots of flaming naptha. Both Marco Polo and Ibn Battūtah commented on the numerous deck cabins and other creature comforts that the big ships offered, and the fact that each of the big Chinese ships was regularly accompanied by smaller ships of various designations that acted as tenders. Neither informs us directly how large the Chinese ships were, though Marco Polo at one point speaks of a draught of about four paces, which one modern authority equates to 20 feet, or five feet per pace. Western three-decked ships of the line carried 800 to 900 men in very crowded conditions; if the large Chinese ships could carry 1,000 sailors and marines, plus passengers, in conditions of comfort, they must have been considerably larger.

Zheng He's treasure ships were thus the culmination of a long tradition of Chinese seafaring in the South China Sea and the Indian Ocean in large, broad-beamed, square-shaped, flat-bottomed ships. These ships appear to have been seaworthy in the conditions normal in the South China Sea and that part of the Indian Ocean north of the Equator, where warm weather and predictable monsoon winds were the rule. But flat-bottomed ships are less seaworthy in rough seas, particularly if their draught is shallow in proportion to their beam. Such ships cannot roll and are thus in danger of taking on water and being swamped by wave action, even in relatively calm seas. For the modern battleships and aircraft carriers mentioned above, the ratio of beam to draught *(b/d)* ranges from three to four, but it had to have been higher for Zheng He's ships.

Calculating draught thus becomes the central issue in estimating the displacement and evaluating the seaworthiness of Zheng He's largest ships. J. V. G. Mills, in his careful translation of Ma Huan, offers the guarded opinion that Zheng He's "largest ships were probably about three hundred feet long and about one hundred fifty feet broad, and displaced about three thousand one hundred tons," an impossibly low number for those dimensions, but nonetheless—as Mills notes correctly—much larger than the three hundred tons of Vasco da Gama's largest ship. Mills continues: "the texts contain no explicit information concerning the draught of [Zheng He's] ships, though it cannot have been any less than the twenty feet drawn by Yuan ships and it might have been considerably more, since the Portuguese carrack *Madre de Dios*, captured by the English in 1592, displaced two thousand tons and drew thirty-one feet." Mills certainly meant to say that the *Madre de Dios* measured two thousand tons. Portuguese carracks could be very large, and this one was comparable in size to the three-decker ships of the line discussed above, all of which were much smaller than the reported dimensions of Zheng He's largest ships. Mills eventually came to "envisage a ship 250 feet long, and 110 feet broad, with 50 cabins. The draught would be 25 feet, the burthen 1,000 tons, and the displacement 1,250 tons." In fact a treasure ship of even these reduced dimensions would displace over ten thousand tons (10,742 tons by the formula given previously, with k set at 64), and neither the written Chinese sources nor the various items of physical evidence provide any basis for reducing the length and beam of the treasure ships to the extent that Mills envisaged.

The subsequent literature has not gone much beyond this, and it has avoided the issue of draught and displacement completely. Yet an important item of evidence has been hiding in plain sight since modern study of Zheng He began. His large treasure ships were built at Nanjing, at the Longjiang Shipyard, on the Qinhuai River that flows around the southern and western walls of the city as refortified by Emperor Hongwu. Dredging the Qinhuai to get to the Yangtze was no doubt a regular part of the ship-building and ship maintenance process, but to get to the ocean they had to sail down the Yangtze, so the draught of even the largest of Zheng He's ships was limited by the depth of the river. Expeditions left and returned at various times of the year, so their ability to sail was not constrained by seasonal variations in the river's depth. The seventh expedition (1431–33), the only one for which there is detailed information on the stages of the voyage, departed Nanjing on 19 January 1431, in winter, when the water level was low.

As recently as 1949 the average depth of the Yangtze at its mouth was 7 meters (23 feet); more recently it has been dredged to 9 meters to accommodate the needs of container ships sailing from Shanghai. The American naval theorist Alfred Thayer Mahan observed in 1900 that battleships, meaning predreadnoughts of 12,000 to 16,000 tons that drew 24 to 26 feet, could sail up the Yangtze as far as Nanjing (and by implication no further). G. R. Worcester, author of the classic *The Junks and Sampans of the Yangtze*, who spent his career on the river and knew it intimately, wrote that "vessels of 24 feet draught can reach Wuhu, 264 miles from Shanghai, at all seasons of the year." We may allow an extra foot or so for the fact that Nanjing is downstream from Wuhu, but J. V. G. Mills's guess of approximately 25 feet is really the upper limit for the draught of Zheng He's largest ships, which were thus very shallow in proportion to their beam.

If the treasure ships actually sailed to Palembang, as opposed to anchoring in the sheltered waters of the Bangka Strait—and the sources are not conclusive on this point, even though the fleet went to Palembang on each voyage—they would have sailed up the wide but shallow Musi River, which in recent years has required regular dredging to maintain a shipping channel 6.5 meters (21 feet, 4 inches) deep. This suggests a lower limit of about 20 feet—Marco Polo's four paces—for the draught of the treasure ships.

It is now possible to estimate the displacement of Zheng He's larger ships. In the tables below, the length of the *chi* is 12 inches and 10.5 inches, and *k* is a conservative 64, though a lower figure (which would yield a higher displacement) could be justified. Both the quoted descriptions and the numbers for *lbd* that we are forced to accept make an extremely rectangular underwater cross section inevitable, since *l/b* is very low and *b/d* very high. Displacements are calculated for draughts of 20 and 25 feet. While the shallower draught reduces the displacements substantially, it does so at the cost of making the ships even less seaworthy.

Dimensions and Displacements of Zheng He's Largest Ships

(*chi* = 12.0 in)

Type	Length	Beam	Calculated displacement (tons) at draughts of	
			(20 feet)	(25 feet)
"large" treasure ships	440	180	24,750	30,938
"next" or "middle" treasure ships	370	150	17,344	21,680

Dimensions and Displacements of Zheng He's Largest Ships

(*chi* = 10.5 in)

Type	Length	Beam	Calculated displacement (tons) at draughts of	
			(20 feet)	(25 feet)
"large" treasure ships	385	157.5	18,949	23,687
"next" or "middle" treasure ships	323.75	131.25	13,279	16,599

Only the dimensions of the two largest classes of ships are given in the authentic historical sources, and both classes are described as "treasure ships." For the description of the second class as "horse ships," for the type names and dimensions of the three smaller classes, and for the numbers of masts, the only source is Luo Maodeng, who cannot be relied on as a primary source for the Zheng He period. Many of the treasure ships whose construction is attested by the historical sources may have been smaller than the two large types whose dimensions are preserved, but no historical source gives the dimensions of such ships. In any case, the naval architectural problems are most severe with the largest types, whose dimensions (length and beam only) are preserved in the sources.

It is clear from the above that our flat-bottomed, shallow-draught ships have sailed into dangerous waters. Even with the reasonable restrictions on draught imposed by the depth of the Yangtze, and the reduction in dimensions called for by the shorter *chi*, the calculated displacements of the treasure ships remain enormous. Even the scaled-down treasure ship envisaged by Mills displaces about three times the 3,500 tons of HMS *Victory*, today the only eighteenth-century ship of the line to survive anywhere in the world, and in its day a large and expensive admiral's flag-ship of a type that was built only in small numbers by those navies well enough developed to afford them. In eighteenth-century Britain, France, and Spain the navy was the largest organized industrial enterprise in the country, and much information survives concerning the organization and costs of each navy's dock-yard infrastructure. (Army and navy expenditures combined constituted the overwhelming majority of state expenditures.) Construction of the *Victory* consumed six thousand trees; each treasure ship would have needed several times that many, even with the shorter *chi*. No balance sheet exists for Zheng He's expeditions, but the authors of the *Mingshi* were unambiguous that "the goods and treasures without name that he acquired were too many to be accounted for, yet they did not make up for the expenditure of the Middle Kingdom." This is the considered judgment of disgruntled and xenophobic Confucians, resentful of whatever hold the "vulgar tradition" of Zheng He's voyages had on the popular imagination, yet it also reflected the reality that Emperor Yongle was unrestrained in his spending and unwilling to establish priorities among his many expensive projects.

Masts and Sails

The treasure ships are described as having nine masts and carrying twelve sails. While this is part of the overly schematic description of Zheng He's fleet invented by Luo Maodeng, it is consistent with the rule of thumb found in other sources, that a ship should have one mast for every five *zhang* of length.

The evidence indicates that Zheng He's largest ships may well have been the largest wooden sailing ships ever constructed. To gain some insight regarding their sails and rig, we must turn again to the better-documented European and American seafaring and consider the largest sailing ships constructed within that tradition, the large merchant sailing ships of the late nineteenth and early twentieth centuries. In this period, coal-fired steam engines were very heavy in proportion to the power they generated, and they consumed fuel that had to be bought and that took up hull space that might otherwise be used for cargo. Masts and sails, on the other hand, did not take up space in the hold, and the wind was free. But these large merchant vessels were nonetheless products of the industrial age: they had steel hulls, and their yards and sails were hoist on steel wires pulled by auxiliary steam engines.

The majority of these ships were bark-rigged, meaning that they had fore-and-aft sails on all the masts except the foremast. Fore-and-aft sails had the same advantage as the lug-and-batten sails standard on Chinese ships: they could be hoist and lowered from the deck, and fewer trained topmen were needed to operate the ship. The largest of all these ships, however, was the five-masted, full-rigged German ship *Preußen*, built in 1902. Her dimensions were 407 feet, 8 inches, by 53 feet, 6 inches, by 27 feet, 1 inch, and she was surveyed at 5,081 gross registered tons (measurement tons). By the conservative formula used above to estimate the displacement of Zheng He's largest ships, the *Preußen* would displace over 9,000 tons; her actual displacement was 11,150 tons. Note that the *Preußen* was as long as Zheng He's largest ships and only a little deeper than the 25-foot maximum draught estimated for them. In the manner of Western sailing ships, her draught is about half her beam, and her beam is about a third of the beam of the largest of Zheng He's treasure ships. The dimensions and displacement of the *Preußen* thus provide a check on the estimated displacements of the treasure ships. But the *Preußen* was a very different type of ship: narrow in proportion to her length and deep in proportion to her beam, she was also fast, once clocked at 13.7 knots in a Force 8 wind. Probably somewhat less than her total 59,770 square feet of sail was spread on that occasion.

The characteristic sail on Chinese ships is the mat-and-batten stiffened lugsail, in which bamboo battens placed at intervals along the sail keep the sail as a whole stiff when hoist. The battens also add to the weight of the sail. The sail is a fore-and-aft sail

A representation of the Keying, mentioned in the text, from *The Boston Evening Transcript* some time in 1847. This drawing illustrates both the lug and batten construction of the sails and the retractable rudder with its well. It also shows that the Keying, which made it to London as well as Boston, had the high sides and deep hull of a seaworthy ship, in contrast to the bargelike dimensions reported for Zheng He's treasure ships. Courtesy of American Heritage Library.

in the Western sense, since it is suspended between a yard and a boom, rather than hung from a yard and sheeted at the bottom corners, in the manner of a Western square sail. When the sail is furled, the yard, battens, and sail sections themselves lie on top of the boom. When the sail is hoist, each sail section lifts the batten beneath so that the lowest raised batten functions temporarily as a boom while the yard is being raised. The higher the yard is raised, the greater the weight of the raised area of sail. Such sails could be of enormous size. Joseph Needham describes the 1848 voyage to London of the junk *Keying* (160 by 33 feet; 750 tons, named after the Manchu statesman Qiying who negotiated the 1842 Treaty of Nanjing). She had three masts, of which the tallest was the 90-foot mainmast, which carried a 67-foot-long mainsail yard. The mainsail, which would have had an area of about 6,000 square feet, weighed nine tons and took a long time to hoist, though it could be lowered quickly because gravity then helped the crew. The British master who sailed her to London described her as "a good sea boat and remarkably dry," though it may be noted that the hull dimensions of the *Keying* (*l/b* about five, draught not stated) are more suggestive of a seaworthy ship than those of the treasure ships.

Zheng He's largest ships are commonly described as having twelve sails on nine masts. Nine sails of the same size as the mainsail of the *Keying* would provide 54,000 square feet of sail area, and the other three sails would add something to that, though they would have been smaller secondary sails on the largest masts. This adds up to about the sail area of the *Preußen* for a ship that may have had more than three times the displacement and whose hull shape was clearly not designed for speed. Yet it is certainly imaginable that Zheng He's ships had enough sail area to sustain the average speeds (nearer to two than to three knots) indicated by the sailing directions in Ma Huan, the *Mingshi*, and other sources. Perhaps the last word on this subject should be that of an English explorer observing Chinese ships in a voyage that started from Macao in 1788. He describes "vessels of a thousand tons burthen" or approximately 1,600 displacement tons, much smaller than Zheng He's largest ships but impressive nonetheless, being comparable to the larger frigates and smaller ships of the line of contemporary Western navies. They have "enormous sails made of matting." Their builders clearly "had not the least idea of our mode of naval architecture," yet even so "these floating bodies of timber are able to encounter any tempestuous weather, hold a remarkable good wind, sail well, and are worked with such facility and care, as to cause the astonishment of European sailors."

Shipbuilding Notices in the Taizong Shilu

Taizong Shilu is the only important source for determining the numbers and types of ships in Zheng He's fleets. It contains 24 entries referring to imperial orders to build a total of 2,868 ships for the years 1403 through 1419, of which 2,339 had been ordered by the end of 1407 and all but 41 by the end of 1413. There are no shipbuilding entries for the Yongle years after 1419. All of the entries are very short, none being more than one line, in a *Taizong Shilu* account of some ten thousand lines for the years mentioned. It is unlikely that all of the shipbuilding entries are related to Zheng He's voyages, since grain transportation to Beijing was an important priority for Emperor Yongle, and the ships dedicated to that mission suffered losses from both storms and pirate attacks. Most other writers on Zheng He have added gratuitous interpretations to these brief entries, thus relating them to Zheng He in a manner that goes beyond the sources themselves.

The 24 *Taizong Shilu* shipbuilding notices are summarized in the table. ZHJ refers to Zhejiang, Huguang, and Jiangxi. The word *deng* functions as "and other" or "et al." The *fu* are prefectures, usually the administrative units directly below the provinces; the five named in the entry for 19 November 1406 were Huizhou, Anqing and Taiping in present-day Anhui province, and Zhenjiang and Suzhou in present-day Jiangsu province.

In Ming times the later provinces of Anhui and Jiangsu together constituted an area "directly controlled by" (Zhili) the capital.

Shipbuilding in the Yongle Reign

Number	Type	Builders	Date of Taizong Shilu entry
137	*haichuan*	Fujian Regional Military Commission (*dusi*)	25 May 1403 (20A.2b)
200	*haiyunchuan*	Capital Guards, ZHJ, Suzhou *deng fu wei*	4 Sept. 1403 (22.4ab)
36	*bu-Wo haichuan*	Guanhai *wei* in Zhejiang	12 Oct. 1403 (23.6b)
188	*haiyunchuan*	ZHJ, conversion (*gaizao*)	1 Nov. 1403 (24.6b)
50	*haichuan*	Capital Guards	1 Mar. 1404 (27.4b)
5	*haichuan*	Fujian, for missions to Western Ocean countries	2 Mar. 1404 (27.4b-5a)
1,180	*haizhou*	Zhejiang *deng dusi*	18 July 1405 (43.3b)

Number	Type	Builders	Date of Taizong Shilu entry
80	*haiyunchuan*	ZHJ, Anqing *deng fu* in Zhili, conversion *(gaizao)*	7 Nov. 1405 (47.3b)
13	*haiyunchuan*	ZHJ, conversion *(gaizao)*	26 Nov. 1405 (48.2a)
88	*haiyunchuan*	ZHJ, 5 named *fu* & other *fu wei* in Zhili	19 Nov. 1406 (60.1b)
249	*haiyunchuan*	*du zhihui* Wang Hao, *gaizao* for Zheng He voyages	5 Oct. 1407 (71.1b)
97	*haiyunchuan*	Guangyang, Huaian *deng wei*	15 Nov. 1407 (72.4a)
16	*haiyunchuan*	ZHJ, conversion *(gaizao)*	6 Dec. 1407 (73. 1b-2a)
48	*baochuan*	Ministry of Works *(gongbu)*	14 Feb. 1408 (75.2b)
33	*haiyunchuan*	Jinxiang *deng wei* in Zhejiang, conversion *(gaizao)*	25 Mar. 1408 (76.3a)
58	*haiyunchuan*	ZHJ, Suzhou & Songjiang *fu* in Zhili	23 Nov. 1408 (85.1b)
35	*haichuan*	ZHJ, Suzhou *deng fu wei*	30 Nov. 1409 (97.4a)
9	*haiyunchuan*	Longhu *deng wei*	17 Dec. 1409 (98.1b)
5	*haichuan*	Yangzhou *deng wei*	14 Jan. 1410 (99.1a)
48	*haichuan*	Linshan, Guanhai, Dinghai, Ningbo, Changguo *wei*	30 Dec. 1411 (120.2ab)
130	*haiyunchuan*	ZHJ, Zhenjiang *deng fu wei*	2 Dec. 1412 (133.3b)
61	*haifengchuan*	Yangzhou *deng wei*	24 Dec. 1412 (134.3b-4a)
61	*haifengchuan*	ZHJ, Zhenjiang *deng fu wei*	19 Oct. 1413 (143.2b)
41	*baochuan*	(place of construction not stated)	2 Oct. 1419 (216.1b)

The Longhu Guard was in Nanjing, subordinated to the General Headquarters of the Army of the Left; the Guangyang Guard, also in Nanjing, was under the Army of the Center, to which the Yangzhou and Huaian Guards, though located in their respective cities, also reported. The Guanhai, Jinxiang, Linshan, Dinghai, Ningbo, and Changguo Guards were all under the

Zhejiang Regional Military Commission. While only the Fujian Regional Military Commission is specified, it is likely that in the case of Zhejiang, Huguang, and Jiangxi it was again the Regional Military Commission, rather than the civilian provincial government, that supervised the building of the ships, and that they were built by personnel of the Guards and Independent Battalions *(shouyu qianhusuo)* that each of these Regional Military Commissions controlled.

The four entries for 1403 give a total of 561 ships; the last entry for 1403 and two for 1405 give a total of 281 ships "converted" *(gaizao)* to "oceangoing transport ships" *(haiyunchuan)*, and three more entries cite a total of 298 more such conversions. Fujian was ordered to build 137 ships in 1403, in the first of the 17 entries relating to shipbuilding in *Taizong Shilu* from 1403 through 1409, but is not mentioned in the later entries, and shipbuilding in Guangdong is not mentioned at all. In 1409 three pirate-hunting squadrons, each of 50 ships and 5,000 men, were created in Fujian and Guangdong waters. One of the squadrons had "firearms" *(huoqi)* as part of its armament, but it is not stated that the ships of these squadrons were newly built; they may have been transferred from other assignments. Most of the shipbuilding entries that refer to provinces cite the three provinces of Zhejiang, Jiangxi, and Huguang (Hunan and Hubei together formed the province of Huguang during the Ming period). The depth of the Yangtze limited the draught of the largest treasure ships, which were built at Nanjing, and would have been an even more important limiting factor for ships built further upstream, in Jiangxi or Huguang. One is struck at the extent to which this immense shipbuilding project was confined to the Yangtze River and the one coastal province—Zhejiang—near its mouth.

The entire text of the last of the entries for 1403 is "[the emperor] ordered Huguang, Zhejiang, and Jiangxi to convert 188 oceangoing transport ships." These ships were probably smaller, shallow-draught vessels, since nothing about this entry suggests the participation of the Longjiang Shipyard, and there is no suggestion in any of the sources that treasure ships were built anywhere else. Once again it is two upstream provinces on the Yangtze and the province of Zhejiang, due south of the

Yangtze's mouth, rather than the coastal provinces in general, that are given the assignment.

Writers on Zheng He frequently cite Yan Congjian's *Shuyu Zhouzilu* (1520), which reports an imperial order of 1403 to build 250 ships for ambassadorial voyages to the Western Ocean. This is a garbled later reference to the order for 200 ships given on 4 September 1403, combined with the order for 50 ships given on 1 March 1404. Both orders refer to the construction of ships by the Capital Guards, and therefore they include the 62 treasure ships of Zheng He's first voyage.

Fully 1,161 of the 2,868 ships tabulated above are called "oceangoing transport ships" *(haiyunchuan)*, and of them 579 are referred to as having been "rebuilt" or "converted" *(gaizao)* as opposed to having been "built" *(zao)*. The term *gaizao* may introduce some double counting. Since many of the *haiyunchuan* were built upriver in Huguang or Jiangxi, and were therefore of even shallower draught than the ships built at Nanjing, they are evidently general-purpose cargo ships adapted from designs suitable for river and canal work, and they were probably built mostly to transport grain to Beijing, though the 249 converted under the supervision of Wang Hao are explicitly said to be "in preparation for the embassies to the countries of the Western Ocean." The 36 *bu-Wo haichuan* ("pirate-catching oceangoing vessels") have an obvious purpose and were probably not part of Zheng He's fleet. The 137 "oceangoing vessels" *(haichuan)* constructed in Fujian starting in 1403, and the five started in 1404, may have included some of Zheng He's ships, but not the largest, which were constructed at Nanjing, the Treasure Ship Yard *par excellence*. The 48 "treasure ships" *(baochuan)* that were built at Nanjing under the direction of the Ministry of Works *(gongbu)*, probably with military labor, were ordered on 14 February 1408 and would have been ready in time for the third voyage, at the earliest. Whatever distinction there was between the 122 "oceangoing sailing ships" *(haifengchuan)* ordered in 1412 and 1413 and the ordinary *haichuan* or *haiyunchuan* is unclear. The largest single order is for the 1,180 *haizhou* on 1 March 1404; the word *zhou* (boat or vessel) is more neutral regarding size than *chuan* (ship), but since the *haizhou* are "oceangoing vessels" built by at least one coastal province, they should be regarded as substantial ships. Similarly, too much should not be made of whatever distinction there is between *haichuan* ("oceangoing ships") and *haiyunchuan* ("oceangoing transport ships"); in other contexts, both *haichuan* and *yunchuan* could be synonyms for *liangchuan*, or "grain (transport) ships." Note that the only type name used in Luo Maodeng's system that is found in these shipbuilding notices is "treasure ship," which is also found in the other historical sources.

Shipbuilding Costs

Given that the reports of shipbuilding programs cited above do not distinguish the types or sizes of ships in any useful manner, it will never be possible to estimate the total cost to the Ming empire of the voyages of Zheng He. There are only scraps of information about shipbuilding costs. One *Mingshi* account states that a ship of unspecified size could cost as much as 1,000 piculs (*shi* or *dan*: in the Ming, a measure of about 107.4 liters of grain that was also used as a unit of account). Another source states that a 600 *liao* ship cost 300 taels (*liang* or Chinese ounces) of silver. A 600 *liao* ship is estimated at 150 measurement tons or 240 displacement tons. The picul typically was worth something less than three taels. At 2.8 taels per picul, these figures work out to 3.5 piculs per displacement ton. With calculated displacements for treasure ships ranging from ten to thirty thousand tons, this gives a range of 35,000 to 105,000 piculs for the cost of an individual treasure ship.

Fully 151 (or 152) treasure ships are attested, the 62 (or 63) that took part on the first voyage, the 48 ordered in 1408, and the 41 ordered in 1419. The first 62 (or 63) are included among the 200 *haiyunchuan* ordered from the Capital Guards in 1403 and the 50 *haichuan* ordered in 1404; the remaining 89 are specifically called *baochuan*, or treasure ships. Rounding the number of treasure ships to 150 and using the range given above suggests that Emperor Yongle spent between 5,250,000 and 15,750,000 piculs for the building of the treasure ships, a figure that does not include operating, upkeep, or any costs associated with the much larger number of smaller ships built during the reign. Since it is nowhere suggested that all the treasure ships were of the largest type, and the sources do not prohibit the existence of treasure ships smaller than the "next" or "middle" category that Luo Maodeng called "horse ships," the actual total is likely to have been at the middle or lower end of the range. It may also never have been calculated precisely; the treasure ships, after all, were merely one of a number of extravagant projects that Emperor Yongle commenced without much consideration of their long-range cost.

The Ming empire could certainly afford this level of expenditure. In 1393 the summer tax assessment of the entire empire had been fixed by Yongle's father, Emperor Hongwu, at 4,712,900 piculs and the autumn tax at 24,729,450 piculs, for a total of 29,442,350 piculs of grain annually. Recorded receipts for the first four years of the reign were 30,459,800 piculs in 1402 (*Taizong Shilu* 15.11a), 31,299,704 piculs in 1403 (*Taizong Shilu* 26.7b), 31,874,371 piculs in 1404 (*Taizong Shilu* 37.4a), and 31,133,993 piculs in 1405 (*Taizong Shilu* 49.4a). These were only the land taxes, which in principle were collected in grain. They accounted for about ninety percent of the empire's revenue, with the salt monopoly and lesser items making up the rest. The problem was that the financial system was already showing signs of the calcification that would last for the rest of the dynasty. Recurring expenditure items were matched against particular sources of revenue, and civil officials (like Minister of Finance Xia Yuanji) were unwilling to contemplate making shipbuilding and voyages regular expenditure items. They were not, after all, part of Emperor Hongwu's system, which ought to be binding on his heirs and successors. Even though the sizes and dimensions of Zheng He's largest ships are difficult to believe in, despite the evidence, and the voyages themselves were certainly not profit-making or even break-even propositions, the enterprise as a whole was affordable for the huge and growing economy of Ming China.

Numbers of Ships in Each of the Voyages

The number of ships present on each of the voyages needs to be reconsidered in light of the information on shipbuilding found in *Taizong Shilu*.

For the first voyage of 1405–07, Zheng He's biography in the *Mingshi* gives him 62 treasure ships crewed by 27,800 men, and Tan Qian's *Guoque* credits him with 63 treasure ships crewed by 27,870 men. There is no point in trying to choose between these specific figures given by two respected sources. The *Zuiweilu* reports 37,000 personnel, which is probably a slip of the pen by a copyist.

Most previous accounts of Zheng He's first voyage have assumed that 255 other ships should be added to the 62 treasure ships, giving the fleet a total of 317 ships. Those 255 were the 250 mentioned in the *Shuyu Zhouzilu* as being built for voyages to the countries of the Western Ocean, plus the five ordered from Fujian for the same purpose on 2 March 1404. Combining the 62 treasure ships attested by the *Mingshi* with the 255 ships attested by other sources as being built for voyages to the countries of the Western Ocean seemed to provide a sound basis for a large but credible fleet of 317 ships.

The problem with this approach is that it introduces double counting by mixing together primary and secondary sources. The first seven of the *Taizong Shilu* references tabulated above record orders for the building or "conversion" of 1,796 ships from early in the Yongle reign (25 May 1403) to 18 July 1405, around the time the first voyage was ordered on 11 July 1405. Shipbuilding cited in later sources must at least be looked for in the *Taizong Shilu* references. This observation applies with special force to the 62 or 63 treasure ships that took part in the first voyage; they are not mentioned as such in any of the *Taizong Shilu* references of 1403–05. The physical evidence that compels belief in the existence of these ships is found only at the Longjiang Shipyard in Nanjing, and they must therefore be included in the 250 ships in two orders (200 on 4 September 1403 and 50 on 1 March 1404) that were built partly or entirely by the Capital Guards. Since these 250 ships are in all likelihood the same 250 ships mentioned in the much later *Shuyu Zhouzilu*, it becomes clear that Zheng He's fleet on the first voyage consisted of at most 255 ships (including the five ships ordered from Fujian on 2 March 1404) and that this number included the 62 or 63 treasure ships, each of which had an average of three smaller ships as tenders. The value of the

Shuyu Zhouzilu reference is that it identifies the 250 ships as being built for voyages to the countries of the Western Ocean, as the original *Taizong Shilu* references do not.

No primary source indicates the number of ships or the number of personnel on the second voyage in so many words. However, the *Taizong Shilu* entry of 5 October 1407 states that "Regional Military Commissioner *(duzhihui)* Wang Hao was ordered to reconstruct (or rebuild or convert: *gaizao*) 249 ocean-going transport ships *(haiyunchuan)* in preparation for embassies to the countries of the Western Ocean." Since this is very near the date that the order for the second voyage is thought to have been given (perhaps 11 October 1407), it seems a logical inference that these 249 ships represent the fleet of the second voyage. If the conclusion that the fleet of the first voyage consisted of 255 ships, including the 62 or 63 treasure ships, is correct, this adds confidence to the view that the fleet of the second voyage consisted of 249 ships, including an unspecified number of treasure ships. In fact, the fleet of the second voyage consisted of substantially the same individual ships as the fleet of the first voyage, with a small allowance for losses and replacements.

On 17 September 1414 Wang Hao, then deputy commissioner *(duzhihui tongzhi,* rank 2b) of the Daning Regional Military Commission in northern China in the vicinity of Beijing, was promoted to assistant chief commissioner *(dudu qianshi,* 2a) of the Rear Army "to be in charge of vessels and warships." This interesting notice in *Taizong Shilu* tells us that Wang Hao was thought of as having expertise in nautical matters, and that this expertise did not prevent him from being assigned to the steppes even in a period of important naval activity. It also indicates that the 1407 entry mentioned above probably abbreviated Wang Hao's rank in that year: a full regional military commissioner held rank 2a, the rank to which Wang Hao was promoted in 1414. More likely he was a deputy (2b) or assistant (3a) commissioner, which may also explain why he is not associated with a particular Regional Military Commission in the 1407 entry.

J. J. L. Duyvendak cites the same order as it appears in the *Ming Dazheng Zuanyao,* which source gives the number of ships as 250 rather than 249. Otherwise the wording is identical, and Duyvendak translates "(the emperor) changed (a previous order and) commanded that vessels for sea-transport be built." This is overtranslation with a vengeance; one might imagine *gaizao* as "converted" (as from civilian to military use) or "reconstructed" (as in a damaged or partially rotted ship receiving new timbers), but in this context *gaizao* is unlikely to mean anything more than that the ships, already in basically sound condition, are to be outfitted and equipped for a new voyage. A corollary of this conclusion is that the large treasure ships are here concealed within the very general category of oceangoing transport ships.

For the third voyage, Fei Xin's *Xingcha Shenglan*, Yan Congjian's *Shuyu Zhouzilu*, and Lu Rong's *Shuyuan Zaji* all say that the fleet consisted of 48 ships. Fei Xin calls them "ocean traders" *(haibo)*, and his figure of "over 27,000" for the personnel of the fleet is preferable to the 30,000 given by the later Ming historian Zheng Xiao. The other two sources refer to the 48 ships as "treasure ships." *Taizong Shilu* records an order dated 14 February 1408 for the building of 48 treasure ships by the Ministry of Works *(gongbu)* at Nanjing, and it is tempting to regard them as the 48 ships of the third voyage. The third expedition left Liujiagang during the ninth month (9 October to 6 November 1409) of the seventh year of Yongle, about twenty months after the building of the 48 treasure ships commenced. This is about the same elapsed time as that taken for the treasure ships of the first voyage, ordered in part on 4 September 1403 and in (smaller) part on 1 March 1404, for a voyage that commenced no earlier than late 1405. It is not possible to be definite on this point; many treasure ships from the first two voyages may have survived in seaworthy condition, and there would have been less pressure to rush the completion of the next batch of treasure ships.

What is more certain is that the 48 refers only to the number of treasure ships, as the majority of the sources state, and that a much larger number of smaller ships attended the treasure ships, as in the first two voyages. The third expedition had the same mission and the same approximate number of personnel as the first two, and it saw the hardest fighting of any of Zheng He's voyages. It is difficult to imagine that it was given a reduced scale of shipping or that the smaller ships that served as tenders and could operate in coastal and river delta waters were omitted.

For the fourth expedition, one of the surviving versions of Ma Huan's *Yingyai Shenglan* says that the fleet was composed of 63 treasure ships. Fei Xin gives a personnel total of 27,670, and another source gives 28,560. There is no point in trying to reconcile the discrepancy between these two personnel figures, but once again the number of personnel and the fact that the 63 ships are explicitly called treasure ships indicates a fleet of the same magnitude and organization as on the earlier expeditions, or about three smaller ships attending each treasure ship for a total of about 250 ships.

There is no specific evidence for the numbers of ships or personnel on the fifth and sixth voyages. On 2 October 1419, after the return of the fifth expedition, 41 new treasure ships were ordered to be constructed. They would have been ready by the time the sixth expedition started, and most writers have interpreted them as the fleet of the sixth voyage. By the time the sixth voyage was ordered in 1421, at least 151 (or 152) treasure ships had been built or were under construction: the 62 (or 63) that had sailed in the first voyage, the 48 ordered on 14 February 1408, and the 41 ordered in 1419. None of the surviving ships was more than fifteen years old. If the ships ordered in 1419 were needed to make up for losses, then the rate of loss was frightening indeed, and the wastefulness of the enterprise all the more pronounced. It seems more likely that the rates of loss were acceptable, that we cannot conclude too much from the way the ships are classified in the *Taizong Shilu* notices, and that the fleets of the fifth and sixth voyages were similar in composition to those that had gone before.

The seventh expedition had "more than a hundred large ships" (*jubo*, literally "great trading vessels") according to the Liujia-gang and Changle inscriptions, a number that might be construed to include most of the still surviving and serviceable treasure ships. Judging from the inscriptions, Zheng He probably realized that this voyage would be his final appearance in active service. The treasure ships were probably attended as before by smaller ships, and the total personnel of the fleet, at 27,550 men, was nearly the same as on the first voyage. Indeed, in both inscriptions Zheng He says explicitly that the seven fleets were similar in composition: "each time [I have] commanded several tens of thousands of government soldiers and over one hundred oceangoing ships."

Personnel

Zheng He commanded a fleet crewed by specified numbers of personnel with definite ranks and functions. One listing of these personnel survives. At the head of the fleet were seventy eunuchs. Seven of them, including Zheng He, held the title of Grand Director (*taijian*, rank 4a) and served as ambassadors and commanders, and their ten highest ranking assistants held the title Junior Director (*shaojian*, 4b). These were the highest ranks that eunuchs could hold, yet there is no doubt that eunuchs were in command of the fleet: this is shown not only by Zheng He himself but by the fact that detached squadrons and separate missions to individual countries were always led by eunuchs.

Below the eunuchs were 302 military officers who held the standard ranks found throughout the Ming military establishment: two regional military commissioners (*du zhihuishi*, 2a; salary 732), 93 guard commanders (*zhihuishi*, 3a; salary 420), 104 battalion commanders (*qianhu*, 5a; salary 192), and 103 company commanders (*bohu*, 6a; salary 120). We know from the details of the rewards given to Zheng He's personnel that his crews also included guard judges (*wei zhenfu*, 5b; salary 168) and battalion judges (*suo zhenfu*, 6b; salary 96). The large number of guard commanders probably included many officers who were actually deputy commanders (*zhihui tongzhi*, 3b; salary 312) or assistant commanders (*zhihui qianshi*, 4a; salary 288), and the even larger number of battalion commanders probably included many battalion vice commanders (*fu qianhu*, 5b; salary 168). (The annual salaries are stated in piculs of grain, like the shipbuilding costs.)

The "judges" adjudicated military offenses, but they were also expected to replace company commanders and battalion commanders and vice commanders when necessary. The fact that the judges, the deputy and assistant guard commanders, and the battalion vice commanders are omitted from the list of officers of Zheng He's fleet suggests that the list abbreviates titles and lumps groups together. Some positions omitted from the list are mentioned in the decrees granting rewards found in *Taizong Shilu*. The list is perhaps also limited to ship captains and squadron leaders rather than a full listing of the total number of officers in the fleet.

The military officers are followed on the list by 190 civilian specialists, including 180 doctors who are ranked with—and rewarded on the same scale as—squad leaders and common soldiers. The other ten civilians were a bureau director from the Ministry of Finance who presumably acted as chief purser for the fleet, two secretaries, two protocol officers from the Court of State Ceremonial that was in charge of the reception of foreign tributary envoys in the capital, and a fortune-telling official and four subordinates. The eunuch directors, military officers, and civilian specialists together total 562.

The rank and file amount to 26,803 men. They include petty officers (called *qixiao* or *guanxiao*, distinct from the officers holding formal ranks that are mentioned above), exceptionally courageous troops or "braves" *(yongshi)*, exceptionally strong soldiers *(lishi)*, regular soldiers referred to as "official soldiers" *(guanjun)* or "flag soldiers" *(qijun)*, supernumeraries *(yuding)*, civilian boatmen (variously *minshi, minshao,* or *shaoshui*), buyers *(maiban)*, and clerks *(shushou)*. Both the "braves" and the strong soldiers were elite categories distinguished from the rank-and-file regulars.

Zhu Yunming, whose *Xia Xiyang* is an important source of detail for the seventh voyage, gives a total fleet personnel of 27,550 including the officers. His categories are officers or petty officers *(guanxiao)*, regular soldiers *(qijun)*, foremen or mess leaders (*huozhang*; a *huo* or "fire" was a ten-man mess unit), rudder operators (*tuogong*; not simply "helmsmen" since the rudder had to be raised and lowered), anchormen (*bandingshou*; the anchors also needed to be raised and lowered), interpreters *(tongshi)*, business managers *(banshi)*, clerks and accountants *(shusuanshi)*, doctors *(yishi)*, blacksmiths for the anchors (*tiemiao*, replacing the character *miao*, "cat," with the homonym meaning "anchor"), caulkers for the hull *(munian)*, sailmakers (*dacai*, literally "hanging materials," referring to sails and rigging), other craftsmen, sailors *(shuishou)*, and civilian boatmen (here *minshaoren*). The sailors are probably the crew proper, while the boatmen operated small boats in harbors or in estuaries such as the approaches to Palembang. The above account, and the accounts of rewards given to fleet personnel that are discussed below, provide a more detailed picture of the

Ming military below the level of formally ranked officers than is present in any Ming account of land campaigns.

Zheng He's armada waged war on a large scale during the first, third, and fourth voyages. On the first expedition Chen Zuyi's fleet was destroyed in the vicinity of Palembang, with ten ships burned, seven captured, and more than five thousand pirates killed. On the third expedition Zheng He led two thousand troops personally by land to capture the capital and the king of Ceylon. On the fourth expedition Zheng He again commanded a landing party, this one capturing the rebel Sekandar in northern Sumatra. The three military actions are emphasized in Zheng He's *Mingshi* biography, and they receive a comparable degree of emphasis in Zheng He's Liujiagang and Changle inscriptions, which are independent sources that the compilers of the *Mingshi* did not know of or use. The ability to conduct operations of this kind was obviously perceived as necessary when the voyages were planned, and this fact refutes any interpretation of the voyages as essentially peaceful in character. Zheng He's armada fought on only three occasions, but it overawed local authorities without fighting on many more. The importance of the military side of the voyages is also shown in the rewards ordered by the emperor for the personnel of the fleet; they are detailed in *Taizong Shilu* and discussed below.

On 29 October 1407 the emperor ordered rewards for the officers and men of Zheng He's forces "who had gained merit capturing bandits at the Old Harbor" of Palembang during the first expedition. Guard Commanders were to receive 100 "ingots" of paper money (*ding*, a unit reflecting the nominal value of the money converted to silver) and four robes and linings of colored silk, Battalion Commanders 80 ingots and three robes and linings, and Company Commanders and Battalion Judges 60 ingots and two robes and linings. Below the officers, doctors and "shift foremen" *(fan huozhang)* received 50 ingots and one robe and lining. Soldiers holding brevet or honorific officer status (the most plausible interpretation of *xiaowei*) also received 50 ingots and three rolls of cotton cloth, while regular troops (here *qijun*), interpreters *(tongshi)*, auxiliary troops *(junban)*, and lower ranks received "paper money and cloth according to their status." Guard Judges, who would normally be placed with Battalion Commanders, are not mentioned here even though the lower ranking Battalion Judges are. The doctors (here *yishi*) occupy the place held by "imperial" or government doctors *(yuyi)* in the more detailed rewards ordered in 1411, in which there is a lower category of "civilian" doctors *(minyi)*.

Also in the 1411 rewards, the "shift foremen" *(fan huozhang)* are distinguished from ordinary foremen *(huozhang)*. The term "foreman" (literally "fire chief") goes back at least to the armies of the Tang Dynasty (618–907), where the *huo* was a squad of ten men, literally a single campfire. The term was used on Chinese ships for a crew unit (a mess in British parlance, but here probably with its own fire for cooking) of similar size.

The personnel of Zheng He's fleet, and the many foreign rulers whom the emperor chose to favor, received much of their rewards in the form of paper money, and therefore one consequence of the voyages was the wide circulation of Chinese paper money outside China. Paper money had been revived in the Hongwu reign; each ingot was nominally equivalent to five strings *(guan)* of copper coins, each string being equal to one picul of husked grain at the official rate of exchange. Unfortunately for the personnel rewarded, Zheng He's voyages coincided with the rapid depreciation of Ming paper currency. In 1385 it took 2.5 strings of paper money to purchase a picul of grain; under Yongle the official exchange rate was 30 strings per picul; and when Xuande became emperor in 1425, the market value of paper money was fluctuating between 40 and 70 strings per picul. The paper money had depreciated in spite of the legal prohibition of the use of copper coins and metallic gold and silver in commercial transactions. In 1435, after the death of both Zheng He and Emperor Xuande, the government permitted the use of copper coins, and traders ignored the prohibition of the use of silver. In 1436 the government began collecting land taxes in silver, and paper money ceased to be important except in small-change transactions. Thus the amounts of the rewards are of importance mostly as indicators of the relative status of the various levels of personnel in Zheng He's fleet.

The battle in Ceylon was the largest-scale and hardest-fought battle of Zheng He's voyages. This is indicated by both the level of generosity and the extreme detail of the rewards approved by the emperor on 13 September 1411, on the joint recommendation of the Ministry of Rites and the Ministry of War. This time both promotions and monetary rewards were granted. For promotions there were the two categories of "extraordinary merit" *(qigong)* and "highest merit" *(tougong)*, the latter being in fact the lower of the two (this was the normal Ming system). For "those who did not wish to be promoted" (*bu yuan sheng zhe,* itself an unusual statement), monetary rewards twice the usual size were authorized (this may be verified for the higher ranks of officers by comparing the amounts authorized in 1411 with those authorized in 1407, above), and a category of "extraordinary merit of the second class" *(qigong cideng)* was inserted between the other two.

All "officers and soldiers" *(guanjun)* were to be promoted two grades for extraordinary merit and one grade for highest merit. In the Ming system each of the nine ranks *(pin)* had two grades *(ji)*, but military officers held only ranks 1a through 6b. Guard commanders, battalion commanders, and company commanders, who already held hereditary rank under this system, were to receive personally the appropriate promotions in grade if still living; if deceased, their sons and heirs should receive them. Below the ranked officers, the standard descriptions of the early Ming military system recognize three categories of personnel: under each company commander were two platoon leaders, each commanding five squad leaders, each of whom in turn commanded ten ordinary soldiers. The regulations on rewards and promotions issued in 1411 show several subdivisions of these categories. Living platoon leaders with extraordinary merit were to be promoted to "substantive" *(shishou)* company commanders; if deceased, their sons were to become "probationary" *(shi)* company commanders, a distinction shared with living platoon leaders of merely highest merit. The sons *and grandsons* of deceased platoon leaders of highest merit were to be promoted to substantive platoon leaders.

There follows the previously unknown category of *zongjia.* A *jia* is a tithing; by analogy with *zongqi*, or platoon leader, a *zongjia* should be the leader of fifty men (conscripts or levies) who are not regular soldiers. Living or dead, *zongjia* of extraordinary merit were to be promoted to probationary company commander and those of highest merit to substantive platoon leader. Note that for the *zongjia*, the reward for merit was always a rank in the regular army.

Living squad leaders of extraordinary merit were to be promoted to acting company commander, the deceased to platoon leader (here the distinction between substantive and probationary is not made), along with living squad leaders of highest merit. The sons of deceased squad leaders of highest merit were to be promoted to substantive squad leaders. These regulations suggest that the unranked petty officer posts of platoon leader and squad leader were regarded in practice as fully inheritable positions, in the same manner as the ranked officer positions from guard commander down to battalion judge, whose hereditary nature has long been understood.

Below the squad leaders was a category of soldiers and sailors who seem to have had the functions of squad leaders without having the specific title, much as the *zongjia* were comparable to platoon leaders. Whether living or dead, they were to be promoted to platoon leader for extraordinary merit and to squad leader for highest merit, and the distinction between substantive and acting is not made in either case. As with the *zongjia*, their reward was a rank in the regular army. First in this category are "military personnel who hold honorific officer status or who are soldiers of exceptional strength"; foremen or mess leaders *(huozhang)* follow, then military personnel with the duties of rudder operators, boatmen, and anchormen are mentioned. This passage concludes by ordering that retainers, extra personnel, overage soldiers, grooms for horses, and petty servants should all be treated in the same way as military personnel who hold honorific officer status.

The financial rewards for those who were "not willing" to be promoted are too involved to be included here, but the classification of personnel is interesting. All personnel were divided into seven rank categories, which overlap, but do not coincide exactly, with the categories given for promotions. All rewards were in the form of a certain number of ingots of paper money plus cloth in the form of robes and linings of colored silk *(caibi)*, rolls of thin silk *(juan)*, or rolls of cotton cloth *(mianbu)*. Each rank category was divided into three categories of merit. For those killed in battle, heirs unwilling to be promoted could claim a death benefit in addition to the other financial rewards.

The first three categories were guard commanders, battalion commanders including guard judges, and company commanders including battalion judges. These categories included most of the hereditary military officers holding formal rank. The fourth-rank category included government doctors *(yuyi)*—a category of medical practitioner distinguished from the civilian doctors *(minyi)* in the lowest rank category—and shift foremen *(fan huozhang)*, who seem to be equivalent to the platoon leaders and *zongjia* (who are not mentioned here) and who are distinguished from the lower-ranking foremen *(huozhang)*. In the fifth-rank category were holders of brevet or honorific officer status. The sixth-rank category listed "regular and conscript soldiers and civilians," interpreters, foremen (probably including the squad leaders who are not mentioned), petty servants, military artisans, and military messengers. The petty servants, here grouped with the lowest-ranking military personnel, seem to be military personnel themselves even though their title does not so indicate. For the seventh and lowest category, the positions all seem to be nonmilitary, including civilian doctors, artisans, kitchen workers, messengers, boatmen, and family members. As already noted, the doctors, artisans, and messengers in this category were distinguished from higher-ranking equivalents.

On 8 August 1419 the emperor, then in Beijing, ordered the Ministry of Rites to give monetary rewards to the personnel of the fleet that had just returned from its fifth voyage. "The officers and men have sailed the oceans for over ten years, and have exhausted their strength traveling thousands of miles visiting dozens of countries, and it is appropriate to encourage them with rewards." As in 1407 and 1411, the amounts of the rewards are given in ingots of paper money. The paper money was by now greatly depreciated in value, since it had been issued for decades without any thought of guarding against inflation; nevertheless the amounts named provide information about the relative rank and status of the personnel of Zheng He's fleet, and they may be compared with the rewards given following the first voyage.

Regional military commissioners, the highest military officers mentioned in the sources as part of the fleet personnel, received 20 ingots. Guard commanders received 18 ingots. Battalion commanders, company commanders, guard judges, and battalion judges received 16 ingots. These were the lowest categories of Ming military officers holding formal rank; the next category, called "foremen *(huozhang)* and those of their class," received 15 ingots. In the Ming army the usual equivalents of the sergeants and corporals of Western armies were the platoon leaders and squad leaders. Here the expression "foremen and those of their class" stands for all noncommissioned or petty officers. At the lowest level, all ordinary soldiers, here "men of the banner army" *(qijunren)*, received 13 ingots. Compensation figures for the "other ranks" in Ming armies are hard to come by, but one or two taels *(liang)* of silver per month is occasionally mentioned in later reigns. The emperor's present, if it had any real value, amounted to no more than a tip for both the officers and the other ranks, yet it provides more evidence that Zheng He's fleet, under its eunuch controllers, functioned as a regular part of the Ming military organization.

Since even Zheng He is elusive as a personality, we know nothing of the men who sailed his ships as individuals. Nevertheless, the material preserved in the sources that relates to shipbuilding and to the rewards given to the crews testifies to the existence of a complex organization that existed continuously throughout the period of the voyages, including the long hiatus between the sixth and seventh. When Emperor Xuande gave the order for the last voyage, the fleet was there to carry it out under its customary commanders and officers.

VII

Zheng He's Career after 1424 and His Final Voyage

Emperor Yongle's death ended the consistent imperial support for the voyages that had been in place since 1403. Hongxi, the new emperor, made permanent the temporary suspension of the voyages that Yongle had ordered in 1421, and he restored Xia Yuanji to his previous position as Minister of Finance. He ordered Zheng He to keep his fleet together as part of the garrison of Nanjing, which he intended to restore as the imperial capital.

Hongxi was dead within nine months, and his successor, Xuande, left these arrangements in place. While the Ming government was accepting defeat and the loss of Vietnam, Zheng He's principal recorded accomplishment was the rebuilding of the Great Baoen Temple at Nanjing. After the death of Xia Yuanji in 1430, Xuande sent Zheng He's fleet on what turned out to be its last voyage to the Western Ocean. Zheng He, now sixty, and his colleagues used the occasion to inscribe the inscriptions at Liujiagang and Changle (see the Appendix) that are the epitaphs of the voyages. The sources include a detailed itinerary of the last voyage, to Hormuz and back, which permits some calculations of the average speeds of the treasure ships.

Emperor Hongxi, Yongle's son and successor, looks imperial rather than obese in this formal portrait, painted in the same style as that of his father (figure 1, p. 19). © ChinaStock

Ming China in the Hongxi (1424–25) and Xuande (1425–35) Reigns

In mid-1424 Zheng He was on a mission to confer upon Shi Jisun his official seal and letter of appointment as Pacification Commissioner or head of the overseas Chinese community at Palembang. By the time he returned, Emperor Yongle was dead. Yongle had been the driving force behind the voyages, and his death on 12 August 1424 at once changed the political situation in China, making further voyages and further Mongolian campaigns less likely and even calling into question the permanence of the transfer of the capital to Beijing and the annexation of Vietnam.

Hongxi, the new emperor, was Yongle's eldest son, the obese and sickly Zhu Gaozhi (1378–1425). Yongle may have preferred his second son, Zhu Gaoxu, Prince of Han, who resembled his father in being tall, physically powerful, and militarily ambitious. Zhu Gaoxu had accompanied Yongle on the five Mongolian campaigns and had used these opportunities to undermine his elder brother. After Hongxi's death, Zhu Gaoxu rebelled in 1426 against the new emperor, Hongxi's son Xuande. The rebellion failed, and Zhu Gaoxu was first imprisoned and then burned to death in 1429 and his family exterminated. Yongle's third and youngest son, Zhu Gaosui, Prince of Zhao, was implicated in the rebellion but nonetheless was pardoned, and his line survived until the end of the dynasty. The troubles that followed Yongle's death echoed the way in which Yongle himself had come to the throne.

During the civil war of 1399–1402, while his father was on campaign, Hongxi as eldest son administered Beiping (the future Beijing) on his behalf, and this relationship continued when Yongle became emperor. Yongle was often absent from the capital, either personally supervising the transformation of Beijing or commanding the Mongolian campaigns; Hongxi served as regent on all those occasions. Yongle left a rather small group of senior civil officials in positions of authority for most of his reign, and Hongxi earned the respect of and worked well with this group. As the cost of Yongle's initiatives escalated, official opposition to them mounted, and the crown prince took the side of the officials and clashed with his father the emperor. Hongxi ascended the throne on 7 September 1424, and on that day ordered the abolition of the treasure ship voyages to the Western Ocean, the tea and horse trade with the Mongols, and purchasing operations in Yunnan and Jiaozhi (the official name of Vietnam as a Chinese province). The next day he ordered the release from prison of Xia Yuanji, who had opposed Zheng He's voyages because of their cost and had been imprisoned late in 1421 for opposing Yongle's third Mongolian campaign. Xia Yuanji resumed his previous position as Minister of Finance.

For modern historians in China and elsewhere, Yongle is the outward-looking and progressive emperor who sponsored Zheng He's voyages, Hongxi the introverted successor who ended them, aided by a supporting cast of backward-looking and xenophobic officials. While the contrast between father and son in personality and policy preferences is as clear as one will ever find in Chinese sources, the picture as usually drawn is too simple. On 14 May 1421, after ordering the sixth voyage but before that voyage had sailed, Yongle had ordered a "temporary" suspension of the treasure ship voyages that lasted for the rest of his reign. The new emperor merely continued an existing state of affairs. The third, fourth, and fifth Mongolian campaigns had consumed both the personal imperial attention and much of the funding that might otherwise have gone to further treasure ship voyages. "Yuanji loved me" the dying Yongle admitted in 1424, and, now in charge of the empire's fiscal system once again, Xia Yuanji had to cope with a crisis whose most visible sign was the collapse of the paper currency that Zheng He had distributed lavishly on his first six voyages.

Zheng He remained in command at Nanjing, and his fleet (ships and personnel) remained in being for the entire period (1422–31) between the return of the sixth voyage and the sailing of the seventh. China's withdrawal from the sea was not an inevitable result of the decisions made in late 1424, but the new emperor and his advisers did confront many problems whose root cause was Yongle's propensity to initiate expensive projects with no apparent consideration of their long-term costs. "Action was his ideology" as Yongle's recent biographer explains, not unkindly.

On 26 September 1424 Emperor Hongxi recalled **Huang Fu** (1363–1440), the civil governor of Jiaozhi (Vietnam). The Ming effort to annex Vietnam had begun almost simultaneously with Zheng He's first expedition, and Ming armies had conquered and reconquered the country in a series of campaigns (1406–08, 1409–10, 1411–13). When Zheng He returned from his third voyage in the summer of 1411, "the prefectures and districts of Jiaozhi had already been destroyed, and the other foreign countries had become increasingly agitated," Zheng He's *Mingshi* biography tells us. By 1414 Jiaozhi seemed adequately pacified, and Yongle recalled the main army and placed the province under civilian rule. The founder of the future Lê Dynasty (1418–1804) rebelled in 1418 and by the winter of 1421 had eliminated his rivals and become the sole rebel leader. Hongxi tried unsuccessfully to co-opt him with an offer to make him

Prefect of Thanh Hoa. Hongxi's recall in 1424 of Huang Fu, the only civil official whom the Vietnamese had ever respected, came to be regarded as the turning point, after which the war in Vietnam became unwinnable.

Early in 1425 Hongxi ordered preparations to move the capital back to Nanjing, but he died (29 May) before this could be accomplished, and the capital remained at Beijing for the rest of the Ming Dynasty. Hongxi's empress survived until 1442 and until her death had close relations with the surviving members of Yongle's core group of conservative civil officials, most of whom had opposed both the naval voyages and the Mongolian campaigns.

Hongxi's eldest son, the new emperor Xuande (Zhu Zhanji, 1399–1435), was a determined and conscientious ruler with strong aesthetic interests. His too-short reign was later regarded as a period of peace and good government despite the emperor's reliance on eunuchs and despite the decay of the hereditary Ming military system that took place on his watch. In addition to the deteriorating situation in Vietnam that he inherited, he had to suppress the rebellion of his uncle Zhu Gaoxu in 1426. In the autumn of 1427, after repeated Chinese defeats, the Ming military commander in Jiaozhi made an unauthorized armistice with the rebel leader and withdrew the remnants of his army from Vietnam. This defeat was the catalytic event that led the emperor and his advisers to cut their losses and make peace in 1427, grudgingly recognizing Lê Dynasty rule in Vietnam. By the midpoint of the Xuande reign, only half of Yongle's policy remained in place: campaigns in Mongolia had ceased, but the capital remained in Beijing; the attempt to conquer Vietnam had been abandoned, but Zheng He and his fleet were to have one final voyage.

Zheng He's Career from 1424 to 1430

When Zheng He returned from his mission to Palembang, Hongxi was emperor. Intending to move the capital back to Nanjing, the new emperor on 24 February 1425 ordered Zheng He to continue to command his fleet (here called the *Xiafan Guanjun*) and to defend *(shou)* Nanjing. "Toward the interior" (referring to administration and civic order in Nanjing) he was to "manage affairs jointly" with three designated eunuchs. "If incidents arose from outside" (alluding to military attack) he was to consult with two designated military noblemen.

Historians cite this order as the origin of the post of commandant (*shoubei*, literally "to defend and prepare") of Nanjing, described in the *Mingshi* as the most important of the three positions that shared the military command at the Ming southern capital. The commandant and the assistant commandant *(xietong shoubei)* were usually members of the Ming military nobility, even though the post originated with the eunuch Zheng He, as stated in his *Mingshi* biography. The third member of the command triumvirate was the Nanjing Minister of War, once the dual capital system became fully institutionalized.

The entry quoted in the *Renzong Shilu*, however, omits the second character of the later title (*bei*, to prepare) and simply assigns Zheng He to *shou* (defend or command a city or other fortified place; the opposite of *gong* or "assault"). His position continues to be the command *(ling)* of the *Xiafan Guanjun* or Foreign Expeditionary Armada. The implication is that the ships of Zheng He's fleet remained in being and its (overwhelmingly military) personnel remained together, with the assignment, originally a temporary one, of providing security for Nanjing until the emperor and the large military establishment that always surrounded the emperor returned from the north. Hongxi's premature death changed things: Xuande did not formally repeal his father's order, but he was plainly in no hurry to carry it out.

Hsu Yü-hu's biography of Zheng He uses the words "commanded the Foreign Expeditionary Armada and served as commandant of Nanjing" *(ling Xiafan Guanjun, shoubei Nanjing)* to describe Zheng He's activities in the years 1425–29 and, after his return from the seventh expedition, again in 1434. His authority for including 1434 is not entirely clear, but his opinion deserves respect. What is clear is the continued existence of the fleet in the years from its return from the sixth expedition in 1422 until 1430, when the seventh expedition was ordered. The *Mingshi* biography of Zheng He confuses the issue somewhat by substituting *zhujun* ("various military forces") for *guanjun* ("government forces" or "imperial forces"), but it also uses the term *xiafan* ("foreign expeditionary") for the troops under

Zheng He's control. Hongxi's long-range intentions were not perfectly clear, despite his seeming eagerness to terminate the voyages and restore their critic Xia Yuanji to high office.

Because the new emperor, Xuande, remained in Beijing, the *ad hoc* arrangements to command and govern Nanjing evolved into permanent institutions. Zheng He continued to have important military authority, and he resumed the role of supervisor of construction projects that he had been performing when Yongle summoned him to command the first naval expedition. When he next appears in the sources he is being reprimanded severely, and there is little background information to explain why.

On 15 May 1426 the Directorate of Ceremonial, the principal eunuch agency, was ordered to send a letter instructing Grand Director Zheng He "not to neglect [regulations] when requesting [permission] to give rewards." Earlier a department director in the Ministry of Works had gone to Nanjing to repair and refurbish government buildings and had given rewards—the term *shangci* suggests something over and above regular wages—to each of the skilled workmen. Returned to Beijing, this official had written a memorial saying that the skilled workmen who had built "temple buildings such as the Nanjing Guoshi" also ought to receive additional rewards. The emperor responded suspiciously and angrily, telling the (unnamed) officials of the Directorate of Ceremonial: "Buddhist temples should be built by the monks themselves—how can these costs be charged to the Court? This official's memorial must have been instigated by Zheng He and his associates, and it will not be enough just to reprimand its author." Emperor Xuande then sent messengers to instruct Zheng He to act strictly in accordance with "propriety and the law" and not to "spy" (using a term for a burglar plotting his next crime) on the Court. Whenever he violated the rules in the future, he would not be permitted to file "wild" (repeated) petitions and appeals.

While this sounds very high-principled, a man of Zheng He's importance would have his agents at court, even though the sources provide no details, and they might include friendly civil officials as well as eunuchs. Zheng He was a capable leader and manager who would try to get any perquisites for his own subordinates that had gone to workmen on other jobs. The emperor's remarks give the impression that Zheng He's behavior on this occasion was the last straw, and we would like to know what had gone on before. In any event, the emperor eventually came to trust Zheng He.

Contradicting his notion that Buddhist temples should be built only by the monks themselves, on 25 March 1428 the emperor ordered Zheng He and "others" (in a later passage four eunuch grand directors are mentioned) to take command of the rebuilding and repair of the Great Baoen Temple at Nanjing, located outside the Qubao Gate (later the Zhonghua Gate) at the southern end of the Ming walled city. Its description occupies the first place in the section on Buddhist and Daoist temples at Nanjing in the official Ming gazetteer *Daming Yitong Zhi*, where its long history going back to the Wu state of the Three Kingdoms period (220–280) is recounted. When Yongle transferred the capital to Beijing, he wanted to "repay the grace" *(baoen)* of his "official" mother, Hongwu's empress, who had raised him and who died not long after he was created Prince of Yan (1380) and moved to his fief in the north. (There are traditions that his birth mother was someone other than Hongwu's empress, and the question cannot be resolved from the surviving sources.)

The construction of the Great Baoen Temple had begun in 1412 and was completed in 1431. Yongle had originally ordered the Ministry of Works to follow a hexagonal (*liujue*, "six cornered") plan for the temple, whose centerpiece was a nine-story octagonal pagoda glazed in five colors, whose height was precisely 32.949 *zhang*. The pagoda was crowned by a gold "windmill" *(fengmo*; here certainly a decorative fixture turned by the wind), and 72 bells hung from eight copper-plated iron chains, and 80 more bells hung from the corners of the pagoda's several stories. Every evening 128 oil lamps were lit on the outer walls of the nine stories. Below, in each of the eight halls corresponding to the eight sides of the pagoda, and in the "heart" *(xin)* of the pagoda itself, there were 12 glazed lamps. At the very top of the pagoda was a "heavenly dish" *(tianpan)* weighing 900 catties (the *jin* or "catty" of 16 *liang* or ounces remained reasonably constant in value from the Tang Dynasty onward, being fixed at one and one-third pounds in the nineteenth century for tariff purposes), and an iron saucepan with two mouths weighing 4,500 catties. The territory occupied by the temple had a circumference of nine *li* and thirteen paces (*bu*; each "pace" was five Chinese feet or half a *zhang*, and a *li* was 360 paces or somewhat more than one-third of a mile). While its official name was Great Baoen Temple, it was also known less formally as the Number One Pagoda *(diyi ta)*. (Reading all of this makes one wish that we had an equivalent amount of descriptive detail about Zheng He's ships.)

At the beginning of the construction of the Great Baoen Temple in 1412, 100,000 "soldiers, skilled craftsmen and miscellaneous laborers" were deployed under the command of three notables designated Officials Supervising Construction. They were a Grand Director of the Directorate of Palace Servants, the eunuch agency that Zheng He had briefly headed before his first voyage; a marquis who was one of the twenty-four generals who had aided Yongle in the war for the throne and who had been rewarded with titles of nobility on 30 September 1402; and a vice minister of works. This triumvirate of a leading eunuch, a member of the military nobility, and an important civil official prefigures the command structure that emerged in 1424 for the Nanjing military forces.

Now, after sixteen years in which the numerous work crews had received salary grain and other rewards, the temple was still incomplete and the emperor was angry. He commanded Zheng He and his colleagues to finish the work and then to hold a Buddhist celebration and vegetarian feast seven days and nights in duration. More than five hundred "licensed monks" and "student monks" were accommodated in the completed temple's 148 cells, and much additional detail is preserved about the Great Baoen Temple, which was a center of Buddhist life in Nanjing until its destruction by the Taiping rebel army when it captured Nanjing in 1856. Some authorities conjecture that the money spent on the Great Baoen Temple came out of the funds that otherwise would have been spent on ocean voyages.

Minister of Finance Xia Yuanji died on 19 February 1430, less than six years after his release from prison and restoration to the office in 1424. Although he had lost the confidence of Emperor Xuande in 1428, around the time that Zheng He was ordered to expedite the construction of the Great Baoen Temple, the prestige he had gained from standing up to Yongle in 1421 was such that he had to be left with his titles and position until he died. One biographer argues that, Xia Yuanji's death having removed the only obstacle, the emperor decided immediately to resume the treasure voyages. In fact the emperor gave orders for the seventh voyage several months later, on 29 June 1430. The *Xuanzong Shilu* reports: "Everything was prosperous and renewed, but the foreign countries, distantly located beyond the sea, still had not heard and did not know. For this reason Grand Directors Zheng He, Wang Jinghong, and others, were specially sent, bearing the word, to go and instruct them into deference and submission."

The foreign embassies who had come to China on the sixth voyage (1421–22) had arrived at court only in 1423 because of the time needed to transit overland or through the Grand Canal to Beijing. They included envoys from Brava and Mogadishu in Africa and from Hormuz and Aden in Arabia. Since then Malacca had sent tribute twice (1424, 1426), Semudera once (1426), Thailand three times (1426–28), Champa—badly affected by Chinese recognition in 1427 of the renewed independence of Vietnam—three times (1427, 1428, 1429), and the declining Majapahit kingdom on Java four times (1426–29). Except for Bengal, whose solitary tribute mission of 1429 was the most distant to arrive by sea in this period, those were all of the embassies from the countries on Zheng He's normal itinerary. The virtual cessation of diplomatic activity after 1422 indicates clearly that the overwhelming military power represented by Zheng He's fleet—the *Xiafan Guanjun*, or Foreign Expeditionary Armada—was the key to maintaining the kind of diplomatic relationships that Emperor Yongle, at least, wanted to have with the countries of Southeast Asia and the Indian Ocean.

The Great Baoen Temple was completed and the seventh voyage embarked in 1431. After the fleet left Nanjing, and while they awaited the monsoon winds, Zheng He and his associates set up two inscriptions, one at Liujiagang on the lower reaches of the Yangtze and one at Changle anchorage in Fujian, that summarized the history of the *Xiafan Guanjun*.

Zheng He's Inscriptions at Liujiagang and Changle

J. J. L. Duyvendak's translation and publication in 1938 of the Liujiagang and Changle inscriptions cleared up the confusion found in *Taizong Shilu*, and magnified in the *Mingshi*, regarding the sequence and dating of the seven voyages. Other information from these inscriptions has found its way, as appropriate, into this narrative. At this point the two inscriptions need to be considered integrally, for they are the nearest thing the sources provide to insight about Zheng He's thoughts and feelings. Zheng He had been born in the fourth year of Hongwu (17 January 1371 to 4 February 1372), a *xinhai* (Metal Boar) year in the cycle of sixty by which both days and years were counted. Both inscriptions were set up in the sixth year of Xuande (12 February 1431 to 2 February 1432), also a *xinhai* year and thus the 61st year of Zheng He's life by Chinese reckoning. The completion of a full sixty-year cycle, which could happen only once in a person's lifetime, was an occasion for personal reflection. At sixty, Confucius's ear was attuned to the truth (*Analects* 2.4), and so we might expect to learn something here of Zheng He's sense of the meaning of his life as he set forth on his seventh and last voyage.

The voyage of 1431–33 is the only one for which a precise itinerary has been preserved: *Xia Xiyang*, or "Down to the Western Ocean." This itinerary has Zheng He's fleet arriving at Liujiagang on 3 February 1431, where the fleet was still present when the Liujiagang inscription was erected on 14 March 1431. The inscription concludes with a reference to the fact that the fleet is once more setting forth for the barbarian countries to communicate the imperial edicts. The fleet arrived at Changle on 8 April 1431 and departed through the Five Tigers Gate of the Min River on 12 January 1432. The Changle inscription is dated only to the eleventh month of the sixth year of Xuande (5 December 1431 to 3 January 1432). It, too, ends by alluding to the fact that the fleet is awaiting a north wind to begin its voyage and imploring divine protection.

Both inscriptions present Zheng He as the leader of the enterprise, but they also mention his principal collaborators. In the Liujiagang inscription Zheng He and Wang Jinghong are both Principal Envoys, while the eunuchs **Zhu Liang,** Zhou Man, **Hong Bao, Yang Zhen,** and **Zhang Da** are Assistant Envoys. All hold the eunuch rank of Grand Director except for Zhang Da, who holds the slightly lower rank of Left Assistant Director (*zuo shaojian,* 4b). In the Changle inscription he has been promoted to Grand Director, and **Li Xing** and **Wu Zhong** have been added to the list of eunuch assistant envoys at the same level. This inscription also lists **Zhu Zhen** and **Wang Heng** as Regional Military Commissioners, and it concludes with a Daoist Resident Priest and Patriarch (*zhengyi,* an official appointment at rank 6a) named **Yang Yichu** begging permission to erect the stone. Wang Jinghong's name in a different form appears with Zheng He's on the trilingual inscription at Galle in Ceylon, and like Zheng He he was venerated by the overseas Chinese community in Indonesia after he lost his life in a shipwreck on the coast of Java in 1434. Ma Huan mentions Li Xing and Zhou Man in connection with the detached squadron of the fleet that went to Aden on the sixth voyage, and Hong Bao as the authority who sent seven men, possibly including Ma Huan himself, to Mecca on the seventh voyage, when the main fleet went no further than Hormuz.

Both inscriptions present the composition of the expeditionary armada and the courses of the individual voyages in the same general terms. The fleet is more than a hundred large ships and several myriads of personnel in both inscriptions. These numbers offer the only figure for the size of the fleet on the seventh voyage; more important, they make the claim that the fleet was similar in numbers of ships and personnel on all seven voyages, which we have seen to be consistent with the other evidence. For the itinerary, the Liujiagang inscription has "from Taicang"—the walled city nearest to Liujiagang—"we have sailed to Champa, Thailand *(Xianluo),* Java, Cochin, and Calicut, finally reaching Hormuz and other countries in the Western Regions, more than thirty countries in all." The Changle inscription lists the same six countries and then adds Aden and Mogadishu to make a total of "more than thirty countries large and small." Each of the two inscriptions also records details of the six voyages already completed.

The first expedition of 1405–07 visited "Calicut and other countries" according to both inscriptions, which then move on promptly to the defeat and capture of Chen Zuyi, labeled in both as a pirate whose forces were in Palembang *(Sanfoqi)*. In the Changle inscription, the secret assistance of "spirit soldiers" *(shenbing)* makes this victory possible.

The second expedition of 1407–09 is described in almost identical language in both inscriptions, as visiting the four countries of Java, Calicut, Cochin, and Thailand, whose rulers sent tribute including rare birds and animals.

The third expedition of 1409–11 is also described in nearly identical language in both inscriptions. Revisiting the same countries as before, their "route took them by" Ceylon, and the war against King Alagakkonara (Alakeshvara) is described. Zheng He's discovery of Alagakkonara's plot against the fleet is attributed to the response of divine power to his prayers.

The description of the fourth expedition of 1413–15 repeats the same pattern. The fleet went to "Hormuz and other countries," and the scene then shifts to Semudera and the conflict with the rebel Sekandar. Again silent divine assistance is given credit for the Chinese victory. Both inscriptions mention that the King of Malacca came in person with his wife and son to present tribute.

For the fifth expedition of 1417–19 both inscriptions mention the six countries of Hormuz, Aden, Mogadishu, and Brava on the Somali coast in Africa, Calicut, and Java. Both give *zulafa* as the native name for the giraffe, which they identify as the Chinese *qilin*, and they name lions, leopards, zebras, horses, and oryxes, as well as an animal called *miligao*, presented by both Java and Calicut, that remains unidentified. All of the countries sent a wide variety of local products as tribute, with members of their royal families serving as ambassadors.

The sixth expedition of 1421–22 was devoted, according to both inscriptions, to returning the ambassadors, and the kings of the various countries are said to have provided tribute even more abundantly than before.

For all three expeditions in which Zheng He's fleet used military force, the inscriptions make the conflict their point of emphasis; for the other three the emphasis is placed on the generous amount of tribute the foreign states offered. Both inscriptions emphasize that the purpose of the expeditions is to enforce the tribute system and to confine trade within it. As the Liujiagang inscription puts it, "barbarian kings who resisted transformation [by Chinese civilization] and were not respectful we captured alive, and bandit soldiers who looted and plundered recklessly we exterminated. Because of this the sea lanes became pure and peaceful, and foreign peoples could rely upon them and pursue their occupations in safety."

Both inscriptions invoke divine protection for a voyage that is about to begin and whose dangers will be familiar and terrifying. The fleet had already sailed over a hundred thousand *li* through seas filled endlessly with waves rising to heaven, and it had encountered thick fogs and high winds. Both inscriptions interpret St. Elmo's Fire, the electrical discharge that occurs at the top of the mast after a storm at sea, as a divine response to their prayers: as soon as the miraculous light appeared, the seas became calm and everyone felt that there was nothing to fear. To whom were they praying? Zheng He's Muslim childhood is well known, and he is claimed to this day by the Chinese Muslim community, including contemporary descendants of his extended family. Yet he is also remembered today with Buddhist rituals by the overseas Chinese community in Southeast Asia. The trilingual inscription at Galle in Ceylon does not help to answer the question: the Chinese text invokes Buddha, the Tamil text an incarnation of Vishnu, and the Persian text Allah. The Galle inscription, of course, honored the competing religious traditions of a foreign land, even though Buddhism and Islam also existed in China. Zheng He's public display of eclecticism seems incompatible with a strict profession of Islam, though the Islam then spreading among the Indonesian islands was an Islam of a tolerant variety.

The Liujiagang and Changle inscriptions were both placed well within the borders of Ming China, and the goddess honored in them represented the true faith of Zheng He's fleet and possibly of Zheng He himself. She was Tianfei, the "Heavenly Princess"—sometimes promoted to Tianhou, the "Heavenly Empress"—the goddess of sailors and seafarers, known popularly in her native Fujian as Mazu or Mazupo, names that mean something like "Old Crone" and do not suggest the affection in which she is held. Duyvendak translated her title as "Heavenly Spouse," but a *fei* is either the spouse of a prince or a secondary consort of an emperor. She was born in 960 in Putian on the coast of Fujian to a family surnamed Lin, and she died on 4 October 987. In life her spirit, in a dream, rescued her brothers from drowning at sea, and after her death her ghost wandered above the sea, wearing a red dress and rescuing endangered mariners. In 1156 she was awarded the title Linghui Furen ("Lady Supernatural Benefactress") and in 1281 she was promoted to Tianfei. Both inscriptions mention the additional honors awarded her in 1409 and the temple erected in her honor at Longjiang near the shipyard at Nanjing. Another temple in her honor had been built at Liujiagang, and that inscription records its repair, which included a new statue of the goddess. "Officials and officers, soldiers and common people all rejoiced and hastened to serve, and there were some who could not contain themselves" because of their happiness.

At Changle the fleet was preparing for imminent departure into the open ocean, which occurred a few days after the inscription was erected, and the inscription has more to say. After mentioning the St. Elmo's fire, the capture of the contumacious kings, the extermination of the pirates, the pacification of the sea lanes, and the building of the Longjiang temple, Zheng He and his colleagues speak of the installations at Changle: The place where the government troops go to pray has been completely refurbished, the once dilapidated and neglected pagoda is now in good condition, and the principal halls and meditation chambers are now much better than before. Zheng He has frequently moored the fleet at Changle, and he has used the time to repair "the halls of the Buddhas and the temples of the gods." Now he promises new and beautiful images of the gods, with a full suite of gongs, drums, and sacrificial utensils, to be housed in grand buildings whose painted beams will seem to fly to the clouds, so that all will gladly hasten to Changle to pray. If men serve their ruler with all their loyalty, they can accomplish anything; and if they can serve the gods with total sincerity, all their prayers will be answered. Zheng He acknowledges the burden of his responsibility for the many personnel of his fleet and the amount of money and cloth entrusted to his care. Facing the violence of the winds and the uncertainty of the nights, and now anchored in the port of Changle awaiting a north wind to take to the sea, Zheng He implores the protection of the divine intelligence.

While these inscriptions were erected with imperial permission, and indeed allude to temples erected and titles bestowed on the goddess by the emperors, they are nonetheless not as closely reflective of the beliefs of the official class as Zheng He's later biography in the *Mingshi*. Instead of a mere eunuch whose voyages were "wasteful expenditures" and seemed to be a "major accomplishment" only in the "vulgar tradition," the inscriptions portray Zheng He as a dedicated servant of his ruler surrounded by fellow officers who are a "band of brothers" and a crew many of whom had sailed on previous voyages with Zheng He and about whose safety and welfare Zheng He cared. The inscriptions also suggest that the voyages by sea had become the activity that defined the meaning of his life for Zheng He, and that devotion to Tianfei, the goddess of seafarers, had become the dominant strand in his eclectic religious heritage. The words of the inscriptions now survive as epitaphs, both for Zheng He and for the voyages themselves.

Zheng He's Seventh and Final Voyage, 1431–33

For the last voyage there is a detailed itinerary, *Xia Xiyang* ("Down to the Western Ocean"), which is preserved in the miscellany *Qianwen Ji* ("A Record of Things Once Heard") of Zhu Yunming (1461–1527), a reclusive scholar of the Soochow (Suzhou) area who became famous for his unconventional views and for his attacks on the Neoconfucianism that had become a stifling orthodoxy in his lifetime. The *Qianwen Ji* in turn was included in the collection *Jilu Huibian* (literally, "Collection of Records," published about 1617), which included many unofficial accounts of military campaigns and related activities in the early part of the Ming. J. V. G. Mills and others have translated the *Xia Xiyang*, and material from this source appears elsewhere in this account of Zheng He's ships and personnel, for the *Xia Xiyang* supplements the other sources.

Mills's careful analysis of Zheng He's routes and their distances, based on the *Xia Xiyang*, remains definitive, and it is used here.

According to the *Xia Xiyang* the fleet of the seventh voyage departed Longwan (Dragon Bay at Nanjing, near the Longjiang Shipyard) on 19 January 1431. Four days later they came to Xushan, an island in the mid-Yangtze whose current identity is uncertain, where they hunted animals by beating them into a circle in the manner made famous by the Mongols. On 2 February 1431 they went by Fuzi Passage (now Baimaosha channel) into the broader waters of the estuarial Yangtze, and on the next day reached Liujiagang. Liujiagang is 184 miles from Nanjing, according to modern charts, and the fleet went slowly on this leg of its voyage. How long they remained there is not certain, but Zheng He and his colleagues were in no hurry, having planned to forfeit the 1430–31 winter monsoon and to spend the rest of 1431 organizing the fleet and—not necessarily a secondary purpose—completing the temples to Tianfei. The hunt on Xushan may have served a purpose as a quasi-military training exercise. The Liujiagang inscription was erected during this period.

The fleet then left Liujiagang and arrived at Changle (here called Changlegang, 402 miles from Liujiagang) on 8 April 1431, where they remained until mid-December. Toward the end of this period Zheng He and his associates erected the Changle inscription, which described the extensive work done on the Tianfei temples while the fleet was in residence. The long layover was dictated by the need to wait for the winter monsoon, but since the decision to begin the overseas voyage with the 1432 winter monsoon was certainly deliberate, it is probable that the fleet left Nanjing essentially empty and was fully provisioned and otherwise fitted out at Changle. This may have been the normal practice for all of the voyages.

The fleet went out through Five Tiger Passage (Wuhumen), the normal route used by the fleet to leave the Min River estuary, on 12 January 1432 and arrived at Zhan City (Zhancheng; the term usually refers to the kingdom of Champa, but here it refers to its capital near present-day Qui Nhon in Vietnam) on 27 January. Zhan City was the first overseas stop of the fleet on all seven voyages. Ma Huan says that it could be reached from Fujian in ten days with a favorable wind, but the *Xia Xiyang* notes that this particular voyage took sixteen days, which we must shorten to fifteen since neither the departure date nor the arrival date can count as a full day of sailing. The distance sailed is 1,046 miles on modern charts, which works out to about 70 miles per day, or an average sustained fleet speed of about 2.5 knots (one knot is 1.15 miles per hour; the nautical mile used for computing these speeds is 6,116 feet).

The fleet left Zhan City on 12 February 1432 and reached Java on 7 March. Here again the 25 recorded sailing days must be reduced to 24 full days. Ma Huan does not give sailing directions, but Fei Xin gives "twenty days and nights from Zhan City" as the duration of a typical voyage to Java. The *Xia Xiyang* notes that the port of destination was Surabaya *(Silumayi)*, well to the east on the island of Java and near the historical heartland of the Majapahit kingdom. The distance sailed on this leg is 1,383 miles on modern sailing charts. The fleet needed to sail west of Borneo before turning east into the Java Sea, and the voyage to Surabaya would require tacking rather than just running before the monsoon winds. The average speed on this leg was about 58 miles per day, or 2.1 knots.

The fleet remained in Java waters for months, setting sail only on 13 July 1432 and arriving at Palembang (Old Harbor) on 24 July. This time the *Xia Xiyang* records the length of the voyage correctly as eleven days, and the distance sailed is 756 miles from Surabaya to the mouth of the Musi River leading to Palembang, for an average speed of about 69 miles per day, or 2.5 knots—or perhaps somewhat faster, since the end phase of the voyage involved moving at least some of the ships up the river to Palembang itself. One of the many unanswered questions of the Zheng He voyages concerns whether his largest ships sailed up the river to Palembang; the silence of the sources on this question argues that they did, which is further indication of their shallow draught. Again Ma Huan gives no sailing directions, but Fei Xin gives "eight days and nights from Java" as the duration of a normal voyage to Palembang.

The fleet did not remain long at Palembang; it departed on 27 July 1432 and arrived at Malacca on 3 August after a voyage that the *Xia Xiyang* reckons as seven days. The distance is 354 miles from the mouth of the Musi River and the average speed about 51 miles per day, or 1.8 knots. This part of the voyage included some difficult navigation: down the river from Palembang, through the narrow Bangka Strait, and past the Lingga and Riau archipelagos, whose piratical maritime populations were normally a threat to shipping but apparently not to Zheng He's armada. Ma Huan's sailing directions to Malacca are eight days with a fair wind from Zhan City to Longya Strait (Singapore Strait), then two days west (actually, northwest). Fei Xin says eight days and nights from Palembang, essentially the duration of the voyage in 1432.

Leaving Malacca on 2 September 1432, the fleet reached Semudera on 12 September after a voyage of (and recorded as) ten days. Semudera is the present Lhokseumawe district in the region of northern Sumatra, now commonly known as Aceh; it is 375 miles northwest of Malacca. The leisurely progression of Zheng He's fleet on this leg of the voyage works out to an average speed of less than 1.4 knots. The winds might have been bad; Ma Huan says five days and nights with a fair wind from Malacca will get a ship to Semudera, but Fei Xin gives nine days and nights, closer to the actual duration of this leg of the voyage in 1432.

Semudera and the little countries that were its neighbors were more important for their location than for their wealth or their products, and Ma Huan wrote that Semudera was "the most important place of assembly [for ships going to] the Western Ocean." On 2 November 1432 Zheng He's fleet set sail from Semudera, and on 28 November it reached Beruwala (*Bieluoli*; given in a note in *Xia Xiyang*) on the west coast of Ceylon after a 26-day voyage that the *Xia Xiyang* incorrectly records as 36 days. This voyage is 1,096 miles for modern ships, and Zheng He's fleet in late 1432 traveled it at an unimpressive average speed of 42 miles per day, or 1.5 knots. This was the most frightening leg of the voyage. Cyclones develop in the Bay of Bengal and the adjoining sections of the Indian Ocean, and voyagers in Zheng He's day had no way to predict them other than by a general awareness of the seasons. The fleet was far from land in all directions, calculating its course by dead reckoning and relying on the help of the Goddess for its safety; the references to immense waterspaces and huge waves

A much later Andaman Islands scene, showing a dugout canoe similar in appearance to those that greeted Zheng He's fleet. Courtesy of ImageWorks/Mary Evans Picture Library.

rising to the sky like mountains in Zheng He's inscriptions were prompted in all likelihood by this leg of the voyage.

An entry preserved only in Fei Xin's book sheds a little light on the delays that could occur on this section of the route. On a date corresponding to 14 November 1432, "because the wind and waves were not cooperating, [the fleet] arrived at *Cuilanxu* (probably Great Nicobar Island) and was tied up at anchor for three days and nights. The natives of the island came out in dugout canoes (*dumuzhou*, 'single-log boats') to trade coconuts. There were both men and women in the canoes, and the fruits were as previously described" in an earlier entry on the primitive Andaman and Nicobar Islands.

The fleet left Beruwala on 2 December 1432 and arrived at Calicut on 10 December. The *Xia Xiyang* reckons the voyage as nine days, which we must shorten to eight. The length of this leg was 408 miles, giving an average speed of 51 miles per day, or 1.8 knots. Ma Huan had called Calicut "the great country of the Western Ocean," but his idea of how to get there was six days and nights from Beruwala to Quilon, followed by one day to Cochin and three days from Cochin to Calicut. Fei Xin allowed ten days and nights with a fair wind from Beruwala to reach Calicut, and he described its eminence in more strictly commercial terms as the "great harbor" of the Western Ocean countries, using the word *matou* (a wharf or jetty). Calicut had been the westward limit of the first three of Zheng He's expeditions.

Four days later, on 14 December, the fleet left Calicut bound for Hormuz, which they reached on 17 January 1433 after a voyage that the *Xia Xiyang* reckons as 35 days, which we must reduce to 34 full days. The elapsed distance was 1,461 miles, which works out to an average speed of 43 miles per day, or 1.6 knots. Ma Huan gives 25 days and nights from Calicut (and Fei Xin an utterly improbable ten days and nights) as the duration of a normal voyage.

Hormuz is the westernmost destination mentioned in the *Xia Xiyang*, and the fleet, or at least the main portion of it, remained there for less than two months, beginning its return voyage on 9 March 1433. However, this is not the whole story. Reference to other sources, primarily the *Mingshi*, makes it seem that at least seventeen countries, other than the eight destinations listed in the *Xia Xiyang*, were visited by ships and/or ambassadors connected with the expedition. In the five cases of *Ganbali* (possibly Coimbatore; see Chapter III), *Lasa*, Djofar, Mogadishu, and Brava, the *Mingshi* explicitly mentions Zheng He in connection with the seventh expedition. For *Ganbali* the language used is "in the 5th Year of Xuande (1430) [Zheng] He again proclaimed [the emperor's] instructions to this country's king Devaraja *(Douwalazha)*, who sent ambassadors with tribute; in the 8th Year (1433) they arrived at the Capital (Beijing)." Whether these words prove that Zheng He went in person to *Ganbali* is a matter of some importance; if he did, then similar language in the *Mingshi* accounts of *Lasa* and Djofar on the southern coast of Arabia and Mogadishu and Brava in Somalia means that he visited those remote locations also. In fact Zheng He did not have time on the seventh voyage to visit Coimbatore, an inland city nearly a hundred miles from Calicut. The fleet stopped only four days at Calicut on the way out, and only nine days there on its return voyage; a 200-mile round trip by land will not fit into either time frame. Either *Ganbali* is some other location in south India or the language of the *Mingshi* does not mean that Zheng He went in person to the countries in Arabia and Africa. The *Mingshi* account of *Lasa* says that the ambassadors of *Lasa*, Aden, and Brava accompanied Zheng He back to China, and we must guess that the ships carrying them rejoined the main fleet at Calicut. *Lasa* sent no tribute missions thereafter, the ending of the voyages having removed both the motive and the means for such a small country to send expensive embassies to China.

The visit of elements of Zheng He's fleet to Thailand on the seventh voyage is not mentioned in the *Mingshi*, but the enduring relationship of Thailand with Ming China paralleled Zheng He's voyages rather than being a part of them in the strict sense. The little countries of Aru, Nagur, Lide, and Lambri were near neighbors of Semudera in northern Sumatra, and they certainly received visits from one or more of Zheng He's ships as the armada passed through. Whether the Andaman and Nicobar island chains should properly be called a "country" might be debated, but the fleet's visit there is solidly attested by Fei Xin's account, dated within the 26-day period of the fleet's passage between Sumatra and Ceylon. Quilon and Cochin are on the way to Calicut, and Coimbatore (if it was *Ganbali*) could be visited only by someone who went overland from Calicut. For other reasons it seems likely that a substantial detachment of the fleet operated from Calicut after Zheng He took the main body to Hormuz, so an overland mission of that kind was possible even if it was not led by Zheng He in person. This accounts for nine of the seventeen countries, in addition to the eight destinations mentioned in the *Xia Xiyang*, that were probably visited by Zheng He's last expedition. The other eight are Bengal, the Laccadive and Maldive island chains, four locations in Arabia (Djofar, *Lasa*, Aden, and Mecca) and two in Africa (Mogadishu and Brava). The eunuch Hong Bao, one of Zheng He's colleagues and collaborators in both the Liujiagang and Changle inscriptions, and the Chinese envoy to Thailand in 1412, was involved with both Bengal and Mecca and perhaps with the others.

One earlier authority argued that Hong Bao and the squadron of the fleet he commanded, including Ma Huan, the author of *Yingyai Shenglan*, did not accompany the main fleet to Java (nor, by implication, to Palembang or Malacca) but was detached by Zheng He after the fleet left Zhan City and went straight to Bengal. This scenario does not exclude a stop at Semudera, since the ocean passage from Sumatra to Bengal was even longer than the voyage to Ceylon. It seemed bizarre to that writer that the chapter on Bengal came near the end of Ma Huan's book, after Aden and before Hormuz and the final chapter on Mecca. This argument adds to the circumstantial evidence supporting a detached role for Hong Bao's squadron, but there is no reason to believe that the breakup of the fleet occurred before Semudera. Hong Bao's squadron, including Ma Huan, went straight from Semudera to Bengal and then back around India to Calicut, arriving there after Zheng He and the main fleet had gone on to Hormuz. It would have to have been a powerful squadron to overawe Bengal, and this might have provided enough ships for later detachments to African and Arabian destinations.

Bengal's king Ghiyath-ud-Din *(Aiyasiding)* had sent a tribute mission to China in 1408; in 1412 another embassy from Bengal announced the death of Ghiyath-ud-Din and the succession of his son Sa'if-ud-Din *(Saiwuding)*. In 1414 his successor Jalal-ud-Din (1414–31)—described merely as "the succeeding king" by the *Mingshi*—had sent the giraffe described as a *qilin* to China, and the following year Emperor Yongle sent **Hou Xian**, a Grand Director who had accompanied Zheng He on his second and third voyages, to confer presents on "the king of this country and his queen (or queens; *fei*) and ministers *(dachen)*." Hou Xian led other difficult and dangerous missions to Tibet and Nepal; in the opinion of the compilers of the *Mingshi* his achievements were comparable to those of Zheng He, whose biography his follows. The *Mingshi* account of Bengal then skips from 1415 to 1438, when they sent another *qilin*; after one more mission in 1439, tribute missions from Bengal ceased. By then Shams-ud-Din Ahmad (1431–42) was king. When Ma Huan visited the country in 1432, he found Bengal hot, wealthy, and densely populated and speaking Bengali *(Banggeli)*. He mentions that two crops of grain could be grown in one year, and he describes as an oddity the Muslim lunar calendar without intercalary months, something one would think that a Muslim like

Ma Huan would have encountered before. He notes with approval government institutions that remind him of China: punishments that include beating with the light or heavy bamboo and banishment, officials with ranks *(guanpin)*, government offices *(yamen)*, and documents bearing seals *(yinxin)*.

Hong Bao and Ma Huan are next seen at Calicut. Ma Huan's chapter on Mecca *(Tianfang)* concludes:

> In the fifth year of Xuande (1430) an order was respectfully received from the imperial court that the Grand Director and eunuch official Zheng He and others were to go to the foreign countries to open and read the imperial commands and bestow gifts and rewards. A detached squadron [of the fleet] came to the country of Calicut. At this time the eunuch official and Grand Director Hong [Bao] saw that the said country had sent men to go there. He thereupon selected an interpreter and others, seven men in all, and sent them bearing as gifts musk, porcelains, and other things. They joined a ship of the said country and went there. They returned after a year, having bought various unusual commodities and rare valuables, including *qilin* (presumably giraffes, as usual), lions, "camel fowl" *(tuoji,* a common term for ostrich), and other such things. Also they painted an accurate representation of the Heavenly Hall. [All of these items] were returned to the capital. The king of this country of Mecca *(Moqie)* also sent official ambassadors with local products, and [these were] accompanied by the interpreter [and the others, in all] seven men who had originally gone there, and these were presented to the Court.

An entry for Mecca, under the same name *Tianfang* ("Heavenly Cube," referring to the Qa'aba) that Ma Huan uses to head his chapter, appears in the very last chapter of the *Mingshi* and is clearly derived from Ma Huan's account, which it repeats in slightly more elegant language. A squadron of the Chinese fleet arrived in Calicut, and men from the squadron joined a Calicut ship already scheduled to travel to Mecca. There they bought strange gems and rare treasures, as well as giraffes, lions, and ostriches for their return. "The king of that country also sent servants to accompany them as ambassadors coming with tribute to the [Ming] court," and the emperor "rejoiced and gave them even more valuable gifts [in return]."

This *Mingshi* passage clears up the references to the "said country" and "there" in Ma Huan's account, and it confirms that the Chinese who went to Mecca did not go on a Chinese ship. Aden therefore is as far as the Chinese fleet, or any part of it, sailed in that direction. It is certainly peculiar that the only strange and rare things that are mentioned by name as having been "bought by" (rather than presented to) the Chinese visitors (who are not described as envoys) are three fauna (giraffe, lion, ostrich) typically associated with Africa rather than Arabia. Yet Ma Huan's description of Mecca contains so much convincing detail that it is difficult to doubt that he saw it in person.

To get to Mecca, Ma Huan relates, one sails three months from Calicut to the port of Jidda and then journeys overland to Mecca. All the people speak Arabic *(Alabi)*. The Great Mosque bears the "foreign" *(fan)* name of Qa'aba *(Kaiabai)*, and near it is the tomb of Ishmael (Isma'il, *Simayi*). The Muslim pilgrimage and its ritual of circumambulating the Qa'aba are described, and the city of Medina is mentioned, though Ma Huan errs in making it only a day's journey from Mecca.

Since Hong Bao from Calicut sent the seven intrepid travelers on their voyage to Mecca, it is probable that he also sent squadrons or detachments of the fleet to Djofar, *Lasa*, and Aden on the south coast of Arabia and to Mogadishu and Brava on the Somali coast. All these locations had been visited previously, beginning with the fifth voyage, and the sailing directions for all of them in the *Mingshi* are various distances from Calicut (Djofar, *Lasa*, Aden), Quilon (Mogadishu), or Ceylon (Brava). The Maldives are also located with reference to Ceylon. One therefore imagines that the fleet, many of whose leading personnel had sailed these waters before, had peeled off detachments as it rounded Ceylon and southern India and had left a substantial squadron in Calicut under Hong Bao while the main body under Zheng He went on to Hormuz. The wording of the *Mingshi* entry for Mecca, the vague sailing directions given for Malindi ("a long way from China"), and the lack of sailing directions for *Zhubu* (located correctly as being near Mogadishu), argue that squadrons of Zheng He's fleet never visited these destinations, even though they were known to exist, and that envoys (or merchants posing as envoys) from these nations made their way to pickup points from which they could be transported to China on Zheng He's ships. It might be noted that the *Mingshi* does have entries on Portugal (*Folangji*, whose location is "near Malacca"), the Netherlands (*Helan*, located "near Portugal"), and Italy (*Yidaliya*, "located in the Great Western Ocean, and not communicated with since antiquity"), none of which was visited by Zheng He's fleet even though a later Chinese reader might think they had been from the description of their locations in the *Mingshi*.

The *Xia Xiyang* says that the main body set sail from Hormuz on 9 March 1433 and arrived in Calicut on 31 March, calling this a voyage of 23 days, which we must reckon as 22, for an impressive average speed of about 66 miles per day (1,461 miles in all), or 2.4 knots. We must infer that the squadrons sent to the other destinations had already assembled at Calicut, for the entire fleet did not remain long. On 9 April it departed Calicut, and on 25 April it reached Semudera. Again the 17 days of the *Xia Xiyang* must be reduced to 16 to account for the arrival and departure dates not being full days of sailing. There is no mention of a stop at Beruwala on Ceylon on the way out, and really no time for a stop there or at any of the other south Indian ports that Zheng He's fleet had visited previously, because now the winds and waves were cooperating and the fleet, no doubt running straight out before the southwest monsoon, averaged 93 miles per day, or 3.4 knots, over a stretch of open ocean that J. V. G. Mills calculated at 1,491 miles. Six days later, on 1 May, the fleet left Semudera and arrived at Malacca on 9 May; once again reducing the length of the 375-mile voyage from nine days to eight, the fleet's average speed was 47 miles per day, or 1.7 knots.

The next entry in the *Xia Xiyang* says "fifth month, tenth day (28 May 1433): returning, [the fleet] arrived at the Kunlun Ocean," referring to the seas around Poulo Condore and the Con Son Islands off the southern tip of present-day Vietnam. The fleet had only reached Qui Nhon or Zhan City sixteen days later, on 13 June. Mills calculates the entire distance from Malacca to Qui Nhon as 983 miles and notes cautiously that "we are not told how many days were taken" on this leg of the voyage. It seems more likely that the fleet left Malacca on 28 May and proceeded to Zhan City at a respectable average speed of 61 miles per day, or 2.2 knots. The word *hui* (returning) had been used to refer to the fleet's departure from Hormuz, and its presence here suggests that the date of the fleet's arrival in the Kunlun Ocean has dropped out in the recopying process. Accepting the text as it stands would require the fleet's leaving Malacca after a stay of only a few days and then spending sixteen days moving up the Champa coast at a much lower than average rate of speed.

The fleet spent only three full days at Zhan City and then set sail on 17 June, the first day of the sixth lunar month. The *Xia Xiyang* records several sightings on the next leg of the voyage, incidentally providing confirmation that the navigators of Zheng He's fleet were happy to sail by landmarks when they could find them, rather than by dead reckoning. The fleet did not anchor until it came to Liujiagang (here called Taicang, from the name of the prefecture) on the 21st day, or 7 July 1433. Mills reckons this leg at 1,429 miles; Zheng He's fleet had accomplished the voyage in 20 days at an average speed of 71 miles per day, or 2.6 knots.

Sailing Data of Zheng He's Fleet on the Seventh Voyage, 1431–33

Leg of Voyage	Days	Mileage	Speed (mpd)	Speed (knots)
Fujian to Champa	15	1,046	70	2.5
Champa to Java (Surabaya)	24	1,383	58	2.1
Java (Surabaya) to Palembang	11	756	69	2.5
Palembang to Malacca	7	354	51	1.8
Malacca to Semudera	10	375	38	1.4
Semudera to Ceylon (Beruwala)	26	1,096	42	1.5
Ceylon (Beruwala) to Calicut	8	408	51	1.8
Calicut to Hormuz (out)	34	1,461	43	1.6
Hormuz to Calicut (return)	22	1,461	66	2.4
Calicut to Semudera	16	1,491	93	3.4
Semudera to Malacca	8	375	47	1.7
Malacca to Champa	16	983	61	2.2
Champa to Liujiagang	20	1,429	71	2.6

The average speed on these thirteen measured legs of the seventh voyage was 58 miles per day, or 2.1 knots. The better performance on the Calicut to Semudera leg of the return voyage probably reflects the full force of the monsoon winds driving the ships. The Chinese term *shunfeng* used in the sailing directions found in the sources, which Mills translates as "with a fair wind," might also be translated as "running before the wind." It implies wind from straight aft or on either quarter, so that the ship is not delayed by tacking.

By the standards of Western navies during the sailing ship era, these speeds are not high. In 1805 Lord Nelson with ten ships of the line—large warships designed for fighting power rather than speed—crossed the Atlantic at an average speed of 135 miles per day, or 4.9 knots. Mid-nineteenth-century clipper ships, during a period in which sail and steam were in serious competition, often achieved sustained speeds in the double digits.

According to the *Xia Xiyang*, the fleet commanded by Zheng He "arrived in the Capital" on 22 July, and five days later its personnel were rewarded with ceremonial robes, other valuables, and paper money. These events are not mentioned in the *Xuanzong Shilu*, but the latter source does have one final entry related to Zheng He's voyages:

> Xuande, eighth year, intercalary eighth month, *xinhai*, the first day of the month (14 September 1433). The king of Semudera *Zainuliabiding* (Zain al-'Abidin) sent his younger brother *Halizhi Han* and others, the king of Calicut *Bilima* sent his ambassador *Gebumanduluya* and others, the king of Cochin *Keyili* sent his ambassador *Jiabubilima* and others, the king of Ceylon *Bulagemabahulapi* (Parakramabahu VI) sent his ambassador *Mennidenai* and others, the king of Djofar *Ali* (Ali) sent his ambassador *Hazhi Huxian* (Hajji Hussein) and others, the king of Aden *Mowukenasier* (Al-Malik az-Zahir Yahya b. Isma'il) sent his ambassador *Puba* and others, the king of Coimbatore *Douwalazha* (Devaraja) sent his ambassador *Duansilijian* and others, the king of Hormuz *Saifuding* (Sa'if-ud-Din) sent the foreigner *(fanren) Malazu* and others, the king of "Old Kayal" *(Jiayile)* sent his ambassador *Aduruhaman* (Abd-ur-Rahman) and others, and the king of Mecca (here *Tianfang*) sent the headman *(toumu) Shaxian* and others. [They all] came to court and presented as tribute giraffes *(qilin)*, elephants, horses, and other goods. The emperor said: "We do not have any desire for goods from distant regions,

but we realize that they [are offered] in full sincerity. Since they come from afar they should be accepted, but [their presentation] is not cause for congratulations."

The emperor's remarks are not as ungracious as they seem; the "congratulations" that he rejects are the flattery of officials and courtiers to the effect that his virtuous rule has attracted yet another *qilin* to China. Yet obviously the emperor's remarks do not have the "full sincerity" that he claimed to detect in the presentation of tribute. The emperor himself had noted that tribute missions from the Western Ocean countries had ceased after the sixth of Zheng He's voyages, and he certainly understood that the tribute missions whose offerings he was disparaging were the result of the reappearance of Zheng He's armada in those waters. This final, if oblique, reference to Zheng He's expeditions in the primary sources is thus added proof that the function of the voyages was to enforce outward compliance with the forms of the Chinese tributary system by the show of an overwhelming armed force. The emperor did not live to see the long-range consequences of this, but the tribute missions from the Western Ocean countries had again ceased, this time forever.

VIII

The Legacy of Zheng He

Zheng He probably died in 1433, during or shortly after the last voyage, and Emperor Xuande certainly died in early 1435. The Ming capital remained at Beijing, Ming rulers concentrated on threats from the north, and both the original Ming military system and the strong presence at sea of the early Ming period decayed rapidly. The elite of civil officials and degree holders that dominated Ming society was consistently hostile to projects associated with eunuchs, and this attitude had negative consequences for the way in which the voyages were remembered. The same elite compiled the official *Mingshi* during the Qing Dynasty, and it continued to regard Zheng He's voyages as having little importance except as examples of imperial waste and extravagance.

Chinese interest in Zheng He revived in the early twentieth century, and Western scholarship followed. Zheng He's achievements gave Chinese history a place in the oceanic narrative of exploration, trade, colonization, and exercise of sea power, even if such portrayals took Zheng He out of the context of early Ming history and viewed his voyages from a Western analytical perspective.

China Turns Away From the Sea After the Death of Zheng He

With the conclusion of the seventh voyage in 1433, or perhaps even before then, Zheng He vanishes from the historical record. A tradition of the contemporary Zheng family, reported by Louise Levathes, has him dying at sea and being buried at sea according to Muslim rites. As we have seen, the effort of the contemporary Zheng family to portray Zheng He as a pious Muslim is not consistent with the evidence of his inscriptions, which show him as worshipping the Sea Goddess Tianfei in China and as being eclectic in his devotions in the inscription erected at Galle in Ceylon. It is also not consistent with the Buddhism suggested by his nickname "Three Treasures."

Xu Yühu, in the year-by-year chronology of Zheng He's life included in his biography, reports that Zheng He served as Commandant of Nanjing and commander of the Foreign Expeditionary Armada (as we have translated *Xiafan Guanjun*) in 1433 and 1434, after the return of the seventh voyage, and that he died in 1435. The evidence he offers for this is twofold but indirect. Because Zheng He was dead, he infers, the position of Commandant of Nanjing was vacant, and therefore Huang Fu was appointed Nanjing Minister of War and Grand Adjutant (*canzan jiwu*, a title regularly conferred on the war minister at Nanjing to indicate his membership in the tripartite military command there), in effect replacing Zheng He in the collective military command at Nanjing that had come into existence during the brief reign of Hongxi. And because Zheng He was dead, he also infers, there was a vacancy in the post of eunuch Grand Director of Ceremonial, to which **Wang Zhen** was appointed in 1435.

Neither of these arguments is absolutely conclusive. The civilian position of Grand Adjutant, normally held as a concurrent title by the Nanjing Minister of War, usually existed alongside the nobles and eunuchs who held the actual military command, and a single military noble shared in the exercise of the military command at Nanjing from 1425 to 1440, during the entire period in which Zheng He was commandant. The death of Zheng He, in other words, did not make a new appointment as Grand Adjutant absolutely necessary, so the appointment of

Huang Fu cannot be used to date Zheng He's death. Huang Fu (1363–1440) had worn himself out before leaving Vietnam in 1424, and he had been Nanjing Minister of Finance since 1432. His career illustrates the Ming tradition of using ministerial appointments at Nanjing as semiretirement positions for deserving senior officials.

The major factor in the appointment of Wang Zhen to the highest eunuch position was the death of Emperor Xuande on 31 January 1435. The new emperor, **Zhu Qizhen** (1427–64; he ruled as Zhengtong from 1435 until 1449 and was restored under the title Tianshun or "Yielding to Heaven" from 1457 until his death), came to the throne as an eight-year-old boy set upon making his particular favorite the head of all the eunuchs. Zheng He was probably dead by this time, but Wang Zhen's appointment as Grand Director of Ceremonial also cannot be used to date his death.

Though the new emperor's mother was still alive, the dominant figure at court during his minority was his grandmother, the consort of Hongxi and the mother of Xuande. She lived until 1442 and became the *de facto* regent during the new emperor's minority, relying on the advice of three grand secretaries, two of whom had served in the Grand Secretariat since its establishment in 1402. As the new emperor's favorite eunuch, Wang Zhen could not be excluded from the decision-making process, and his influence grew as the emperor approached his majority.

The ending of the Zheng He voyages is usually seen in personal and cultural terms. Hongxi is described as hostile to, and perhaps jealous of, his active and dominant father, and he sided with civil officials whose opposition to Yongle's policies stemmed, it is supposed, largely from cultural factors. We noted earlier that the story is more nuanced. After ordering the sixth expedition to take place, Yongle had temporarily suspended the voyages in 1421, on the eve of his third expedition into Mongolia, and Hongxi's order, on his accession to the throne in 1424, merely confirmed and continued a suspension that had then been in place for three years. Hongxi apparently had no personal hostility to Zheng He; on the contrary, he kept the fleet together under the designation Foreign Expeditionary Armada *(Xiafan Guanjun)* and used it to garrison Nanjing, a disposition that certainly left open the possibility of further voyages. The civil officials Hongxi had sided with, and on whom his empress depended during her regency after 1435, might indeed oppose the voyages on cultural grounds: hostility to the acquisition of strange and useless things from foreign countries had been a staple of Neoconfucian doctrine for centuries. But the voyages could also be justified on cultural grounds: foreign princes and ambassadors coming to present tribute enhanced the legitimacy of the Chinese emperor.

Civil official opposition to the voyages also had political and institutional dimensions. Commanded by eunuchs and crewed by military personnel, Zheng He's fleet obviously enhanced the standing of elements traditionally in competition with the civil officials for influence within the state system. Nevertheless, the political crisis of 1421 that had led to the suspension of the voyages was, at least on the surface, an argument about what the Ming empire could afford. Xia Yuanji and the officials punished with him were confronting the costs of a continuing war in Vietnam, a sixth Zheng He voyage that had just been ordered, and the creation of a new imperial capital at Beijing that was complete only in 1421. Their protest concerned the cost of a third Mongolian expedition piled on to these other expenses.

By the time Hongxi became emperor in 1424, the third, fourth, and fifth Mongolian expeditions had taken place with no discernible gain to the Ming empire, and the war in Vietnam had gone bad. While Hongxi's order terminating the voyages in practice merely continued the suspension ordered in 1421, one may see a cost-saving element in the fact that civilian sailors—presumably hired or conscripted for the voyages—were now told to go back to their families even though the military personnel of the fleet were all to return to the capital. The "capital" here is Nanjing, to which city Hongxi in 1425 ordered the capital to return. Hongxi died before he could carry out his intention, and his son Xuande took no action to implement the move; Nevertheless, from 1425 to 1441 the term "Capital" (usually *Jingshi*) in Ming documents refers to Nanjing, Beijing being designated the "temporary" *(xingzai)* capital. There was a cost-saving element in this decision also: even though the city of Beijing had now been fully constructed, maintaining the capital there required large annual expenses to operate the Grand Canal and to transport grain via the canal to the impoverished north.

Hongxi's decision to return the capital to Nanjing, had it been carried out, would have enhanced the prospects for further voyages by placing the emperors and their officials within sedan-chair distance of the Longjiang Shipyard, or Treasure Ship Yard, where the ships were built and near where the voyages commenced. Hongxi's decision regarding the capital, then, was hardly a sign of hostility to the voyages. His empress at least kept the policy of moving the capital back to Nanjing on the books, and its reversal in 1441, the year before her death, is probably a sign of her waning influence. By leaving the capital in Beijing, the Ming chose an enhanced presence on the Mongolian frontier at the price of diminished influence on the ocean and, indeed, on its own coast. Luckily for the Ming, the consequences of this tradeoff would be deferred until the Japanese pirate crisis of the next century. The new emperor, egged on by Wang Zhen, developed a desire to imitate the Mongolian, rather than the ocean-going, aspects of his ancestor Yongle's legacy.

As the capital remained in the north, and as the directors of government policy were at first Hongxi's widow and her long-serving grand secretaries, followed in 1441–42 by the new emperor and his favorite eunuch, the imperial interest that had sponsored the voyages in the Yongle reign, and to a lesser extent in the Xuande reign, vanished. The processes described by Jung-Pang Lo in his article "The Decline of the Early Ming Navy" reflect a fundamental shift in Ming society in which the political power of civil officials grew at the expense of the nobles and military officers who had been such important members of the ruling elite in the Hongwu and Yongle reigns. The so-called eunuch dictators, of whom Wang Zhen was the first, stood for imperial arbitrariness and extravagance, but they could seldom mobilize enough support outside the palace to attempt policy initiatives opposed by the majority of civil officials. They did occasionally encourage Ming emperors to emulate the achievements of Yongle, and so the prospect of a revival of naval voyages in the manner of Zheng He continued to haunt Ming civil officials.

To speak of a Ming "navy" and its decline is to introduce an anachronism into the Zheng He story. While Zheng He's fleet seems to have had a permanent composition and organizational structure, Ming warships in general were assigned to the regular *weisuo* units of the Ming military system, all of which were commanded by the Five Army Headquarters and administered by the civilian Ministry of War. There was no institution in Ming China that could be called a Navy Department; thus there was no vested interest to argue the case for sea power or for a blue water strategy, nor did China exercise what later naval theorists would call "control of the seas" even during the period of Zheng He's voyages. Early Ming leaders occasionally had flashes of insight regarding a sea power strategy. In 1385 the commander of the fleet that subdued the South China coast in the year the Ming was founded argued that "the Japanese come on the sea and should be opposed on the sea," but his remark is also further evidence of the pervasiveness of piracy even during this period of Ming China's greatest military and naval strength.

Grain transported from the south on the new Grand Canal, which had opened for service in 1415, supported the new capital at Beijing. The canal was preferred because both storms and piracy plagued the sea route. In 1417 the eunuch **Zhang Qian**, returning from an embassy to the Western Ocean, had to fight his way through a Japanese pirate fleet on the China coast. For J. P. Lo this proved that "during the early years, the morale of the men was high and their spirit militant." It also demonstrates that while the Ming empire was sending a powerful fleet as far as the coast of Africa, it had not taken what seems to be the next logical step of creating a similarly powerful fleet to ensure the safety of its own coastal cities and coastal trade. The "efficient navy of thirty-five hundred ships" identified by the same authority is a fantasy based on the idea that each *wei* possessed the fifty warships mandated for it by a decree of 1370. Even if it had, a collection of coast guard vessels, responsible to individual local commands, is not a fleet in the modern sense or even in the sense of Zheng He's *Xiafan Guanjun*.

Despite these reservations about Chinese sea power during the Zheng He era, there is no doubt that Ming China's presence at sea declined precipitously after 1435. As the civil official mentality grew dominant, the expense of replacing ships was regularly represented as a burden on the people, and the ships were not replaced. In 1436 the building of seagoing ships was banned, and the number of smaller vessels built was reduced. By the early 1500s only one or two warships were left of every ten that were supposed to be present, and the largest warships were 400 *liao* vessels crewed by 100 men. A 400 *liao* ship was perhaps 100 measurement tons or 160 displacement tons by western reckoning, tiny in comparison to Zheng He's treasure ships, whose plans and dimensions had by then been lost. For seagoing ships of any size "the designs and dimensions could not be ascertained" laments the *Longjiang Chuanchang Zhi*, the official history of the shipyard that once had built the treasure ships, which also notes that the ships then being built were shoddily constructed, mostly with timber salvaged from older ships. Since the treasure ships were the largest of the seagoing ships and are often included with the seagoing ships *(haichuan)* in the brief shipbuilding notices in *Taizong Shilu*, this statement in the *Longjiang Chuanchang Zhi* indicates that the plans for the treasure ships were included among the "designs and dimensions" that had been lost.

Dealing with the Memory of Zheng He's Voyages

Louise Levathes refers to the disappearance of the "logs" of Zheng He's voyages. Joseph Needham believes that Zheng He "and his associates must certainly have presented the fullest records of their voyages to their imperial master" and that "before the century ended these were burned and destroyed" by perpetrators "in the service of the Confucian anti-maritime party." Other accounts refer to the missing plans of Zheng He's treasure ships. The logs of Zheng He's voyages survive in part in the sailing directions found in Ma Huan, Fei Xin, and the *Mingshi*, as well as in the *Xia Xiyang* that formed the basis for the account of the seventh voyage presented in Chapter VII. The plans of the ships are another matter. As we saw in Chapter VI, there is good nonliterary physical evidence for the length, beam, and draught of Zheng He's largest ships, and this evidence forces us to accept the conclusion that these ships may have been the largest wooden ships ever built. They were also proportionately expensive, and they were the product of eunuch activity. It is therefore understandable that civil officials opposed to any resumption of the voyages would wish to destroy the plans, and Chinese popular opinion, at least, certainly held them guilty of that crime. But while the plans of the treasure ships vanished, it is less clear what documents were deliberately destroyed, and such evidence as exists points to anti-eunuch rather than anti-maritime thinking, even though the result was to turn China from the sea.

In 1449 the twenty-two-year-old emperor Zhu Qizhen led an army said to be half a million strong into Inner Mongolia in pursuit of the Oirat Mongols, who had become dominant in the grasslands since Yongle's death. The Ming army was trapped at Tumu postal station in northern Shanxi. The emperor was captured, and much of the army and numerous senior commanders were killed. Wang Zhen, the emperor's favorite eunuch, was also killed, and he was made the scapegoat for this catastrophe. The emperor's younger brother, **Jingtai** (Zhu Qiyu, born 1428, ruled 1450–57), assumed the throne and refused to yield it even when the Mongols returned the captured emperor. The pillar of Jingtai's government was Minister of War **Yu Qian** (1398–1457), an archetypal civil official and foe of the eunuchs. There is a tradition that Yu Qian used his period in power to destroy the plans of Zheng He's ships and other documents related to the voyages, but most authorities feel that this tradition merely assigns the later destruction of documents to the more prominent figure of Yu Qian.

Another eunuch, **Cao Jixiang**, was instrumental in overthrowing Jingtai and restoring Zhu Qizhen under the title Tianshun. Cao Jixiang was the second Ming eunuch to exercise quasi-dictatorial power for a few years until his armed rebellion led to his death in 1461. Zhu Qizhen died in 1464 and was succeeded by his son, the introverted and stammering Emperor **Chenghua** (Zhu Jianshen, born 1447, ruled 1464–87). In 1471, during his reign, Vietnam finally conquered and absorbed Champa, the country that had been the first overseas port of call in all of Zheng He's voyages. During the years 1476–81 a third eunuch dictator, **Wang Zhi**, exercised power through his control of a secret police agency known as the Western Depot.

In 1480 Wang Zhi took some sort of initiative that met with resistance from **Liu Daxia** (1437–1516), then Director of either the Bureau of Regional Military Organization or the Bureau of Military Equipage, two of the four bureaus into which the Ministry of War was divided. Liu Daxia lived long enough, and was successful and principled enough, to become Minister of War (1501–06) and to suffer persecution from the next of the eunuch dictators, so his credentials as an opponent of eunuch influence are not in doubt.

The *Kezuo Zhuiyu*, a work by Gu Qiyuan published in 1628, states that sometime in the Chenghua reign the emperor issued an order to search for documents concerning the expeditions to the Western Ocean that were kept in the archives of the Ministry of War. Liu Daxia extracted these documents from the files and burned them, describing their contents as "deceitful exaggerations of bizarre things far removed from the testimony of people's ears and eyes" (Duyvendak's translation). Zheng He's voyages had brought back nothing but betel nuts, bamboo staves, grape vines, pomegranates, ostrich eggs, and similar curious things. "The account of the *Xingcha Shenglan* is rare and cannot be examined"—that is, the things it described were both unusual and unverifiable. The *Shuyu Zhouzilu* also reports an order of Emperor Chenghua to search out the itinerary of Zheng He's expeditions. Minister of War **Xiang Zhong** (in office 1474–77) had a clerk search for them, but they had been removed by Liu Daxia, described in this source as Director of the Bureau of Military Equipage. Liu Daxia later gave Xiang Zhong an often quoted justification for his actions, saying that "the expeditions of Sanbao"—referring to Zheng He—"to the Western Ocean wasted tens of myriads of money and grain, and moreover the people who met their deaths [on these expeditions] may be counted by the myriads. Although he returned with wonderful precious things, what benefit was it to the state? This was merely an action of bad government of which ministers should severely disapprove. Even if the old archives were still preserved they should be destroyed in order to suppress [a repetition of these things] at the root." Xiang Zhong was so impressed with this that he predicted Liu Daxia's eventual rise to be Minister of War.

Duyvendak felt that study of the *Mingshi* biographies of Xiang Zhong and Liu Daxia "considerably clarifies the situation and confirms the essentials of the story." In fact the biography of Liu Daxia states that Wang Zhi wanted to gain reputation through warfare on the frontier, and that he felt that Vietnam was vulnerable because of recent defeats by Laos. He had therefore caused the emperor to order the examination of the "old archives" of the Vietnam war during the Yongle reign. Liu Daxia hid these documents and secretly reported his action to Minister of War **Yu Zijun** (in office 1477–81), saying "once military conflict begins, the Southwest will be burned and laid waste." The *Mingshi Jishi Benmo*—unofficial, but the first comprehensive history of the Ming to be published (1658)—dates the same event to 1480 and identifies Liu Daxia as Director of the Bureau of Regional Military Organization, whose responsibilities were maps and charts, the military system, walls and moats, garrisons, conscription and training, and military campaigns, and which therefore would have had records of the Vietnam war. The duties of the Bureau of Military Equipage, on the other hand, concerned imperial insignia and guards, the military courier service, and horse administration; its director seems less likely to have had access to the kinds of records Liu Daxia allegedly hid and/or burned. The *Shuyu Zhouzilu*, quoted above on the destruction of the Zheng He documents, also includes a 1475 memorial by Xiang Zhong opposing war with Vietnam.

Both the *Mingshi* and the *Mingshi Jishi Benmo* (along with the *Xianzong Shilu* that covers the Chenghua reign) relate the document suppression and/or destruction strictly to Wang Zhi's desire to make war on Vietnam. The *Kezuo Zhuiyu* and the *Shuyu Zhouzilu* are both later sources. Liu Daxia does not seem to have been in a position to destroy archival material related to Zheng He's voyages, and the remarks attributed to him in the *Shuyu Zhouzilu* may be apocryphal. Nevertheless, the feeling that all principled officials should frustrate the schemes of eunuchs was real, and even though in his lifetime Zheng He seems to have been respected throughout the Ming elite, he later became just another eunuch as far as Confucian opinion was concerned. Whether by Liu Daxia's hand or by the act of someone else, the plans for the treasure ships and much else about the voyages did disappear. When the scholar Gu Yingtai compiled his *Mingshi Jishi Benmo* in 1658, he devoted none of its eighty topically arranged chapters to Zheng He's voyages, which by then had largely been forgotten.

While these events went on, China became increasingly inward looking—and northward looking toward the Mongols where foreign policy was concerned. The prohibition against building oceangoing ships and conducting foreign trade remained in force, and Chinese private citizens who violated this prohibition went beyond the borders of the Ming empire and ceased to be objects of government solicitude. This Chinese attitude was the opposite of that taken by the Portuguese, Dutch, and other European sea and colonial powers. Champa, the first stop on the outward leg of all of Zheng He's voyages, had been annexed by Vietnam in 1471, and seagoing trade from its former territory suffered as a result. Another of Zheng He's major ports of call, Malacca, had prospered. After the third ruler of Malacca converted to Islam in 1436, Malacca attracted to its port an increasing amount of the Indian Ocean and South China Sea trade, much of which was carried on ships sent by Muslim merchants and crewed by Muslim sailors. Malacca also became a major center for the propagation of Islam throughout Indonesia. Malacca thus served as an eastern terminus of the same system of Indian Ocean trade through which Zheng He's fleets had sailed. This system included the northern regions of Sumatra that later became the sultanate of Aceh, the island of Ceylon, Cochin and Calicut and other locations on the west coast of India, Hormuz and Aden on the Arabian peninsula, and other locations on the east coast of Africa. Despite China's failure to send more government fleets into these seas after the death of Zheng He, this pattern of trade, now largely in Muslim hands, persisted until the arrival of the Portuguese.

The Portuguese voyages and conquests during what is called, from the European perspective, the Age of Discovery, are well known. Comparing the course of Portuguese expansion to that of Zheng He's voyages indicates the extent to which both Portuguese and Chinese were attracted by an already functioning trading system. Vasco da Gama's first voyage left Portugal in July 1497 and stopped at Mombasa and Malindi before sailing from the latter port directly to Calicut (May 1498), which had been Zheng He's ultimate destination on his first three voyages and which he had visited on all seven. By the time of Pedro Cabral's voyage (1500–01) the Portuguese had become involved in conflict in Calicut and had shifted their operations to Cochin, a smaller rival of Calicut that Zheng He's fleets had also visited regularly. Vasco da Gama on his second voyage set up a Portuguese factory at Cochin and attempted unsuccessfully to capture Aden at the mouth of the Red Sea, another port that Zheng He's fleet or squadrons of it had visited. The Portuguese were also roughly handled at Mogadishu, the African Somali-coast port of which the *Mingshi* says "the customs of the people are bigoted and insincere, and they spend their time drilling their soldiers and practicing archery"—words suggesting that Zheng He's fleet encountered hostility on its visits there.

In 1505 Francisco de Almeida became the first Portuguese Viceroy of the Indies. The factory at Cochin had grown into a fort by 1506, and the conquest of the island of Socotra in 1507 allowed the Portuguese to interdict the flow of spices into the Red Sea. Also in 1507 the Portuguese conquered Hormuz at the mouth of the Persian Gulf, which had been Zheng He's ultimate destination on his fourth and seventh voyages and which had been visited by Chinese ships on the fifth and sixth voyages. The goal of the Chinese voyages had been to force the maritime countries they visited into compliance with the norms of the Chinese tribute system of foreign relations; the more radical Portuguese goal was to force the spice trade away from its traditional Red Sea and Persian Gulf routes and onto a route around Africa that the Portuguese would control. Egypt and the other affected Muslim countries opposed this project by outfitting a large fleet in the Indian Ocean. Francisco de Almeida destroyed that fleet in 1509, his last year of office.

Afonso de Albuquerque served (1509–15) as the second and even more famous Viceroy of the Indies, moving his base from Cochin to Goa in 1510. As the capital of the Portuguese State of the Indies in its period of strength and wealth, Golden Goa eclipsed Calicut, Cochin, and the other trading cities of the Indian Malabar coast. In 1511 the Portuguese conquered Malacca, the trading city that owed its rise in large measure to its use as a base by Zheng He's fleets. And just as Zheng He and his officers regarded Ceylon as less important than Calicut and the other cities on the west coast of India, the Portuguese bypassed Ceylon in their rush to Malacca and did not build a fort at Colombo until 1519, though they were interested in profiting from the cinnamon grown in Ceylon. Despite their small numbers, the Portuguese prevailed in this period because of a firearms technology superior to that of all the enemies they encountered (significantly not including the Chinese) and a ruthless determination to bring the "commerce, trade and navigation" of the Indies under their sole control.

Ming China during the sixteenth century faced endemic piracy by the Chinese-Japanese gangs known collectively as *Wokou*, or dwarf pirates, and occasional violence by the Portuguese. Against the *Wokou* China's defenses included the brilliant small-unit tactics of **Qi Jiguang** (1528–88), but naval defenses were confined to small patrol craft, and there was no creation of a new fleet like that of Zheng He's. The Portuguese settlement at Macao, established semi-legally by the collaboration of Chinese provincial authorities, dates from 1557. By the time the Dutch moved in during the following century, the familiar trading patterns of Zheng He's day had been destroyed or transformed by the actions of the Portuguese.

In 1597 Luo Maodeng published his fantastic novel *Xiyang Ji*, which recounts the exploits of Zheng He and Wang Jinghong and the men they commanded. It is full of elaborately described scenes of fighting and magic. In one episode Zheng He and his companions descend into the underworld, and at many of their ports of call they must outfight and outwit the natives. In contrast, the *Taizong Shilu* entries and Zheng He's two inscriptions of 1431 emphasize the size and power of Zheng He's armada, but they describe only three battles during the first six voyages. Luo Maodeng's reason for writing was to recall the military exploits of the Yongle reign, of which the voyages were a part; for him, the fact that "over thirty" countries came to present tribute is itself a tribute to the military power exerted by the Chinese fleet. It was a different situation in the 1590s, when China was victorious in fighting a war with Japan in Korea: the war demonstrated Chinese military decline because Japan should

have been too awed by China's military power to attack another vassal (Korea) in the first place. "Suppose the two leaders
Wang [Jinghong and] Zheng [He] were to reappear—wouldn't
the authorities once again think about slapping their knees"
with enthusiasm, says the preface to the novel, and the author's
imaginary interlocutor agrees.

J. J. L. Duyvendak, in his article "Desultory Notes on the
Xiyang Ji" (1953), argues that the novel could have some use as
a source for material relating to Zheng He's voyages: Luo Maodeng "does not lack didactic historical intent and so makes a
sedulous use of the data found in the descriptions of these voyages." In addition to passages from Ma Huan and Fei Xin, the
novel contains detailed lists of tribute items and other matter-of-
fact geographical description, which Duyvendak felt may have
come from the then unavailable *Xiyang Fanguo Zhi* of Gong
Zhen. The latter book may in turn have been used by the compilers of the *Mingshi*, which was first issued in 1739 after a long
period of preparation, and whose geographical chapters we
have quoted extensively. Duyvendak discusses five other topics
concerning which he feels that information found only in the
Xiyang Ji makes a contribution to the historical record. Three of
them are peripheral to the main themes of the voyages and have
not been discussed in this book; on a fourth issue (the location
of *Lasa*) I have followed J. V. G. Mills's arguments. The fifth
topic—the use of guns or bombards mounted on wooden siege
towers during otherwise unknown Chinese attacks on *Lasa* in
Arabia and on Mogadishu in Africa—I discussed in Chapter V
and rejected it. Careful reading of Duyvendak's careful analysis,
in other words, calls Duyvendak's own conclusions into question and allows us to add nothing from the *Xiyang Ji* to the account provided from the authentic sources.

In *On the Ships of Cheng Ho*, Pao Tsun-peng goes much further in using the *Xiyang Ji*, which is his source for both the
numbers and the dimensions of the five largest classes of Zheng
He's ships. Thus we read of 36 nine-masted treasure ships, no
fewer than 700 eight-masted horse ships that are almost as large,
240 seven-masted grain ships, 300 six-masted accommodation
ships, and 180 five-masted combat ships. This information is
presented in tabular form in Hsu Yü-hu's *Zheng He Pingzhuan*

and repeated by the usually very careful J. V. G. Mills without Hsu Yü-hu's qualifying statement that, except for the length and beam of the treasure ships proper, none of Luo Maodeng's numbers are recorded in any other source. These numbers need to be rejected, and in Chapter VII presented a different picture of the numbers and dimensions of Zheng He's ships. A more recent writer notes that "the true historic value of the novel has not been determined" and that it should be used "cautiously." In practice, many writers on Zheng He have accepted whatever Luo Maodeng material that Pao Tsun-peng endorsed, even though that material is historically unfounded.

After the fall of the Ming, the Qing Dynasty took their time compiling an official history of their predecessor. The long delay before the appearance of the *Mingshi* in 1739 was caused in part by Manchu delicacy in dealing with the persistence of Ming loyalism among the scholar-gentry class that produced the officials: many men of that class would work on a historical project even if they were unwilling to accept a substantive office under the regime that had destroyed the Ming. The compilers of the *Mingshi* biography of Zheng He worked from the *Taizong Shilu*, which conflated the second and third voyages, and from the *Renzong Shilu* and the *Xuanzong Shilu*. They also had the surviving works of Ma Huan and Fei Xin, and perhaps the work of Gong Zhen that adds little to the text of Ma Huan. Obviously they did not make use of Luo Maodeng; to do so would have been a gross violation of orthodox historiographical convention. And they did not know of Zheng He's Liujiagang or Changle inscriptions, let alone the trilingual inscription at Galle, but they were aware of the tradition that Zheng He had made seven voyages.

Their solution was to compose Zheng He's biography so that readers would treat the voyage to Palembang that Zheng He was ordered to take in 1424 as the sixth voyage. In the *benji* (annals) section of the *Mingshi* this is made explicit: the 1424 voyage is described as a voyage to the Western or Indian Ocean, even though Palembang is in eastern Sumatra. They also incorporated some of the geographical information stemming from the voyages into the accounts of the various foreign countries in the *liezhuan* (biographies) section, but they clearly had little sense of where the places were. Thus Portugal is near Malacca, and Malindi in Africa is "a long way from China." Zheng He's biography is placed at the head of the section devoted to biographies of eminent eunuchs, and while he is praised with reservations, later eunuchs receive much of the blame for the misfortunes of the Ming Dynasty.

The compilers of the *Mingshi* got one central point right. The expeditions of Zheng He were sent because his emperor "wanted to display his soldiers in strange lands in order to make manifest the wealth and power of the Middle Kingdom," so Zheng He's fleet "went in succession to the various foreign countries, proclaiming the edicts of the Son of Heaven and giving gifts to their rulers and chieftains. Those who did not submit were pacified by force." Three hundred years after the voyages, the fact that they were about getting recognition of China's preeminent position from countries that could be reached only by sea was apparent to historians who were poorly informed about Zheng He but for whom the tribute system was still a living reality. For the next two centuries the record in the *Mingshi* and its surviving sources defined the story of Zheng He and his voyages for the few who cared.

The Rediscovery of Zheng He

China's nineteenth-century humiliations were strongly related to her weakness and failure at sea. At the start of the Opium War, China had no unified navy and no sense of how vulnerable she was to attack from the sea; British forces sailed and steamed wherever they wanted to go, and they forced China's surrender by occupying Zhenjiang and interdicting grain shipments to the north via the Grand Canal. In the Arrow War (1856–60), the Chinese had no way to prevent the Anglo-French expedition of 1860 from sailing into the Gulf of Zhili and landing as near as possible to Beijing. Meanwhile, new but not exactly modern Chinese armies suppressed the midcentury rebellions, bluffed Russia into a peaceful settlement of disputed frontiers in Central Asia, and defeated French forces on land in the Sino-French War (1884–85). But the defeat of the fleet, and the resulting threat to steamship traffic and to Taiwan, forced China to conclude peace on unfavorable terms.

China spent much of the next decade developing the outwardly impressive and modern-looking Beiyang Fleet. In the (First) Sino-Japanese War (1894–95) the new Imperial Japanese Navy, run by the descendants of the dwarf pirates who had troubled the Ming, destroyed the Beiyang Fleet before the admiring eyes of foreign naval observers, making China a laughingstock in naval circles around the world. This defeat, which deprived China of Taiwan and what was left of her influence in Korea, was also a catalytic event in Chinese domestic history. The leaders of the Hundred Days Reform made the creation of a modern navy a major item of their agenda when they were briefly in power in 1898.

In 1905 one of those leaders, **Liang Qichao** (1873–1929), now in exile following the reaction against the reform movement, published the article "Zheng He: A Great Navigator of Our Mother Country" in the influential journal *Xinmin Congbao*, which he had founded. Liang Qichao was a major player in the early-twentieth-century debates about how and to what extent China needed to Westernize; not knowing much about Zheng He, his approach was to compare him to Columbus as an explorer. The timing of the article indicates its subtext. Also in 1905 Britain escalated the naval arms race by laying down the *Dreadnought*, a battleship of a new and revolutionary design, and the Imperial Japanese Navy destroyed Russia's last fleet to give Japan a narrow victory in the Russo-Japanese War (1904–05). China was held in such contempt that the two powers fought their land war entirely on her territory. Western and westernized powers, in other words, had to injure China from the sea before the Chinese could alter their perspective and view Zheng He's achievements as important.

By then the West had created two powerful narratives within which ships and seafaring were major components of world history. The first was that of exploration and colonial expansion. North and South America, Africa, and Asia were "discovered" by European explorers, leading to the creation of European-derived societies in the Americas and the imposition of European rule over most of Africa and much of Asia. The second narrative was the theory of sea power derived in the 1890s by Alfred Thayer Mahan from his understanding of British naval history: fleets command the seas and promote the commerce of the nation while destroying the commerce of its enemies. Military navies, civilian shipping, and colonial expansion all fit together in Mahan's thinking, which has been highly influential since its origins in the years prior to World War I. Zheng He's story could be dusted off and used to give China an honorable place in both narratives, and the size of Zheng He's ships seemed to refute any suggestion that China was forced to give up the sea.

The narrative of exploration was taken up by J. J. L. Duyvendak, who argued in *China's Discovery of Africa* that obtaining giraffes (equated to the mythical *qilin* whose appearance was a primary indicator of good government) was the reason for the voyages. Joseph Needham echoed the exploration theme enthusiastically in several passages we have quoted in other chapters. J. V. G. Mills was judicious, as a retired judge should be, regarding the motives that inspired the voyages, but his interest in and careful identification of all the place names in the Chinese accounts may leave a careless reader with the impression that Zheng He's mandate was to explore. We have noticed that Zheng He's destinations were prosperous commercial ports located on regularly traveled trade routes and that his voyages used navigational techniques and details of the monsoon wind patterns that were known to Chinese navigators since the Song Dynasty (960–1276) and to Arab and Indonesian sailors for centuries before that.

Nevertheless, the idea of Zheng He as explorer refuses to die, and it has recently been revived by Gavin Menzies in *1421: The Year China Discovered America*. Menzies's thesis is that the sixth voyage somehow sailed through the South Atlantic and around Cape Horn, nearing the coast of Antarctica before sailing up the west coast of the Americas as far as San Francisco Bay, and then returning to China across the Pacific. There is no evidence for any of this is the Chinese sources, which do document the return of the sixth expedition in 1422, and we have reason to doubt that Zheng He's ships were seaworthy enough for the rough waters off Cape Horn and near Antarctica. Menzies's book nonetheless indicates that the idea of Zheng He as an explorer comparable in achievement to Columbus, da Gama,

Cabral, or Magellan is still part of the popular perception of the Grand Director of the Three Treasures.

While the Yuan Dynasty sent naval forces to invade Japan, Java, and Ceylon, those invasions all resulted in failure, and had been undertaken at the initiative of the non-Chinese Mongol ruler Khubilai. Zheng He has thus become the symbol of China's sea power in a period of China's historical greatness under indigenous Chinese rule. Bruce Swanson's *Eighth Voyage of the Dragon: A History of China's Quest for Seapower* (1982) makes this point explicitly.

> In the early Ming period seven magnificent voyages (1405–1433) were authorized that extended Chinese seapower southward into the Indian Ocean and on to Africa. However, pressure was exerted by the continentalists, and almost as suddenly as they began, the voyages were terminated. In the ensuing centuries laws were frequently enacted that retarded naval and maritime development to the extent that navies and merchant fleets were ineffective and unable—even sometimes forbidden— to sail on the open sea.

Here, in a work of real sensitivity and historical sophistication whose emphasis is China's nineteenth- and twentieth-century naval history, we find Zheng He interpreted through the eyes of Mahan: Zheng He "extended Chinese seapower southward" but in opposition "pressure was exerted by the continentalists," just as, in Mahan's opinion, France was always torn between sea power and continental ambitions and therefore lost out on the sea to Britain. The "eighth voyage" of the book's title is China's current effort to develop a powerful modern navy, a voyage whose end was not in sight when Swanson wrote and that continues today.

What Zheng He and his fleet did was more like the exercise of sea power than exploration, but because Zheng He and his colleagues lacked a theory of sea power, and vested interests in support of one, the results of the voyages were likely to be ephemeral. Mahan's later writings welded together command of the sea exercised by a fleet of warships, trade carried by merchant ships, and overseas colonies to support far-flung naval operations into a coherent theory that could become national policy. We saw that what Ming China did during the period of Zheng He's voyages did not conform to Mahan's doctrines. Instead of commanding the sea in a naval sense, Zheng He's armada could land a powerful army at the seaport of any small state the Chinese wished to intimidate. While Zheng He's armada was thus occupied, pirate fleets, often composed largely of Chinese, operated on the Chinese coast and in Southeast Asia. Zheng He suppressed the fleet commanded by Chen Zuyi, but then he continued on his primary mission of enforcing the tribute system on the countries of the Western Ocean, while in Chinese waters piracy continued to interfere with grain shipments to the north. Ming China also had no intention of promoting civilian overseas shipping during the period of Zheng He's voyages. On the contrary, both Hongwu and Yongle saw only danger in Chinese merchants going abroad, and they made serious efforts to suppress the Chinese shipping that had flourished under both Song and Yuan.

Spanish, Portuguese, Dutch, British, and French sea power all expanded through the acquisition of distant colonial bases, but the only entity that might be called a Ming colony was Palembang under the rule of the Chinese merchant community. The Ming court recognized the Chinese rulers of Palembang but not as kings, giving them instead the same relatively low-ranking title that was conferred on aboriginal tribal chieftains in southwestern China. The Ming government also lost track of Palembang after conferring a seal on its ruler in 1425. The next mention of Palembang, in 1577, is revealing: the "Old Harbor" was visited by merchants who observed that Zhang Lian, a Guangdong pirate previously (ca. 1566) defeated by government forces, had made himself the chief of the "foreign shippers" (fanbo), and that many people from Zhangzhou and Quanzhou in Fujian, who should not have been there given the Ming prohibition against sailing overseas, had attached themselves to him. Chinese shipping officials (shiboguan, presumably officials of the maritime trade superintendency or shibo tijusi at Canton, then the only such office in the Ming empire) commented that "this place" was an important assembly point for various foreigners. Palembang, then, was both a commercial entrepôt and a pirate's lair, but it was not a Chinese colony, and

Chinese authorities did not contemplate going after the pirate Zhang Lian or the Fujian merchants who had sailed there illegally and joined him. Overseas meant out of mind, as far as official China was concerned. Mahan's doctrines may not be the only possible theory of sea power, but Ming China did not have an alternative theory, only a desire to avoid the ocean, a desire that was powerful even during the reigns of Hongwu and Yongle, when China was performing its greatest deeds at sea.

Whether Zheng He is mislabeled as an admiral, misidentified as an explorer, or misunderstood as the fifteenth-century embodiment of a Chinese sea power of the Alfred Thayer Mahan variety, he is likely to sail on forever in our imaginations. This is because he is a highly visible symbol of a course not taken by world history, one in which Chinese rather than Europeans discovered the Americas and/or established an empire of sea power and colonies throughout Southeast Asia and the lands of the Indian Ocean. Despite the sparse historical record of Zheng He's voyages, there is no doubt that the seven expeditions took place with thousands of Chinese troops and with ships that were in all likelihood the largest wooden ships ever built anywhere. Had China behaved as expected, which is to say as the western European sea powers behaved, Vasco da Gama and his successors would have found a powerful navy in control of the Indian Ocean, and—though this is much less likely—Christopher Columbus might have encountered Chinese junks exploring the Caribbean. Our present world might not be a better place, but it would certainly be a very different one.

Instead China withdrew from the sea. The present book has attempted to show that this decision is less of a mystery when the specific context of early Ming history is understood, but the enigma of Zheng He's career nevertheless illustrates an important truth about historical causes and processes. Zheng He built his fleet and set sail because his emperor ordered him to, and he ceased sailing and resumed sailing because of further imperial orders. The same emperors who ordered the voyages were also implementing policies that had the long-term effect of turning China away from the sea. It is impossible to understand Zheng He's career without being aware of the deliberate decisions made by rulers, and it is also impossible to interpret his career through any reductionist lens such as technological determinism or the class interests of merchants. Zheng He's first six voyages took place because Emperor Yongle wanted to force the countries of the Western Ocean into tributary relations with China. Zheng He's seventh voyage took place because Emperor Xuande was concerned that tribute missions from these countries had ceased to arrive. None of the eleven Ming emperors who succeeded Xuande cared about the Western Ocean and its countries, and their eunuchs did other things.

Appendix: Translations of Primary Sources

These translations, and all other translations of Chinese sources in this book, are mine. The words in square brackets are words that have to be supplied by the translator to make the translation read smoothly in English. The words in parentheses are notes to the text.

I. Zheng He's Biography in Mingshi 304.2b–4b

Zheng He, a native of Yunnan, is the one whom the world calls the Grand Director of the Three Treasures. Originally he served the Prince of Yan in the palace of his princely fief. He followed [when the prince] raised troops, accumulated merit [in his service, and] was promoted to Grand Director. [Emperor] Chengzu suspected that Emperor Hui had fled beyond the sea and wanted to track him down; moreover, he wanted to display his soldiers in strange lands in order to make manifest the wealth and power of the Middle Kingdom. In the sixth month of the third year of Yongle *(27 June to 25 July 1405)* [the Emperor] ordered Zheng He, along with his associates Wang Jinghong and others, to go as envoys throughout the Western Oceans. They led over 27,800 officers and men and were well supplied with gold and silk for gifts. Sixty-two great ships had been built, [each] 44 *zhang* long and 18 *zhang* wide. [The fleet] departed from Liu Family Harbor in Suzhou [prefecture] and sailed the sea to Fujian [province]. From Five Tiger Gate in Fujian they spread their sails and went straight to Champa. Then they went in succession to the various foreign countries, proclaiming the edicts of the Son of Heaven and giving gifts to their rulers and chieftains. Those who did not submit were pacified by force.

In the ninth month of the fifth year *(1 to 30 October 1407)* [of Yongle, Zheng] He and the rest [of his fleet] returned, and the envoys sent by the various countries accompanied Zheng He to an audience at court. Zheng He presented the [pirate] chieftain of the Old Harbor, whom he had captured. The Emperor was delighted, and [rewarded the officers] with titles and gifts according to [their deserts]. Old Harbor was the former country of Sri Vijaya. Its chieftain Chen Zuyi was a pirate who plundered merchant shipping. Zheng He sent an envoy to summon and instruct him. Chen Zuyi promised to surrender but secretly planned to intercept and ambush [Zheng He's fleet. Zheng] He heavily defeated his forces, took Chen Zuyi prisoner, and presented his captive to be beheaded in the capital marketplace.

In the ninth month of the sixth year *(20 September to 18 October 1408)* [of Yongle, Zheng He set sail] once again and went to the country of Ceylon. The King [of Ceylon] Alagakkonara lured Zheng He into the interior of the country, demanded gold and silk, and sent troops to plunder Zheng He's ships. Zheng He's scouts observed that, since the main army of the bandits had gone out [to plunder the ships, the] interior of the country was empty, so [Zheng He] led forth over two thousand men of those he commanded, assaulted [the capital] by surprise, breached [the walls, and] took prisoner Alagakkonara along with his wives, children, officials, and subordinates. Those who were plundering Zheng He's ships heard about this and returned to come to the rescue themselves, [but the Ming] Imperial Army heavily defeated them once again. In the sixth month of the ninth year *(21 June to 20 July 1411)* [of Yongle, Zheng He] presented his captives to the court, but the Emperor pardoned them, did not execute them, and freed them to return to their country. As of this time the prefectures and districts of Vietnam had already been captured and destroyed, and the many other foreign countries had become increasingly agitated. [The number of embassies] coming to verify this increased day by day.

In the eleventh month of the tenth year *(4 December 1412 to 2 January 1413)* [of Yongle, the emperor] again ordered Zheng

He and the others to go as envoys, [this time] to Semudera. Before this, Sekandar, who pretended to be the son of a king, had been plotting to murder his lord and set himself up [as king, and he] was angry that Zheng He did not present him with [imperial] gifts. Leading his troops in person, he confronted and attacked the Imperial Army. Zheng He battled him forcefully, pursued him to Lambri, and took him prisoner, also capturing his wives and children. When [the expedition] returned to the Imperial Court in the seventh month of the thirteenth year *(5 August to 2 September 1415)* [of Yongle, the] emperor was very pleased and rewarded the officers and men according to their deserts.

In the winter of the fourteenth year *(21 October 1416 to 17 January 1417)* [of Yongle] Malacca, Calicut, and others, nineteen countries in all, sent ambassadors to the Imperial Court with tribute. When the emperor dismissed them to return to their home countries, he again commanded Zheng He and his associates to accompany them, bringing gifts to their rulers and chieftains. In the seventh month of the seventeenth year *(23 July to 20 August 1419)* [of Yongle, the expedition] returned.

In the spring of the nineteenth year *(2 February to 1 May 1421)* [of Yongle, Zheng He] went forth again, returning in the eighth month *(17 August to 15 September 1422)* of the following year.

In the first month of the twenty-second year *(1 to 29 February 1424)* [of Yongle, the] paramount chieftain of the Old Harbor, Shi Jisun, asked for imperial assent to succeed to the office of Pacification Commissioner, [and Zheng He] was entrusted with the official seal and imperial commission and sent to confer them. When he returned Chengzu had already passed away.

In the second month of the first year of Hongxi *(18 February to 19 March 1425)*, Renzong *(Emperor Yongle's son and successor)* ordered Zheng He to use the military forces [that he had led] down to the foreign [countries] and to take command at Nanjing. The establishment of [the post of] Commandant of Nanjing thus originates with Zheng He.

In the sixth month of the fifth year of [Yongle's grandson Emperor] Xuande *(21 June to 19 July 1430)*, the emperor reflected on the fact that, though it had been several years since he ascended the eastern steps [on becoming emperor], those foreign countries that were distant had still not sent tribute to the

Imperial Court. Thereupon Zheng He and Wang Jinghong again received the imperial order to sail to Hormuz *(Hulumosi)* and elsewhere, seventeen countries in all, and return.

Zheng He served three emperors in his career, and from beginning to end he accepted credentials as an ambassador on seven occasions. He sailed to over thirty countries in all, including Champa *(Zhancheng)*, Java (here *Guawa*, but usually written *Zhaowa*), Cambodia *(Zhenla)*, the Old Harbor (*Jiugang*, Palembang on Sumatra), Thailand *(Xianluo)*, Calicut *(Guli)*, Malacca *(Manlajia)*, Brunei *(Poni)*, Semudera (*Sumendala*, on the north coast of Sumatra), Aru (*Alu*, also transcribed *Yalu*, on the east coast of Sumatra), Cochin *(Gezhi)*, "Greater Quilon" *(Da Gelan*, somewhere on the west coast of India), "Lesser" Quilon (*Xiao Gelan*, the actual Quilon), "Chola of the Western Ocean" (*Xiyang Suoli*, uncertain but from the name somewhere on the east coast of India), Chola (*Suoli*, Negapatam on the east coast of India), *Abobadan* (a country bordering on Coimbatore in southern India), Lambri (*Nanwuli*, also transcribed *Nanpoli* and also rendered Lamuri; Aceh in Sumatra), *Ganbali* (perhaps Coimbatore in Southern India), Ceylon *(Xilanshan)*, Lambri (again; this time transcribed *Nanpoli* but not recognized as the same country by the compiler), Pahang *(Penghang)*, Kelantan *(Jilandan)*, Hormuz *(Hulumosi)*, *Bila* (probably Bitra Atoll in the Laccadives), *Liushan* (the Maldive and Laccadive Islands collectively), *Sunla* (probably Chetlat Atoll in the Laccadives), Mogadishu *(Mugudushu)*, Malindi *(Malin)*, *Lasa* (near Mukallah on the southern coast of the Arabian peninsula), Djofar (*Zufaer*, also on the southern coast of the Arabian peninsula), *Shaliwanni* (perhaps Cannanore on the west coast of India), *Zhubu* (Giumbo on the Somali coast south of Mogadishu), Bengal *(Banggela)*, Mecca (*Tianfang* or "Heavenly Square"), Lide (*Lifa*, error for *Lidai*), and Nagur (*Naguer*; Lide and Nagur were small states in northern Sumatra). The goods and treasures without name that he acquired were too many to be accounted for, yet they did not make up for the wasteful expenditures of the Middle Kingdom. From the time that [Zheng He] returned from distant regions in the Xuande period (1425–35), the most urgent priorities have been different from those of the Yongle period (1402–24). Moreover, Zheng He grew old and eventually died, and after Zheng He, of all those who received orders to transmit imperial letters by sea, none failed to praise Zheng He lavishly in order to boast to the foreigners. Thus, in the vulgar tradition [the story of] the Grand Director of the Three Treasures sailing down to the Western Ocean [is seen as] a major accomplishment of the early years of the Ming.

II. Zheng He's Liujiagang Inscription of 1431

Zheng He and his associates set up inscriptions engraved on stones at the port of Liujiagang on the Yangtze and at the anchorage at Changle in Fujian as the fleet was preparing to sail on its seventh and last voyage (1431–33). The compilers of Taizong Shilu *and the* Mingshi *were unaware of these inscriptions, and their publication by J. J. L. Duyvendak in 1938 solved the question of the "true dates" of the voyages that had baffled earlier scholars. The translations below are mine, but I am much indebted to Duyvendak's work.*

Inscription on Stone in the Temple of the Heavenly Princess at Liujiagang in Eastern Lü, Recording the History of Contacts with the Barbarians

Zheng He

On the first day [of the second month of] spring in the sixth year of Xuande of the Ming, the Metal Boar *(xinhai)* year of the [sixty-year] cycle *(14 March 1431)*, the principal envoys Grand Directors Zheng He and Wang Jinghong and the deputy envoys Grand Directors Zhu Liang, Zhou Man *(corrected from Zhou Fu)*, Hong Bao, and Yang Zhen and Senior Assistant Director Zhang Da, and others, have set up these words, which say:

The divine majestic spirit of the Heavenly Princess, [who is] titled by imperial edict "[she who] defends the country and shelters the people, [whose] miraculous spirit responds visibly [to prayers, and whose] vast benevolence saves all," spreads across the oceans, and her merits and virtues are recorded with honor at the Bureau of Sacrificial Worship. [We, Zheng] He and the others, have been commissioned as envoys to the various barbarians on seven occasions from the beginning of Yongle until now. Each time we have commanded several tens of thousands of government troops and over a hundred seagoing ships. From Taicang we have sailed to Champa *(Zhancheng)*, Thailand *(Xianluo)*, Java (correcting *Guawa* to *Zhaowa*), Cochin *(Kezhi)* and Calicut *(Guli)*, finally reaching Hormuz *(Hulumosi)* and other countries in the Western Regions, more than thirty *(correcting 'thousand' to 'ten')* countries in all. [We have] traversed over a hundred thousand *li* of vast ocean [and have] beheld great ocean waves, rising as high as the sky and swelling and swelling endlessly. Whether in dense fog and drizzling rain or in wind-driven waves rising like mountains, no matter what the sudden changes in sea conditions, we spread our cloudlike sails aloft and sailed by the stars day and night. [Had we] not trusted her divine merit, how could we have done this in peace and safety? When we met with danger, once we invoked the divine name, her answer to our prayer was like an echo; suddenly there was a divine lamp which illuminated the masts and sails, and once this miraculous light appeared, then apprehension turned to calm. The personnel of the fleet were then at rest, and all trusted they had nothing to fear. This is the general outline of the goddess' merit.

When we arrived at the foreign countries, barbarian kings who resisted transformation [by Chinese civilization] and were not respectful we captured alive, and bandit soldiers who looted and plundered recklessly we exterminated. Because of this the sea routes became pure and peaceful and the foreign peoples could rely upon them and pursue their occupations in safety. All of this was due to the aid of the goddess.

We have previously reported the meritorious deeds of the goddess in a memorial to the court, in which we asked that a temple be erected on the banks of the Dragon River at Nanjing, where sacrificial worship may be continued in perpetuity. We have respectfully received an imperially composed inscription, whose words display her spirit and also praise her as the ultimate in goodness. However, there is nowhere one can go where the spirit of the goddess does not reside. Thus the branch temple at Liujiagang was built years ago, and we have repaired it every time we have come back here. In the winter of the fifth year of Xuande (1430), having once more accepted commissions as ambassadors to the barbarian countries, we moored our ships beneath the shrine, and the personnel of the expeditionary force have been reverent in ritual and diligent in sincerity, performing sacrifices without interruption. We have repaired and added to the main hall of the temple, enlarging it greatly beyond its former scale, and we have also reconstructed the divine shrine of the "Younger Sister of Mt. Qu" behind the temple. We have made the statue of the goddess in the main hall shine as though it were new. Officials and officers, soldiers and common people all rejoiced and hastened to serve, and there were some who could not contain themselves [for joy]. How could it have come to this, if not for the merit and virtue of the goddess being felt in people's hearts? Therefore, we have engraved an inscription on [this] stone, both to record the years and months of our going to and returning from the foreign countries, and to make [these things] known forever and ever.

[I] In the third year of Yongle (1405) we went in command of the fleet to Calicut *(Guli)* and other countries. At that time the pirate Chen Zuyi and his gang had gathered together at Palembang *(Sanfoqi)*, where they plundered the foreign merchants. We captured their chieftains alive and returned in the fifth year (1407).

[II] In the fifth year of Yongle (1407) we went in command of the fleet to Java (written *Guawa* in error for *Zhaowa*), Calicut, Cochin *(Kezhi)*, Thailand *(Xianluo)*, and other countries, whose kings each presented tributes of local products, precious birds, and [rare] animals. In the seventh year (1409) we returned.

[III] In the seventh year of Yongle (1409) we went in command of the fleet to the afore[mentioned] countries, passing by the island of Ceylon *(Xilanshan)* on our way. The king of that country, Alagakkonāra *(Yaliekunaer*, correcting *ruo* to *ku)*, trusted to his own strength and plotted to do harm to the fleet. Trusting to a divine manifestation of the spirit of the goddess, we perceived and understood this, and in consequence captured that king alive and presented him [to the emperor] on our return in the ninth year (1411). Afterward he received the favor of a pardon and was returned again to [his own] country.

[IV] In the twelfth year of Yongle (1414) we went in command of the fleet to Hormuz *(Hulumusi)* and other countries.

In the country of Semudera *(Sumendala)* a pretender to the throne, Sekandar *(Suganla)*, had invaded and plundered his own country, whose [legitimate] king had sent an envoy to the gates [of the Ming imperial palace] to lodge a complaint and ask for assistance. Therefore we led imperial troops to attack and exterminate [those rebels, and] silently aided by the merit of the goddess we then captured the pretender alive and presented him [to the emperor] on our return in the thirteenth year (1415). In the same year the king of the country of Malacca *(Manlajia)* came in person, with his wife and son, to present tribute at court.

[V] In the fifteenth year of Yongle (1417) we went in command of the fleet to the Western Regions, whose country of Hormuz presented lions *(shizi)*, leopards *(jinqianbao)*, and Arabian horses *(xima or "western" horses)*, [while the] country of Aden *(Adan)* presented *qilin*, whose foreign name is *zulafa* *("zarafa" is the Arabic word from which "giraffe" is derived)*, along with the long-horned *maha* animal *(oryx)*, the country of Mogadishu *(Mugudushu)* sent zebras *(huafulu)* as well as lions, the country of Brava *(Bulawa)* presented thousand-*li* camels *(luotuo)* as well as ostriches *(tuoji)*, and the countries of Java and Calicut both presented *miligao* animals *(unidentified)*. Each presented local products, none of which had ever been heard of before, and sent a son or younger brother of the king, bearing a memorial of submission written on gold leaf, to court with the tribute.

[VI] In the nineteenth year of Yongle (1421) we went in command of the fleet to conduct the ambassadors of Hormuz and all the other countries, who had been in attendance in the capital for a long time, back to their respective countries, and the kings of those countries presented tribute in local products even more abundantly than before.

[VII] Now, in the fifth year of Xuande (1430), we go once again to the foreign countries to proclaim [the emperor's] edicts, and the fleet has made anchor beneath this shrine. Recalling how, on all of the several previous occasions, we have relied on the merit of the protection and assistance of the divine illumination, this time we have carved this text on this stone.

III. Zheng He's Changle Inscription of 1431

Record [of Prayers] Answered by the Divine Spirit of the Heavenly Princess

The Imperial Ming [Dynasty] has unified [the lands within the four] seas [and under the] canopy [of Heaven], excelling the Three Dynasties and surpassing the Han and Tang. From the edge of the sky to the ends of the earth there are none who have not become subjects and slaves. To the most western of the Western Regions and to the most northern of the northern extremities, the length of a journey may be calculated, and thus the barbarians from beyond the seas, even those who are truly distant, [so that their languages require] double translation *(into another language that can then be translated into Chinese)*, all have come to court bearing precious objects and presents.

The Emperor has delighted in their loyalty and sincerity and has ordered [Zheng] He and others to take command of several tens of thousands of imperial officers and soldiers, embarked in over a hundred great ships, to go to their countries and confer presents on them, so as to transform them by displaying our power *(a pun on the emperor's reign name Xuande)* while treating distant peoples with kindness. From the third year of Yongle until now we have seven times received commissions as ambassadors to the countries of the Western Ocean. The foreign countries that we have visited are: going by way of Champa *(Zhancheng)*, Java *(Zhaowa)*, Palembang *(Sanfoqi)*, and Thailand *(Xianluo)*, [we then went] straight over the ocean to the countries of Ceylon *(Xilanshan)*, Calicut *(Guli)* and Cochin *(Kezhi)* in southern India *(Tianzhu)*, [before] going on to Hormuz *(Hulumusi)*, Aden *(Adan)*, and Mogadishu *(Mugudushu)* in the Western Regions *(Xiyu)*, in all more than thirty countries large and small. [We have] traversed over a hundred thousand *li* of vast ocean [and have] beheld rolling billows in the great ocean and huge waves like mountains rising as high as the sky, and we have set eyes on distant foreign regions dimly perceived as though veiled in mist and fog, and yet [throughout] we spread our cloudlike sails aloft and sailed by the stars day and night, riding those savage waves as though we were traveling on a public highway. Truly this was due to the majesty and good fortune of the Imperial Court, and moreover to our trust in the divine protecting power of the Heavenly Princess.

The spirit of the goddess, having appeared in previous times, has been abundantly manifest in the present generation. When, [already in] heavy seas, we suddenly encountered great wind-driven waves, suddenly there was a divine lamp which illuminated the masts and sails, and once this miraculous light appeared, then apprehension turned to calm, and even in danger of foundering we all trusted we had nothing to fear. When we arrived at the foreign countries, barbarian kings who resisted transformation [by Chinese civilization] we captured alive and barbarian bandits who invaded and plundered we wiped out. Because of this the sea routes became pure and peaceful and the foreign peoples could rely upon them. All of this was the gift of the goddess.

It is not easy to enumerate completely all the cases in which the goddess has answered our prayers. We have previously memorialized the court, asking that her merits be recorded at [the Bureau of] Sacrificial Worship, and that a temple be erected on the banks of the Dragon River at Nanjing, where sacrificial worship may be continued in perpetuity. We have respectfully received an imperially composed inscription, whose words display her spirit and also praise her as the ultimate in goodness. However, there is nowhere one can go where the spirit of the goddess does not reside. As for the branch temple on the southern hill at Changle, I have several times stayed at that shrine with the fleet, [awaiting a favorable] wind to set sail upon the ocean, and thus in the tenth year of Yongle (1412) I memorialized reporting that the place constructed for the government troops to sacrifice and pray was already completely in order. On the right (*west*) side of the southern hill there was a pagoda temple of great antiquity that had become neglected and dilapidated. On each visit we made repairs, and now after several years the main hall and meditation chambers have been enlarged greatly beyond their former scale. Having started once again for the foreign countries in the spring of this year, I moored the ships in this anchorage and again repaired the halls of the Buddhas and the temples of the gods with even more splendor, and moreover resolved to spend whatever was needed to construct a Precious Hall for the Three Pure ones *(Daoist gods)* to the left of the temple, to repair and decorate the statues of the gods so they were like new, and to provide all the bells, drums, and sacrificial utensils necessary. Thereupon all declared they would serve the heart of the divine intelligence of Heaven and Earth with utmost reverence, and vowed that it should be so, and all rejoiced and hastened to serve. The grand and beautiful buildings will be completed soon, their painted beams rising up to the clouds like bright-colored birds in flight, with green pines and emerald bamboos giving a pleasant shade on either side. With the gods at rest and men rejoicing, this truly is a remarkable place. In this ground and with these people, would not all receive happiness and prosperity? If men serve their prince with utmost loyalty there is nothing they cannot do, and if they worship the gods with utmost sincerity there is no prayer that will not be answered.

We, [Zheng] He and the rest, have been favored with a gracious commission from our Sacred Prince to convey to the distant barbarians the favor [earned by their] respectfulness and good faith. While in command of the personnel of the fleet, and [responsible for the great] amount of money and valuables [embarked, our] one concern while facing the violence of the winds and the dangers of the nights was that we would not succeed. Would we then have served the nation with utmost loyalty, and worshipped the divine intelligence with utmost sincerity? None of us could doubt that this was the source of aid and safety for the fleet in its comings and goings. Therefore we have made manifest the virtue of the goddess with this inscription on stone, which records the years and months of our going to and returning from the foreign [countries] so that they may be remembered forever.

[I] In the third year of Yongle (1405) we went in command of the fleet to Calicut *(Guli)* and other countries. At that time the pirate Chen Zuyi and his gang had gathered together at Palembang *(Sanfoqi)*, where they plundered the foreign merchants. When he came to attack our fleet, supernatural soldiers came secretly to our assistance, and we annihilated him in one beat of the drum. We returned in the fifth year (1407).

[II] In the fifth year of Yongle (1407) we went in command of the fleet to Java, Calicut, Cochin *(Kezhi)*, Thailand *(Xianluo)*, and other countries, whose kings each presented tributes of precious objects, precious birds, and rare animals. In the seventh year (1409) we returned.

[III] In the seventh year of Yongle (1409) we went in command of the fleet to the afore[mentioned] countries, passing by the island of Ceylon *(Xilanshan)* on our way. The king of that country, Alagakkonāra *(Yaliekunaer)*, trusted to his own strength and plotted to do harm to the fleet. Trusting to a divine manifestation of the spirit of the goddess, we perceived and understood this, and in consequence captured that king alive and presented him [to the emperor] on our return in the ninth year (1411). Afterward he received the favor of a pardon and was returned again to his own country.

[IV] In the eleventh year of Yongle (1413) we went in command of the fleet to Hormuz *(Hulumusi)* and other countries. In the country of Semudera *(Sumendala)* a pretender to the throne, Sekandar *(Suganla)*, had invaded and plundered his own country, whose king Zain al-'Abidin *(Zainuliabiding)* had sent an envoy to the gates [of the Ming imperial palace] to lodge a complaint. Therefore we led imperial troops to attack and exterminate [those rebels, and] silently aided by the merit of the goddess we then captured the pretender alive and presented him [to the emperor] on our return in the thirteenth year (1415). In the same year the king of the country of Malacca *(Manlajia)* came in person, with his wife and son, to present tribute at court.

[V] In the fifteenth year of Yongle (1417) we went in command of the fleet to the Western Regions, whose country of Hormuz presented lions *(shizi)*, leopards *(jinqianbao)*, and large Arabian horses *(daxima)*, [while the] country of Aden *(Adan)* presented *qilin*, whose foreign name is *zulafa*, along with the long-horned *maha* animal *(oryx)*, the country of Mogadishu *(Mugudushu)* sent zebras *(huafulu)* as well as lions, the country of Brava *(Bulawa)* presented thousand-*li* camels *(luotuo)* as well as ostriches *(tuoji)*, and the countries of Java and Calicut both presented *miligao* animals. There were none who did not vie to present gems hidden in the mountains or submerged in the ocean, or pearls buried in the sand or cast up on the shore, and each sent a son, paternal uncle, or younger brother of the king, bearing a memorial of submission written on gold leaf, to court with the tribute.

[VI] In the nineteenth year of Yongle (1421) we went in command of the fleet to conduct the ambassadors of Hormuz and all the other countries, who had been in attendance in the capital for a long time, back to their respective countries, and the kings of those countries presented tribute in local products even more abundantly than before.

[VII] [Now, in the] sixth year of Xuande (1431) once again, in command of the fleet, we go to the foreign countries to proclaim and read [the emperor's edicts and to] confer gifts [upon their rulers, and we have] anchored at this harbor while we await the north wind to take to the sea. Remembering the many occasions where we have benefited from the help and protection of the divine intelligence, we have recorded this inscription in stone.

Xuande, sixth year, the Metal Boar *(xinhai)* year of the [sixty-year] cycle, on an auspicious day in the second winter month (5 December 1431 to 3 January 1432), the principal envoys Grand Directors Zheng He and Wang Jinghong and the deputy envoys Grand Directors Li Xing, Zhu Liang, Zhou Man, Hong Bao, Yang Zhen, Zhang Da, and Wu Zhong, and the Regional Military Commissioners Zhu Zhen and Wang Heng, and others, have composed this, which the [Daoist] Patriarch in Residence Yang Yichu, knocking his head, begs [permission] to erect.

Chronology

1274 Zheng He's great-great-grandfather Saiyid Ajall Shams al-Din (1211–79) appointed governor of Yunnan by Mongol emperor Khubilai Khan (born 1215, ruled 1260–94)

1368 (23 January) to 24 June 1398: reign of **Hongwu** (Zhu Yuanzhang, born 1328; posth. Taizu), the first Ming emperor

1371 Zheng He born as Ma He in Kunyang, Yunnan, then under the rule of Prince Basalawarmi, a descendant of Khubilai Khan

1380 Zhu Di (born 11 June 1360), fourth son of Hongwu and future Emperor Yongle, created Prince of Yan and sent to live in Beiping

1381 Ming conquest of Yunnan; Ma He captured, castrated, and afterward consigned to the household of the Prince of Yan

1398 (30 June) to 13 July 1402: reign of **Jianwen** (Zhu Yunwen, born 1377; posth. Emperor Hui conferred in 1736), son of Zhu Biao and grandson of Hongwu, the second Ming emperor

1399 (August) Prince of Yan rebels; Ma He wins battle at Zheng Family Dike near Beiping

1402 (July) Defection of river fleet under Chen Xuan permits Prince of Yan to capture Nanjing

1402 (17 July) to 12 August 1424: reign of the former Prince of Yan as **Yongle** (posth. Taizong, changed 1538 to Chengzu), the third Ming emperor; Beiping renamed Beijing in 1403

1402–1405 Ma He (renamed Zheng He on 11 February 1404) is Director of Palace Servants with the highest eunuch rank; extensive shipbuilding begins in 1403

1405–1407 Zheng He's **First Voyage** (orders given 11 July 1405), to Calicut and back, defeating Chen Zuyi at Palembang on its return (recorded on 2 October 1407, rewards ordered 29 October)

1407–1408 Ming invasion and annexation of Vietnam

1407 Enlargement of Beijing as an imperial capital begins

1407–1409 Zheng He's **Second Voyage** (orders probably given 23 October 1407), again to Calicut and back

1409–1410 Yongle travels from Nanjing to Beijing (23 February to 4 April 1409), and, after a Ming army is defeated in Mongolia (23 September), he conducts his **First Mongolian Campaign** (15 March to 15 July 1410) and returns from Beijing to Nanjing (31 October to 7 December)

1409–1411 Zheng He's **Third Voyage** (returns 6 July 1411), to Calicut and back, with the campaign in Ceylon

1411 Song Li completes canal from Beijing to Yellow River

1412–1415 Zheng He's **Fourth Voyage** (ordered 18 December 1412) to Hormuz, with the campaign against Sekandar on its return (recorded on 12 August 1415)

1415 Song Li completes canal from Yellow River to Yangtze River; from this time grain transport to Beijing is entirely by canal

1413–1416 Yongle travels from Nanjing to Beijing (16 March to 30 April 1413), conducts his **Second Mongolian Campaign** (6 April to 15 August 1414), and returns from Beijing to Nanjing (10 October to 14 November 1416)

1416–1417 Yongle's last period of residence in Nanjing, to which no Ming emperor ever returns; he travels from Nanjing to Beijing (12 April to 16 May 1417)

1417–1419 Zheng He's **Fifth Voyage** (ordered 28 December 1416) reaches Arabia and Africa and returns (dated 8 August 1419)

1417–1421 Main period of building in Beijing

1418 Founder of Lê Dynasty (1418-1804) rebels in Vietnam

1421 Yongle inaugurates Beijing as primary capital (2 February), orders a sixth voyage (3 March), and then orders a temporary suspension (14 May) of the voyages; later he orders a third Mongolian campaign (6 August) and sends Xia Yuanji and others to prison (11 December); in Vietnam, founder of Lê Dynasty eliminates local rivals

1421–1422 Zheng He's **Sixth Voyage** (return recorded 3 September 1422)

1422 Yongle's **Third Mongolian Campaign** (12 April to 23 September)

1423 Yongle's **Fourth Mongolian Campaign** (29 August to 16 December)

1424 Yongle's **Fifth Mongolian Campaign** (1 April to 12 August) and his death, while Zheng He is on a diplomatic mission to Palembang (ordered 27 February)

1424 (7 September) to 29 May 1425: reign of **Hongxi** (Zhu Gaozhi, born 16 August 1378; posth. Renzong), son of Yongle, the fourth Ming emperor; Hongxi recalls Huang Fu from Vietnam

1424–1430 Zheng He is commandant *(shoubei)* at Nanjing, in association with Huang Fu, and his fleet remains at Nanjing as part of the garrison

1425 (27 June) to 31 January 1435: reign of **Xuande** (Zhu Zhanji, born 16 March 1399; posth. Xuanzong), son of Hongxi, the fifth Ming emperor

1431–1433 Zheng He's **Seventh Voyage** (ordered 29 June 1430) and his death

1433–1436 Books by Ma Huan (*Yingyai Shenglan*, 1433), Gong Zhen (*Xiyang Fanguo Zhi*, 1434), and Fei Xin (*Xingcha Shenglan*, 1436) appear, describing the countries visited by Zheng He's fleets

1597 Luo Maodeng's novel about Zheng He, *Xiyang Ji,* appears

1905 Liang Qichao's article begins modern interest in Zheng He and his voyages

Glossary

When a proper name other than a book title is given in *italics*, it is the name as it appears in Chinese transcription. In some cases, this is the only form of the name that is known.

Abobadan, small country in southern India, described as bordering *Ganbali* in the entry for that country in *Mingshi* 326.15a

Aden (*Adan* in *Mingshi* 326.11a–12a, also sometimes *Hadan*), still a city in Yemen

Alagakkonara, *see* Alakeshvara

Alakeshvara, king of Ceylon from the Alagakkonara (*Yaliekunaier*) family, who attacked Zheng He and was captured by him on the third voyage; father of Nayanar

Aru (*Alu* in *Mingshi* 325.17ab, which gives the alternative reading *Yalu*), small country in the Deli district in northern Sumatra, east of Semudera

Bayan, son of Saiyid Ajall Shams al-Din, great-grandfather of Zheng He and father of Hajji (I)

Basalawarmi, Mongol prince descended from Khubilai, ruler of Yunnan at the time of the Ming conquest in 1381

Bengal (*Banggela, Mingshi* 326.7b–9a), now Bangladesh, in Zheng He's day also a Muslim state at the mouth of the Ganges

Bila (*Mingshi* 326.14ab), possibly Bitra Atoll in the Laccadive Islands

Brava (*Bulawa, Mingshi* 326.10b–11a), still a town in Somalia, now usually spelled Braawe

Brunei (*Poni, Mingshi* 325.1b–6a), small, now wealthy, country on the northern coast of Borneo

Calicut (*Guli* in both Ma Huan and *Mingshi* 326.1b–3a), major trading city on the southwestern coast of India, visited by Zheng He on all of his voyages

Cambodia (*Zhenla, Mingshi* 324.12b–14b), still a kingdom in Southeast Asia

Cao Jixiang d. 1461, second of the eunuch dictators, restored Zhu Jichen as emperor in 1457

Ceylon (*Xilan* or *Xilanshan*, now formally Sri Lanka; *Mingshi* 326.5b–7b)

Champa (*Zhancheng*, literally "Cham City," *Mingshi* 324.1a–12b), kingdom in present-day southern Vietnam, first stop outbound and last stop homebound on all of Zheng He's voyages

Chen Shiliang, son of the pirate leader Chen Zuyi (q.v.)

Chen Xuan (1365–1433), naval commander whose timely defection in 1402 earned him the title Earl of Pingjiang since it enabled Yongle to cross the Yangtze River and become emperor; Chen Xuan later commanded the fleets that brought grain from the south to Beijing and also erected a temple to Tianfei

Chen Zuyi, Chinese leader at Palembang, sent to Nanjing for execution after Zheng He destroyed his pirate fleet on the first voyage

Cheng Ho, older transcription of the characters for Zheng He

Chenghua (Zhu Jianshen, born 1447, ruled 1464–87), eighth Ming emperor, son of Zhu Jichen

Chola: Dynasty on the eastern coast of India that reached the peak of its maritime strength under King Rajendra Chola (ruled 1014–42), who sent a fleet to raid Palembang in 1025; also as *Suoli* (*Mingshi* 325.14b), a small south Indian state in Zheng He's time described as "near" to Chola of the Western Ocean and "about as small." The two Cholas because of their names should be placed on the Coromandel or Chola (east) coast of India; J. V. G. Mills put Chola at Nagapattinam (Negapatam) and Chola of the Western Ocean somewhat further north.

Chola of the Western Ocean (*Xiyang Suoli, Mingshi* 325.14ab), a small south Indian state; *see* Chola

Cochin (*Kezhi* in both Ma Huan and *Mingshi* 326.3b–5a), city state in southern India

Da Gelan or **"Greater" Quilon,** described in the entry on "Lesser" Quilon (*see* Quilon) in *Mingshi* 326.5b. "There is also Greater Quilon, to which ships cannot sail because of billowing waves and strong currents, so merchants seldom arrive there. The earth is black and fertile and it is easy to grow wheat" and other grains, which made the people lazy, but local "customs and products are mostly the same" as those of "Lesser" Quilon. The waves and currents are probably no more than an allusion to the difficulty of loading and unloading on the harborless coast of southern India, where goods had to be put on lighters and rowed through the breakers. One may infer that the two Quilons were close to one another.

Djofar (*Zufaer, Mingshi* 326.9b–10a), east of *Lasa* on the southern coast of Arabia; also spelled Dhafar, Dhufar, Zafar, and other ways in English-language works

Fang Guozhen (died 1374), leader of the maritime rebellion on the Zhejiang coast that contributed to the fall of the Yuan and the rise of the Ming

Faxian, Chinese Buddhist monk whose voyage to India in 413 documents the early existence of very large ships, accompanied by smaller ships as tenders, on the routes later sailed by Zheng He

Fei Xin, soldier who sailed on the third, fifth, and seventh voyages and later wrote the *Xingcha Shenglan* ("Overall Survey of the Star Raft"), a primary source for the voyages

Ganbali, a small country in southern India described merely as "a small country in the Western Ocean" in *Mingshi* 326.15a

Gong Zhen, soldier who served as Zheng He's private secretary on the last voyage, author of the *Xiyang Fanguo Zhi* ("Monograph on the Foreign Countries of the Western Ocean"), whose text is largely identical with that of Ma Huan

Hajji (II: 1343–81), Zheng He's father, was the son of another Hajji (I), who was the son of Saiyid Ajall Shams al-Din's son Bayan

Hayam Wuruk (ruled 1350–89) Rajasanagara, the greatest king of the Majapahit dynasty (1222–1451) on Java

Hong Bao, eunuch associate of Zheng He, whose name appears on both of the 1431 inscriptions; despatched Ma Huan to Mecca while in command at Calicut on the seventh voyage

Hongxi (Zhu Gaozhi, born 1378, ruled 1424–25), fourth Ming emperor, son of Yongle and father of Xuande, posthumous name Renzong

Hongwu (Zhu Yuanzhang, born 1328, ruled 1368–98), first Ming emperor, grandfather of Jianwen and father of Yongle, posthumous name Taizu

Hormuz (*Hulumosi, Mingshi* 326.13a–14a), trading port whose name is still preserved in the Straits of Hormuz; visited on the fourth and subsequent voyages

Hou Xian, eunuch associate of Zheng He, afterward envoy to Tibet and Nepal

Hu Weiyong, Ming chancellor or *chengxiang,* whose execution in 1380 began a purge of Hongwu's original supporters and a fundamental restructuring of Ming government

Huang Fu (1363–1440), Ming civil governor of Jiaozhi (Vietnam as a Ming province) whose recall in 1424 preceded a swift collapse of Ming authority in Vietnam

Ibn Battūtah, Muslim world traveler whose account of his 1347 visit to China includes a description of large ships with crews of 1,000 men, accompanied by smaller ships as tenders

Iskandar Shah, *see* Paramesvara

Jambi, port in Sumatra, north of and rival to Palembang

Java (*Zhaowa*, sometimes incorrectly written *Guawa*, *Mingshi* 324.20a–24b), the Chinese term usually referring to the Empire of Majapahit, the most powerful Javanese state in Zheng He's time

Jaya Sinhavarman V, King of Champa 1400–41

Jianwen (Zhu Yunwen, born 1377, ruled 1398–1402), the second Ming emperor, posthumously named Emperor Hui in 1736; son of Hongwu's eldest son, Zhu Biao (1355–92)

Jingtai (Zhu Qiyu, born 1428, ruled 1450–57), the seventh Ming emperor, son of Xuande

Jiayile, a small country in southern India described as "a small country in the Western Ocean" in *Mingshi* 326.14b–15a. J. V. G. Mills identified *Jiayile* with "Old Kayal" or Cael, ruins on the shore of the Gulf of Mannar near present-day Tuticorin; this location is supported by a *Jiayicheng* or *Jiayi* City that appears on the Mao Kun map in the later Ming compendium *Wubei Zhi.*

Kelantan (*Jilandan* in *Mingshi* 326.15ab), still a state in Malaysia

Khubilai, born 1215, brother of Möngke, son of Tolui, and grandson of Chinggis ("Genghis") Khan; ruled as Mongol Emperor 1260–94 and proclaimed the Yuan Dynasty in China in 1271; patron of Marco Polo

Lambri (*Nanwuli* in *Mingshi* 326.14b), Aceh, at the northern end of Sumatra; in English-language works called Aceh, Atjeh, Acheh, Lamuri, or Lambri and appearing as both *Nanwuli* and *Nanpoli* in the list of 37 countries visited by Zheng He that appears in his *Mingshi* biography

Lasa (*Mingshi* 326.12ab), the Mukalla region, now in southern Yemen

Li Xing, eunuch associate of Zheng He whose name appears on the Changle inscription of 1431

Liang Daoming, Guangdong native and headman of the Chinese community at Palembang

Liang Guanzheng, nephew of Liang Daoming

Liang Qichao (1873–1929), major intellectual figure in modern Chinese history who revived Chinese interest in Zheng He

Lide (*Lidai, Mingshi* 325.16b miswrites *Lifa*), small coastal kingdom in Sumatra

Liu Daxia (1437–1516), Minister of War 1501–06, allegedly involved in the destruction of Zheng He material in 1477

Liushan (*Mingshi* 326.14ab), includes both the Maldive and the Laccadive islands

Luo Maodeng, author of the 1597 novel *Sanbao Taijian Xia Xiyang* ("The Grand Director of the Three Treasures Goes Down to the Western Ocean") about Zheng He's voyages; material from this novel is often but without justification cited as evidence for aspects of the voyages

Ma He, Zheng He's name for the first half of his life

Ma Huan, a Chinese Muslim who accompanied Zheng He as an interpreter and translator on the fourth, sixth, and seventh voyages and afterward wrote the *Yingyai Shenglan* ("Overall Survey of the Ocean's Shores"), a major source for information about the voyages

Malacca (*Manlajia, Mingshi* 325.6a), still Malacca today, a state in Malaysia

Malindi *(Malin),* on the Kenya coast still has the same name; the entire account of this country in *Mingshi* 326.12b–13a describes it as the source of the *qilin* or giraffe

Marco Polo, Venetian merchant and traveler, present in China 1275–92; he traveled by sea from China to Iran, and his account of the trip describes large Chinese ships constructed with transverse bulkheads and accompanied by smaller ships as tenders

Mas'ud, son of Saiyid Ajall Shams al-Din and governor of Yunnan

Mecca (*Tianfang* in both Ma Huan and *Mingshi* 332.2b–27b, some of which is based on Ma Huan's account) was visited in a private capacity by seven Chinese from Zheng He's fleet, possibly including Ma Huan, but there is no evidence that the fleet or any squadron of it entered the Red Sea

Mogadishu *(Mugudushu)* In Somalia; *Mingshi* 326.10ab

Möngke (born 1209, ruled 1251–59), Khubilai's brother and predecessor as Mongol emperor

Nagur (*Naguer*, *Mingshi* 325.16b), small coastal kingdom in Sumatra

Nasir-al-Din, son of Saiyid Ajall Shams al-Din and governor of Yunnan

Nayanar, son of Alakeshvara (q.v.)

Pahang (*Pengheng*, *Mingshi* 325.15b–16a), still a state in Malaysia

Pajajaran (*Baihua*, *Mingshi* 325.15ab), in western Java

Palembang, in Sumatra, transcribed as *Sanfoqi* or "Shri Vijaya" in *Mingshi* 324.24b–27b, and also referred to as *Jiugang* ("Old Harbor")

Paramesvara, also known as Iskandar Shah, ruler of Palembang who migrated to Singapore before founding the sultanate of Malacca

Pulau Sembilan, literally "nine islands" and now a tourist destination off the coast of Malaysia; Fei Xin alone reports that Zheng He's fleet stopped here in 1409 to cut incense logs

Qi Jiguang (1528–88), Ming military leader and theorist

Qiu Yancheng, envoy sent by Shi Jisun (q.v.) to petition for his succession to the office of Pacification Commissioner *(xuanweishi)* of the Chinese community at Palembang

Qui Nhon, in present-day southern Vietnam, was called Xinzhou ("new department") harbor by the Chinese; the port for the capital city of the kingdom of Champa

Quilon (*Xiao Gelan* or "Lesser Quilon" in both Ma Huan and *Mingshi* 326.5b, which appends a description of *Da Gelan* or "Greater" Quilon), city and state in southern India

Rajasanagara, *see* Hayam Wuruk

Saiyid Ajall Shams al-Din (1211–79), great-great-grandfather of Zheng He, governor of Yunnan after the Mongol conquest, and father of Bayan, Nasir al-Din, and Mas'ud (qq.v.)

Sekandar *(Suganla),* pretender to the throne of Semudera, captured by Zheng He on his fourth voyage

Semudera (*Sumendala*, the same as *Xuwendana* according to both Ma Huan and *Mingshi* 325.10a–13a), the Lhokseumawe district on the northern coast of Sumatra

Shaliwanni (*Mingshi* 326.15b), small country in southern India. J. V. G. Mills located it at Cannanore, north of Calicut on the west coast but still in the southern part of the Indian peninsula.

Shi Erjie, daughter and first successor of Shi Jinqing at Palembang, according to Ma Huan

Shi Jinqing, head of the Chinese merchants at Palembang, appointed Pacification Commissioner by the Ming after the overthrow of Chen Zuyi

Shi Jisun, son and last known successor of Shi Jinqing at Palembang

Shi Lang (1621–96), Chinese admiral who defeated the heirs of Zheng Chenggong in 1683

Shri Vijaya, *see* Palembang

Singosari and Majapahit, *see* Java

Song Li, Minister of Works from 1404 until his death in 1422, central figure in shipbuilding, the rebuilding of Beijing, the reopening of the Grand Canal, and the transport of grain by canal

Sultan Muhammad Shah, grandson of Paramesvara, third ruler of Malacca (ruled 1423–44)

Sunla (*Mingshi* 326.14ab), possibly Chetlat Atoll in the Laccadive Islands

Thailand (*Xianluo, Mingshi* 324.14b–20a), still an independent kingdom

Tianfei or "Heavenly Princess," also called Tianhou or "Heavenly Empress" and Mazu or Mazupo, a Fujian woman (960–987) deified as the goddess of sailors

Wang Hao, Ming military officer involved in building and fitting out Zheng He's ships

Wang Heng, military officer associated with Zheng He; his name appears on the Changle inscription

Wang Jinghong (died 1434), eunuch associate of Zheng He whose name appears variously as Wang Guitong or Wang Qinglian; listed directly after Zheng He on both of the 1431 inscriptions

Wang Zhen (died 1449), favorite of Zhu Jichen and first of the Ming eunuch dictators

Wang Zhi, third of the Ming eunuch dictators, in power 1476–81

Wu Zhong, eunuch associate of Zheng He; his name appears on the Changle inscription of 1431

Xia Yuanji (1366–1430), Minister of Finance 1402–21 and 1424–30, imprisoned 1421–24 for his opposition to the escalating costs of Yongle's projects, including the voyages

Xiang Zhong, Minister of War 1474–77, Liu Daxia's superior in 1477

Xiafan Guanjun, the official designation of Zheng He's fleet, literally the "government troops [assigned] to go down to the foreign [countries]," or Foreign Expeditionary Armada

Xuande (Zhu Zhanji, born 1399, ruled 1425–35), fifth Ming emperor, son of Hongxi, posthumous name Xuanzong

Yang Yichu, Daoist priest whose name appears on the Changle inscription of 1431

Yang Zhen, eunuch associate of Zheng He; his name appears on both of the 1431 inscriptions

Yin Qing, eunuch sent as envoy to Paramesvara in 1404

Yongle (Zhu Di, born 1360, Prince of Yan 1380–1402, emperor 1402–24), third Ming emperor, son of Hongwu, father of Hongxi, patron of Zheng He, posthumous name Taizong changed to Chengzu in 1538

Yu Qian (1398–1457), Minister of War and supporter of Emperor Jingtai

Yu Zijun, Minister of War 1477–81, Liu Daxia's superior in 1477

Zain al-'Abidin (*Zainuliabiding*), the king of Semudera (ca. 1405–33) recognized by the Chinese, whom Zheng He defended against Sekandar (q.v.)

Zhang Da, eunuch associate of Zheng He; his name appears on both of the 1431 inscriptions

Zhang Funama, otherwise unknown envoy from the Chinese community at Palembang in 1425

Zhang Qian, eunuch commanding a squadron that fought a Japanese pirate fleet in 1417

Zheng Chenggong (Koxinga, 1624–62), Ming loyalist and pirate leader

Zheng He (1371–1433), originally named Ma He, eunuch organizer and commander of the seven Ming naval expeditions undertaken in the Yongle and Xuande reigns

Zhou Man, eunuch Grand Director and associate of Zheng He, who commanded the squadron that went to Aden on the sixth voyage; listed as Zhou Fu on the Liujiagang inscription and as Zhou Man on the Changle inscription

Zhubu (*Mingshi* 326.11a), now overshadowed by Kismayu (Chisimayo) at the mouth of the river shown as the Webi Jubba on recent maps, and as the Giuba on maps dating from the Italian colonial period

Zhu Liang, eunuch associate of Zheng He; his name appears on both of the 1431 inscriptions

Zhu Qizhen (born 1427), son of Xuande, sixth Ming emperor and the only one with two distinct reigns, as Zhengtong, 1435–49, and restored as Tianshun, 1457–64

Zhu Zhen, military officer associated with Zheng He; his name appears on the Changle inscription

A Note on the Sources

Since the story of Zheng He is closely related to the manner in which perceptions of the voyages have evolved, a great deal of discussion of the sources has found its way into the text. And because so many earlier writers on Zheng He have credited him with intentions and achievements for which there is simply no evidence, I have tried to base this account closely on what the sparse written sources actually say. In fact, much of the Chinese source material is included in the text, in translation, at the appropriate places.

Two of the earliest primary sources are the inscriptions set up by Zheng He and his associates in 1431, on the eve of their last voyage, which are given in new translations in the Appendix. They were first presented to the world in J. J. L. Duyvendak's "The True Dates of the Chinese Maritime Expeditions in the Early Fifteenth Century" (*T'oung* Pao XXXIV [1938], 341–412). The inscriptions settled the issue of the dates of the seven voyages, which is confused in the official written sources, and which had baffled the great French sinologist Paul Pelliot, whose "Les Grands Voyages Maritimes Chinois au Début du XVe Siècle" (*T'oung Pao* XXX [1933], 237–452) and "Notes Additionelles sur Tcheng Houo et sur ses Voyages" (*T'oung Pao* XXXI [1935], 274–314) dealt authoritatively with the identification of the place names and technical terms in the sources known to him. Duyvendak viewed Zheng He as an explorer, and his books *Ma Huan Re-Examined* (Amsterdam, 1933) and *China's Discovery of Africa* (London, 1949) developed this theme.

The most important official sources for the voyages are the "veritable records" or *shilu* (literally, "true records") of the period. In the highly formalized process of official historiography, items presented to or issued by the emperor in his daily court sessions were summarized into a *shilu* of the reign after his death. After the fall of the dynasty, the *shilu* served as the primary sources for the official history compiled by the successor dynasty, and then they were usually destroyed. Since the *Mingshi*, the Qing-compiled official history of the Ming Dynasty, was issued only in 1739, long after the fall of the dynasty, unauthorized copies of the *shilu* of the Ming period had a long time to circulate, and some have survived down to the present.

Zheng He lived in the reigns of five Ming emperors, four of whom had *shilu* composed for their reigns. The *Taizu Shilu* covering the Hongwu reign is not cited, but it is the ultimate source for much of the action described in Chapter II; see my *Early Ming China: A Political History, 1355–1435* (Stanford, 1982). The *Taizong Shilu* compiled after Yongle's death includes the period of Emperor Jianwen's reign, and since the first six voyages took place under Emperor Yongle, this is the richest source of Zheng He material. The *Renzong Shilu* of the brief Hongxi reign and the *Xuanzong Shilu* covering the Xuande reign also have notices relating to Zheng He. The *shilu* and other traditional Chinese sources are paginated by chapter *(juan)*, and each page number refers to a folio (sheet), with "a" and "b" indicating the front and back pages respectively. Sometimes the same chapter number is used for two consecutive chapters, which are then cited as "A" and "B."

Specific references to the *Taizong Shilu* are given in Chapter VI for the shipbuilding notices discussed there. In Chapters IV and V the following passages from the same source are quoted: 43.3a (11 July 1405), 56.7b (12 August 1406), 71.1ab (2–3 October 1407), 71.6a–7a (23 and 29–30 October 1407), 83.3b (under the date corresponding to 17 October 1408, which probably should be corrected to 23 October 1407, as discussed in the text), 116.2ab (6 July 1411), 118.3a–4a (13 September 1411), 134.3a (18 December 1412), 162.3b (29 April 1415), 166.1a (12–13 August 1415), 182.1a (19 November 1416), 183.1ab (28 December 1416), 214.3a (8 August 1419), 233.5b (3 March 1421), 236.3a (14 May 1421), 250.8b (3 September 1422), and 267.3a (25 and 27 February 1424). The quoted passages from the *Renzong Shilu* are 1A.8ab (7 September 1424) and 7A.3b (24 February 1425), and those from the *Xuanzong*

Shilu are 7.5a (17 September 1425), 67.3b–4a (29 June 1430), and 105.1a (14 September 1433). Chapter VII also quotes material from pages 176–177 and 181 of Hsu Yü-hu's *Zheng He Pingzhuan* [A Critical Biography of Zheng He] (Taipei, 1958). Yongle's recent biographer is Henry Shih-shan Tsai, *Perpetual Happiness: the Ming Emperor Yongle* (Seattle and London: University of Washington Press, 2001); the quotation regarding the emperor's character is on page 211.

The major unofficial written sources are the *Yingyai Shenglan* [Overall Survey of the Ocean's Shores] of Ma Huan (1433), the *Xingcha Shenglan* [Overall Survey of the Star Raft] of Fei Xin (1436), and the *Xiyang Fanguo Zhi* [Monograph on the Foreign Countries of the Western Ocean] of Gong Zhen (1434), the text of which mostly repeats that of Ma Huan word for word. These are best approached through Ma Huan, *Ying-Yai Sheng-Lan: 'The Overall Survey of the Ocean's Shores' [1433], Translated from the Chinese text edited by Feng Ch'eng-chün with introduction, notes and appendices by J. V. G. Mills*, "formerly Puisne Judge, Straits Settlements" (Cambridge: Cambridge University Press, 1970). This is actually Mills's work; by making Ma Huan its author and putting the main title in Chinese, Mills has caused some confusion for students. The book includes a complete annotated translation of Ma Huan, a critical discussion of the other two works, and a glossary (with Chinese characters) of all the place names associated with Zheng He, plus numerous appendices. I have checked Mills's translations against the original text, but I have usually followed them. Duyvendak's "Sailing Directions of Chinese Voyages" (*T'oung Pao* XXXIV [1938], 230–237) should be read in conjunction with Mills. The Chinese texts of the *Xingcha Shenglan* and the *Yingyai Shenglan* were republished in Taipei in 1969 by Kuang-wen Shu-chü, and the quote from Fei Xin regarding Pulau Sembilan is on page 30 of that edition. As Mills notes (page 56), a full Chinese text of Gong Zhen was first published in Beijing in 1961, with annotations by Xiang Da.

In addition to the inscriptions, the *shilu*, and the three travel accounts, other Ming sources add information to the Zheng He story. Lu Rong's *Shuyan Zaji* [Bean Garden Miscellany] of 1475 is an additional source for the size of the fleet on the third voyage. The *Shuyu Zhouzilu* [Record of Despatches Concerning the Different Countries] of Yan Congjian (1520) tells us that 250 ships were built specifically for Zheng He's voyages, and, less certainly, that Zheng He was nine feet tall. It and the *Kezuo Zhuiyu* [Boring Talks for My Guests] of Gu Qiyuan (ca. 1628) provide unofficial information about later attempts to deprecate the memory of the voyages. Duyvendak cites the *Ming Tazheng Zuanyao* [Compendium on Ming Government] of Tan Xisi (1619) for material that came originally from the *shilu*. The *Daming Yitong Zhi* (compiled on imperial order in 1462) is a gazetteer of the Ming empire that includes an entry on the Great Baoen Temple. The *Xia Xiyang* [Down to the Western Ocean] is described in Chapter VII. The military encyclopedia *Wubei Zhi* published by Mao Yuanyi in 1628 includes the Mao Kun map, based in large part on material from Zheng He's voyages, that has been studied by Mills and others.

Moving on to Zheng He's ships, I argued in the text that Luo Maodeng's 1597 novel *Sanbao Taijian Xia Xiyang Ji Tongsu Yanyi* [The Grand Director of the Three Treasures Goes Down to the Western Ocean], usually cited by the short title *Xiyang Ji*, has no value as a source.

Duyvendak's "Desultory Notes on the Hsi-Yang Chi" (*T'oung Pao* XLII [1953], 1–35) argued the contrary position, that the novel might contain nuggets of historical material missing from the official sources, and gave specific examples, one of which I criticized. Pao Tsen-peng's *On the Ships of Cheng Ho* (Chinese title *Zheng He Xia Xiyang zhi Baochuan Kao* [An Examination of the Treasure Ships that Zheng He Sailed to the Western Ocean]; Hong Kong and Taipei: Chung-hua shu-chü, 1961), published in both an English and a Chinese version, of which the Chinese is significantly more complete, goes much further, using the *Xiyang Ji* as the source for several categories of large ships that are unattested elsewhere. Pao's classification of ships has, unfortunately, been followed by most subsequent writers, including recently Louise Levathes in *When China Ruled the Seas: the Treasure Fleet of the Dragon Throne* (New York: Simon & Schuster, 1994). Yet Li Zhaoxiang's *Longjiang Chuanchang Zhi* [Record of the Dragon River Shipyard], preface dated 1553, notes that the plans for Zheng He's treasure ships had already vanished from the yard in which they were built.

Joseph Needham frequently refers to Zheng He's ships and voyages in his influential multivolume work *Science and Civilization in China*, particularly in Volume 4, "Physics and Physical Technology, Part III: Civil Engineering and Nautics" (Cambridge: Cambridge University Press, 1971), where Section 29 (pages 379–699) is devoted to "Nautical Technology" in the broadest sense. Needham quotes the observations of Marco Polo and Ibn Battūtah, as well as two Song period accounts: the *Lingwai Daida* [Information on What is Beyond the Passes] of Zhou Qufei (1178) and the *Zhufan Zhi* [Records of Foreign Peoples] of Zhao Rugua, dated 1225 by Pelliot and between 1242 and 1258 according to Friedrich Hirth and W. W. Rockhill, whose translation is *Chau Ju-Kua: His Work on the Chinese and Arab Trade in the twelfth and thirteenth Centuries, entitled Chu-fan-chï* (St. Petersburg, 1911; repr. New York: Paragon, 1966). Some of Needham's observations were due to the work of Jung-Pang Lo, whose "The Decline of the Early Ming Navy" (*Oriens Extremis* V:2 [1958], 149–168) has been quoted in the text. Recently Christopher Wake, "The Myth of Zheng He's Great Treasure Ships" (*International Journal of Maritime History* XVI:1 [June 2004], 59–75) has argued against the commonly accepted large dimensions. I am grateful to my colleague Michael Miller for calling this helpful reference to my attention.

G. R. Worcester's *The Junks & Sampans of the Yangtze* is a classic; his remarks on the navigability of the Yangtze are on page 3 of the reprinted edition (Annapolis: Naval Institute Press, 1971). Alfred Thayer Mahan first expounded his theories in *The Influence of Sea Power upon History, 1660–1783*, which has been reprinted numerous times since its first publication in 1890; his remark about battleships ascending the Yangtze is on page 61 of *The Problem of Asia and Its Effect upon International Policies* (London, 1900). Bruce Swanson, *Eighth Voyage of the Dragon: A History of China's Quest for Seapower* (Annapolis: Naval Institute Press, 1982) is quoted (page 1) in Chapter VIII. The quotation regarding Galle harbor is from George Davidson Winius, *The Fatal History of Portuguese Ceylon: Transition to Dutch Rule* (Cambridge: Harvard University Press, 1971), page 43. O. W. Wolters, *The Fall of Shrivijaya in Malay History* (Ithaca: Cornell University Press, 1970) includes much material, some of it from Chinese sources, on the interaction of the Palembang/Malacca royal dynasty with Zheng He's voyages.

In the near-century between the fall of the Ming in 1644 and the publication of the official *Mingshi* [Ming History] in 1739, numerous unofficial histories (*waishi* or "outside histories," as opposed to *zhengshi* or "orthodox histories") appeared. They vary in quality, but they were based on the same sources later used for the official history, and some of them are very useful. The first comprehensive history of the Ming was Tan Qian's *Guoque* [National Assessment], which was completed some time before its author's death in 1658 and survived in manuscript form for three centuries until its first publication in 1958. The *Guoque* mentions Zheng He's voyages, occasionally with slightly different details that have been noted in the text. On the other hand, Gu Yingtai's *Mingshi Jishi Benmo* [Ming History by Topics Narrated from Beginning to End], published in 1658, does not deal with Zheng He's voyages. The nature of the *jishi benmo* format, in which individual topics are selected and all relevant material is arranged chronologically under each topic, imposes the necessity of choice upon the historian, and the fact that Gu Yingtai did not make Zheng He one of his topics is, in its own way, an important commentary on the way that later educated Chinese regarded his voyages.

The long delay in producing the *Mingshi* was due in part to the Qing desire to use the historical project to win the loyalties of the Chinese educated class, so it is not surprising that the final product, while regarded as one of the best of the later dynastic histories, also represents the views of that class in a rather homogenized manner. Zheng He's *Mingshi* biography is translated in the Appendix. In addition, much Zheng He material found its way into the geographical chapters of the *Mingshi*, which are referenced country by country in the Glossary.

Continuing interest in Zheng He has produced a large secondary literature in Chinese, a recent taste of which may be found in Wan Ming, "Reflections on the Study of Zheng He's Expeditions," *Ming Studies* 49 [Spring 2004], 17–33. All of this work depends, as does this book, on the same restricted body of primary sources, and unless and until more source material appears the answers to many of the questions that interest us about Zheng He, his ships, and his voyages will continue to be beyond our reach.

Character List

Abobadan 阿撥把丹

Adan 阿丹

Alu 阿魯

Baihua 百花

bandingshou 班碇手

Banggela 榜葛剌

banshi 辦事

baochuan 寶船

baochuanchang 寶船廠

Bayan 拜顏

Basalawarmi 把匝剌瓦爾密

Bila 比剌

Bulawa 不剌哇

bu-Wo haichuan 捕倭海船

bu yuan sheng zhe 不願陞者

caibi 綵幣

Cao Jixiang 曹吉祥

Chen Shiliang 陳士良

Chen Xuan 陳瑄

Chen Zuyi 陳祖義

Chengzu 成祖

Chenghua 成化

chengxiang 丞相

chi 尺

Da Gelan 大葛蘭

dacai 搭材

Daming Yitong Zhi 大明一統志

ding 錠

duogong 舵工

Emperor Hui 惠帝

fan huozhang 番火長

Fang Guozhen 方國珍

Faxian 法顯

Fei Xin 費信

gaizao 改造

Ganbali 甘巴里

Gong Zhen 鞏珍

Great Baoen Temple 大報恩寺

Gu Qiyuan 顧起元

Gu Yingtai 谷應泰

guan 貫

guanjun 官軍

guanxiao 官校

Guawa 瓜哇

Guli 古里

Guoque 國榷

Hadan 哈丹

haibo 海舶

haichuan 海船

haifengchuan 海風船

haiyunchuan 海運船
haizhou 海舟
Hajji 哈只
Hong Bao 洪保
Hongxi 洪熙
Hongwu 洪武
Hou Xian 侯顯
Hsu Yü-hu 徐玉虎
hu 斛
Hu Weiyong 胡惟庸
Huang Fu 黃福
Hulumosi 忽魯謨斯
huoqi 火器
huozhang 火長
ji 級
Jianwen 建文
Jiaozhi 交趾
Jingtai 景泰
Jiayicheng 加異城
Jiayile 加異勒
Jilandan 急蘭丹
Jiugang 舊港
juan (chapter) 卷
juan (thin silk) 絹
jubo 巨舶
junban 軍伴
Kezhi 柯枝
Kezuo Zhuiyu 客座贅語

Lasa 剌撒
Li Xing 李興
Li Zhaoxiang 李昭祥
liang 兩
Liang Daoming 梁道明
Liang Guanzheng 梁觀政
Liang Qichao 梁啟超
liangchuan 糧船
liao 料
Lidai 黎代
Lifa 黎伐
Lingwai Daida 嶺外代答
lishi 力士
Liu Daxia 劉大夏
Liushan 溜山
longgu 龍骨
Longjiang Chuanchang Zhi 龍江船廠志
louchuan 樓船
Lu Rong 陸容
Luo Maodeng 羅懋登
Ma He 馬和
Ma Huan 馬歡
machuan 馬船
maiban 買辦
Malin 麻林
Manlajia 滿剌加
Mao Kun 茅坤

Mao Yuanyi 茅元儀
Mazu 媽祖
Mazupo 媽祖婆
mianbu 綿布
miligao 糜里羔
Ming Tazheng Zuanyao 明大正纂要
Mingshi 明史
Mingshi Jishi Benmo 明史紀事本末
minshao 民稍
minshaoren 民稍人
minshi 民士
minyi 民醫
Mugudushu 木骨都束
Naguer 那孤兒
Nanpoli 喃渤利
Nanwuli 南巫里
Pao Tsen-peng 包尊彭
Pengheng 彭亨
pin 品
Poni 淳泥
qijun 旗軍
qijunren 旗軍人
qigong 奇功
qigong cideng 奇功次等
qilin 麒麟
qixiao 旗校

Qi Jiguang 戚繼光
Qiu Yancheng 丘彥成
Renzong 仁宗
Renzong Shilu 仁宗實錄
Sanbao Taijian Xia Xiyang 三寶太監下西洋
Sanbao Taijian Xia Xiyang Ji Tongsu Yanyi 三寶太監下西洋記通俗演義
Sanfoqi 三佛齊
shachuan 沙船
Sumendala 蘇門答剌
Shaliwanni 沙里灣泥
shaoshui 稍水
shi 試
Shi Erjie 施二姐
Shi Jinqing 施進卿
Shi Jisun 施濟孫
Shi Lang 施琅
shishou 實授
shushou 書手
shusuanshou 書算手
Shuyu Zhouzilu 殊域周咨錄
Shuyuan Zaji 菽園雜記
Song Li 宋禮
Suganla 蘇幹剌
Sunla 孫剌
Suoli 瑣里

Taizong 太宗
Taizong Shilu 太宗實錄
Taizu 太祖
Taizu Shilu 太祖實錄
Tan Qian 談遷
Tan Xisi 譚希思
Tianfang 天方
Tianfei 天妃
Tianhou 天后
Tianshun 天順
tiemao 鐵錨
tongshi 通事
tougong 頭功
waishi 外史
Wang Guitong 王貴通
Wang Hao 汪浩
Wang Heng 王衡
Wang Jinghong 王景弘
Wang Qinglian 王清濂
Wang Zhen 王振
Wang Zhi 汪直
Wu Zhong 吳忠
Wubei Zhi 武備志
Xia Xiyang 下西洋
Xia Yuanji 夏原吉
Xiang Zhong 項忠
Xianluo 暹羅
Xiafan Guanjun 下番官軍

Xiao Gelan 小葛蘭
xiaowei 校尉
Xilan 錫蘭
Xilanshan 錫蘭山
Xingcha Shenglan 星槎勝覽
Xinzhou 新州
Xiyang Fanguo Zhi 西洋番國志
Xiyang Suoli 西洋瑣里
Xuande 宣德
Xuanzong 宣宗
Xuanzong Shilu 宣宗實錄
Yaliekunaier 亞烈苦奈兒
Yalu 啞魯
Yan Congjian 嚴從簡
Yang Yichu 楊一初
Yang Zhen 楊真
Yin Qing 尹慶
Yingyai Shenglan 瀛涯勝覽
yishi 醫士
Yongle 永樂
yongshi 勇士
Yu Qian 于謙
Yu Zijun 余子俊
yuding 餘丁
yuyi 御醫
yunchuan 運船
Zainuliabiding 宰奴里阿必丁

Zhancheng 占城

zhanchuan 戰船

zhang 丈

Zhang Da 張達

Zhang Funama 張佛那馬

Zhang Qian 張謙

Zhao Rugua 趙汝适

Zhaowa 爪哇

Zheng Chenggong 鄭成功

Zheng He 鄭和

Zheng He Pingzhuan 鄭和平傳

Zheng He Xia Xiyang zhi Baochuan Kao 鄭和下西洋之寶船考

zhengshi 正史

Zhengtong 正統

Zhenla 真臘

Zhou Fu 周福

Zhou Man 周滿

Zhou Qufei 周去非

Zhu Biao 朱標

Zhu Di 朱棣

Zhu Fan Zhi 諸藩志

Zhu Gaozhi 朱高熾

Zhu Jianshen 朱見深

Zhu Liang 朱良

Zhu Qiyu 朱祁鈺

Zhu Qizhen 朱祁鎮

Zhu Yuanzhang 朱元璋

Zhu Yunming 祝允明

Zhu Yunwen 朱允炆

Zhu Zhanji 朱瞻基

Zhu Zhen 朱真

Zhubu 竹步

zongjia 總甲

zongqi 總旗

Zufaer 祖法兒

zulafa 祖剌法

zuochuan 坐船

Index